Ben Hellman and Andrei Rogachevskii

FILMING THE UNFILMABLE

Casper Wrede's 'One Day in the Life of Ivan Denisovich'

With a foreword by Ian D. Thatcher

ibidem-Verlag
Stuttgart

Bibliografische Information der Deutschen Nationalbibliothek
Die Deutsche Nationalbibliothek verzeichnet diese Publikation in der Deutschen Nationalbibliografie; detaillierte bibliografische Daten sind im Internet über http://dnb.d-nb.de abrufbar.

Bibliographic information published by the Deutsche Nationalbibliothek
Die Deutsche Nationalbibliothek lists this publication in the Deutsche Nationalbibliografie; detailed bibliographic data are available in the Internet at http://dnb.d-nb.de.

Front Cover Picture: Tom Courtenay as Ivan Denisovich. Photograph by © Sven Åsberg 1970

Second, Revised and Expanded Edition

∞

Gedruckt auf alterungsbeständigem, säurefreien Papier
Printed on acid-free paper

ISSN: 1614-3515

ISBN-13: 978-3-8382-0044-6

© *ibidem*-Verlag
Stuttgart 2014

Alle Rechte vorbehalten

Das Werk einschließlich aller seiner Teile ist urheberrechtlich geschützt. Jede Verwertung außerhalb der engen Grenzen des Urheberrechtsgesetzes ist ohne Zustimmung des Verlages unzulässig und strafbar. Dies gilt insbesondere für Vervielfältigungen, Übersetzungen, Mikroverfilmungen und elektronische Speicherformen sowie die Einspeicherung und Verarbeitung in elektronischen Systemen.

All rights reserved. No part of this publication may be reproduced, stored in or introduced into a retrieval system, or transmitted, in any form, or by any means (electronical, mechanical, photocopying, recording or otherwise) without the prior written permission of the publisher. Any person who does any unauthorized act in relation to this publication may be liable to criminal prosecution and civil claims for damages.

Printed in Germany

CONTENTS

FOREWORD TO THE SECOND EDITION by Ian D. Thatcher — VII

PREFACE TO THE SECOND EDITION — 1

INTRODUCTION — 7

1. A FILM IN THE CAREER OF CASPER WREDE — 13
2. COSTINGS AND FUNDING — 25
3. PRE-PRODUCTION — 29
4. FILMING — 41
5. THE BOOK – THE SCRIPT – THE FILM: A COMPARISON — 57
6. RECEPTION — 87

EPILOGUE AND CONCLUSIONS — 135

ACKNOWLEDGEMENTS — 143

SELECTED FILMOGRAPHY AND BIBLIOGRAPHY — 145

APPENDICES

I	Casper Wrede's "Russia on My Mind" and "Letter to a Young Actor"	159
II	Student feedback after the viewing of *One Day in the Life of Ivan Denisovich*	184
III	Mikhail Demin's drawings for the set	188
IV	Other illustrations	216
V	Staging the Unstageable: Casper Wrede's Production of *Hope Against Hope* (1983)	229
	INDEX	249

Soviet and Post-Soviet Politics and Society (SPPS)
ISSN 1614-3515

Founded in 2004 and refereed since 2007, SPPS makes available affordable English-, German-, and Russian-language studies on the history of the countries of the former Soviet bloc from the late Tsarist period to today. It publishes between 5 and 20 volumes per year and focuses on issues in transitions to and from democracy such as economic crisis, identity formation, civil society development, and constitutional reform in CEE and the NIS. SPPS also aims to highlight so far understudied themes in East European studies such as right-wing radicalism, religious life, higher education, or human rights protection. The authors and titles of all previously published volumes are listed at the end of this book. For a full description of the series and reviews of its books, see
www.ibidem-verlag.de/red/spps.

Editorial correspondence & manuscripts should be sent to: Dr. Andreas Umland, DAAD, German Embassy, vul. Bohdana Khmelnitskoho 25, UA-01901 Kyiv, Ukraine.
e-mail: umland@stanfordalumni.org

Business correspondence & review copy requests should be sent to: *ibidem* Press, Leuschnerstr. 40, 30457 Hannover, Germany; tel.: +49 511 2622200; fax: +49 511 2622201; spps@ibidem.eu.

Authors, reviewers, referees, and editors for (as well as all other persons sympathetic to) SPPS are invited to join its networks at
www.facebook.com/group.php?gid=52638198614
www.linkedin.com/groups?about=&gid=103012
www.xing.com/net/spps-ibidem-verlag/

Recent Volumes

116 Valerio Trabandt
Neue Nachbarn, gute Nachbarschaft?
Die EU als internationaler Akteur am Beispiel ihrer Demokratieförderung in Belarus und der Ukraine 2004-2009
Mit einem Vorwort von Jutta Joachim
ISBN 978-3-8382-0437-6

117 Fabian Pfeiffer
Estlands Außen- und Sicherheitspolitik I
Der estnische Atlantizismus nach der wiedererlangten Unabhängigkeit 1991-2004
Mit einem Vorwort von Helmut Hubel
ISBN 978-3-8382-0127-6

118 Jana Podßuweit
Estlands Außen- und Sicherheitspolitik II
Handlungsoptionen eines Kleinstaates im Rahmen seiner EU-Mitgliedschaft (2004-2008)
Mit einem Vorwort von Helmut Hubel
ISBN 978-3-8382-0440-6

119 Karin Pointner
Estlands Außen- und Sicherheitspolitik III
Eine gedächtnispolitische Analyse estnischer Entwicklungskooperation 2006-2010
Mit einem Vorwort von Karin Liebhart
ISBN 978-3-8382-0435-2

120 Ruslana Vovk
Die Offenheit der ukrainischen Verfassung für das Völkerrecht und die europäische Integration
Mit einem Vorwort von Alexander Blankenagel
ISBN 978-3-8382-0481-9

121 Mykhaylo Banakh
Die Relevanz der Zivilgesellschaft bei den postkommunistischen Transformationsprozessen in mittel- und osteuropäischen Ländern
Das Beispiel der spät- und postsowjetischen Ukraine 1986-2009
Mit einem Vorwort von Gerhard Simon
ISBN 978-3-8382-0499-4

122 Michael Moser
Language Policy and the Discourse on Languages in Ukraine under President Viktor Yanukovych (25 February 2010–28 October 2012)
ISBN 978-3-8382-0497-0 (Paperback edition)
ISBN 978-3-8382-0507-6 (Hardcover edition)

123 Nicole Krome
Russischer Netzwerkkapitalismus
Restrukturierungsprozesse in der Russischen Föderation am Beispiel des Luftfahrtunternehmens "Aviastar"
Mit einem Vorwort von Petra Stykow
ISBN 978-3-8382-0534-2

Soviet and Post-Soviet Politics and Society (SPPS) Vol. 94
ISSN 1614-3515

General Editor: Andreas Umland,
Kyiv-Mohyla Academy, umland@stanfordalumni.org

Commissioning Editor: Max Jakob Horstmann,
London, mjh@ibidem.eu

EDITORIAL COMMITTEE*

DOMESTIC & COMPARATIVE POLITICS
Prof. **Ellen Bos**, *Andrássy University of Budapest*
Dr. **Ingmar Bredies**, *FH Bund, Brühl*
Dr. **Andrey Kazantsev**, *MGIMO (U) MID RF, Moscow*
Dr. **Heiko Pleines**, *University of Bremen*
Prof. **Richard Sakwa**, *University of Kent at Canterbury*
Dr. **Sarah Whitmore**, *Oxford Brookes University*
Dr. **Harald Wydra**, *University of Cambridge*

SOCIETY, CLASS & ETHNICITY
Col. **David Glantz**, *"Journal of Slavic Military Studies"*
Dr. **Marlène Laruelle**, *George Washington University*
Dr. **Stephen Shulman**, *Southern Illinois University*
Prof. **Stefan Troebst**, *University of Leipzig*

POLITICAL ECONOMY & PUBLIC POLICY
Prof. em. **Marshall Goldman**, *Wellesley College, Mass.*
Dr. **Andreas Goldthau**, *Central European University*
Dr. **Robert Kravchuk**, *University of North Carolina*
Dr. **David Lane**, *University of Cambridge*
Dr. **Carol Leonard**, *University of Oxford*
Dr. **Maria Popova**, *McGill University, Montreal*

FOREIGN POLICY & INTERNATIONAL AFFAIRS
Dr. **Peter Duncan**, *University College London*
Dr. **Taras Kuzio**, *Johns Hopkins University*
Prof. **Gerhard Mangott**, *University of Innsbruck*
Dr. **Diana Schmidt-Pfister**, *University of Konstanz*
Dr. **Lisbeth Tarlow**, *Harvard University, Cambridge*
Dr. **Christian Wipperfürth**, *N-Ost Network, Berlin*
Dr. **William Zimmerman**, *University of Michigan*

HISTORY, CULTURE & THOUGHT
Dr. **Catherine Andreyev**, *University of Oxford*
Prof. **Mark Bassin**, *Södertörn University*
Prof. **Karsten Brüggemann**, *Tallinn University*
Dr. **Alexander Etkind**, *University of Cambridge*
Dr. **Gasan Gusejnov**, *Moscow State University*
Prof. em. **Walter Laqueur**, *Georgetown University*
Prof. **Leonid Luks**, *Catholic University of Eichstaett*
Dr. **Olga Malinova**, *Russian Academy of Sciences*
Prof. **Andrei Rogatchevski**, *University of Tromsø*
Dr. **Mark Tauger**, *West Virginia University*
Dr. **Stefan Wiedekehr**, *BBAW, Berlin*

ADVISORY BOARD*

Prof. **Dominique Arel**, *University of Ottawa*
Prof. **Jörg Baberowski**, *Humboldt University of Berlin*
Prof. **Margarita Balmaceda**, *Seton Hall University*
Dr. **John Barber**, *University of Cambridge*
Prof. **Timm Beichelt**, *European University Viadrina*
Dr. **Katrin Boeckh**, *University of Munich*
Prof. em. **Archie Brown**, *University of Oxford*
Dr. **Vyacheslav Bryukhovetsky**, *Kyiv-Mohyla Academy*
Prof. **Timothy Colton**, *Harvard University, Cambridge*
Prof. **Paul D'Anieri**, *University of Florida*
Dr. **Heike Dörrenbächer**, *DGO, Berlin*
Prof. **John Dunlop**, *Hoover Institution, Stanford, California*
Dr. **Sabine Fischer**, *SWP, Berlin*
Dr. **Geir Flikke**, *NUPI, Oslo*
Prof. **David Galbreath**, *University of Aberdeen*
Prof. **Alexander Galkin**, *Russian Academy of Sciences*
Prof. **Frank Golczewski**, *University of Hamburg*
Dr. **Nikolas Gvosdev**, *Naval War College, Newport, RI*
Prof. **Mark von Hagen**, *Arizona State University*
Dr. **Guido Hausmann**, *University of Freiburg i.Br.*
Prof. **Dale Herspring**, *Kansas State University*
Dr. **Stefani Hoffman**, *Hebrew University of Jerusalem*
Prof. **Mikhail Ilyin**, *MGIMO (U) MID RF, Moscow*
Prof. **Vladimir Kantor**, *Higher School of Economics*
Dr. **Ivan Katchanovski**, *University of Ottawa*
Prof. em. **Andrzej Korbonski**, *University of California*
Dr. **Iris Kempe**, *"Caucasus Analytical Digest"*
Prof. **Herbert Küpper**, *Institut für Ostrecht Regensburg*
Dr. **Rainer Lindner**, *CEEER, Berlin*
Dr. **Vladimir Malakhov**, *Russian Academy of Sciences*

Dr. **Luke March**, *University of Edinburgh*
Prof. **Michael McFaul**, *US Embassy at Moscow*
Prof. **Birgit Menzel**, *University of Mainz-Germersheim*
Prof. **Valery Mikhailenko**, *The Urals State University*
Prof. **Emil Pain**, *Higher School of Economics, Moscow*
Dr. **Oleg Podvintsev**, *Russian Academy of Sciences*
Prof. **Olga Popova**, *St. Petersburg State University*
Dr. **Alex Pravda**, *University of Oxford*
Dr. **Erik van Ree**, *University of Amsterdam*
Dr. **Joachim Rogall**, *Robert Bosch Foundation Stuttgart*
Prof. **Peter Rutland**, *Wesleyan University, Middletown*
Prof. **Marat Salikov**, *The Urals State Law Academy*
Dr. **Gwendolyn Sasse**, *University of Oxford*
Prof. **Jutta Scherrer**, *EHESS, Paris*
Prof. **Robert Service**, *University of Oxford*
Mr. **James Sherr**, *RIIA Chatham House London*
Dr. **Oxana Shevel**, *Tufts University, Medford*
Dr. **Eberhard Schneider**, *University of Siegen*
Prof. **Olexander Shnyrkov**, *Shevchenko University, Kyiv*
Prof. **Hans-Henning Schröder**, *SWP, Berlin*
Prof. **Yuri Shapoval**, *Ukrainian Academy of Sciences*
Prof. **Viktor Shnirelman**, *Russian Academy of Sciences*
Dr. **Lisa Sundstrom**, *University of British Columbia*
Dr. **Philip Walters**, *"Religion, State and Society", Oxford*
Dr. **Zenon Wasyliw**, *Ithaca College, New York State*
Dr. **Lucan Way**, *University of Toronto*
Dr. **Markus Wehner**, *"Frankfurter Allgemeine Zeitung"*
Dr. **Andrew Wilson**, *University College London*
Prof. **Jan Zielonka**, *University of Oxford*
Prof. **Andrei Zorin**, *University of Oxford*

* While the Editorial Committee and Advisory Board support the General Editor in the choice and improvement of manuscripts for publication, responsibility for remaining errors and misinterpretations in the series' volumes lies with the books' authors.

FOREWORD TO THE SECOND EDITION

I first watched *One Day in the Life of Ivan Denisovich* as a seventeen year old A-level History student. I had read Solzhenitsyn's novella, borrowing my teacher's Penguin paperback copy. Shortly afterwards BBC2 aired the movie. The family had recently acquired a new TV and video recorder from my dad's redundancy money (this was early Thatcherism and this was the industrial north east of England), so I was able to save a copy on videocassette. Years later, as a university academic specializing in Russian history, I wanted to use movies as a historical source, to give students a visual insight into the knowledge normally acquired through the study of texts. For 'authenticity' my inclination was to draw upon Soviet movies through the usual suspects – *The Battleship Potemkin* (early Soviet period), *The Cranes Are Flying* (Khrushchev), *Moscow Does Not Believe in Tears* (Brezhnev), and *Little Vera* (Gorbachev). The exception was this favourite Western cinematic adaptation of a crucial text of Khrushchev's de-Stalinisation. Despite the English and despite the non-Soviet setting, there is honesty to this dramatization that conveys authenticity. When videocassette was becoming technologically obsolete in the classroom, the university technicians transferred it to DVD. After a chance meeting in Glasgow and an accidental academic conversation about current teaching topics and methods, I lent my copy to colleague Andrei Rogachevskii to use in his own teaching. Subsequently he let it slip that he had gone on to co-author a book on filming the impossible, of which the current text is the second edition.

Why does *One Day* remain, for me, a crucial teaching tool? Why not just use the book? It does not make easy viewing, especially for a younger audience embedded in a culture of fast moving action and instant news. It challenges by its pace, by its silence, by the drama of non-drama. Rogachevskii and his co-author Ben Hellman note that for some critics this left them cold, without a sense of emotional involvement. Exactly – numbness, ambiguity, confusion are appropriate responses. Above all, I show *One Day* in class because this is a remarkable film that takes a text to a new level of visual art. It speaks directly to the audience as individuals and as a collective about that most difficult of questions: what was life like in the camps? From Tom Courtenay's narration to the high quality acting in a brilliant and believable set, I defy anyone not to be moved by circumstances in which all, guards and prisoners, are entrapped by life in the camp. Through this movie we feel alternatively the boredom, the drabness, the friendship, the fear, the hope, and the taste of sausage or of tobacco. The editor of *Novyi Mir*, the Soviet journal that published *One Day*, praised Solzhenitsyn for encapsulating the contradictions of a complex time in the history of the USSR through well-rounded characters. In this *One Day* the film more than captures the spirit of *One Day* the book.

First, it establishes an individual point of view. This is history not as the result of class forces or organisations such as the Communist Party. It is the validity of first-hand experience that is incredibly difficult for us, 'non-camp inmates', to question. As Rogachevskii and Hellman point out, Solzhenitsyn felt that the camp was insufficiently realistic – clothes are too fine, prisoners are too well fed. The understandable ex-*zek* sensitivity will not be shared by most viewers for whom the stark conditions will be apparent.

Second, despite the prominence given to Ivan Denisovich, there is no dominant narrative as there are as many experiences of camp life as there are individuals. Each inmate lives Ivan's day in his own fashion: one avoids the cells, another ends up in them; one enjoys a comfortable office job and conversations about art, another picks at ice in the open air to help lay the foundations of what will be the People's Centre for Cultural Activities.

Third, it illustrates the complexity of a range of camp relationships, prisoner-prisoner, prisoner-guard, and guard-guard. There could be collaboration in breaking rules between prisoner and guard, for example, in order to make conditions a little more bearable – as when Ivan is let off punishment for getting up late so that a floor can be cleaned.

Fourth, despite the evidently horrible conditions (barrels as latrines, boiled grass as porridge, cramped sleeping arrangements, and a plethora of rules and regulations), this is a story about life. Death is largely absent; the imperative is to survive and to leave the camps. The arch survivor is Ivan Denisovich, able to take pleasure from building a wall to the extent that he works overtime, risking time in the cells to finish off the last of the cement. The Christian character Alyosha even raises a seemingly impossible consideration: why would one wish to leave the camps for the whirlwind of freedom when in the camps one is free to examine one's soul? (Saul Bellow reaches a similar conclusion in *A Dangling Man*).

Fifth, the movie brings out the dilemmas of reform communism. Openness was required and encouraged to face up to the difficult recent Stalinist past. Stalin is linked to the camp system: it is his, not Lenin's portrait that hangs in the officer's rest room. That the lies and distortions of socialism Stalin style were an open secret is clear from a prisoner checking the thermometer to see if the temperature is so low that a non-work day would be declared, and a fellow inmate interjecting: 'Do you think that they would hang one up that gives the real temperature?' Such talk could produce the system's downfall. When a supervisor asks Ivan Denisovich why he is laying cement so thinly he replies: 'Because, citizen, if I lay it on any thicker when the spring comes the whole wall will collapse'. This is the victory of the small man over the bureaucracy. There are limits, though. It is precisely when a commissar's communist honour is brought into public question during a morning search for 'illegal garments' that a harsh punishment is meted out: 'Ten days in the cells (starting this evening)'. One could say so much more about this movie's insights into life in a Stalinist camp and how the topic was tackled under Khrushchev. The point to stress is that *One Day* the movie is not just a historical relic from a Cold War cinematic past. It remains relevant as a celluloid pathway into that past.

Outwith a peculiar and particular Soviet experience, this movie speaks to individual actions and responsibility much more generally and universally. As Wrede himself noted: 'we are what we do; that is not what we do but how we do it that makes us what we are'. Themes that here are presented in a historical camp context are also relevant in peaceful, ordinary, mainstream society, including the most affluent. *One Day* is not cheap Cold War rhetoric, for it has challenging and uncomfortable thoughts that transcend political divisions. The key question, repeated twice, is 'how can we expect someone who is warm to understand someone who is cold?' When this imaginative leap is taken, when true empathy rules, then one hopes that GULAG camps will not be constructed, that dialogue and charity will replace exclusion and violence in all guises, whether harsh or comparatively mild. This is the essence of a humanistic education. Ultimately and paradoxically, *One Day* also remains relevant as a hymn to humanism. We should all be grateful to Hellman and Rogachevskii for this fascinating insight into the making and reception of this remarkable filming of the unfilmable. If I were asked to recommend one movie about the camps, this would be it.

Ian D. Thatcher
Professor of History at the University of Ulster
Helsinki, November 2013

PREFACE TO THE SECOND EDITION

Since the publication of the first edition of our book, several reviews have come out, aimed at the general public,[1] as well as professional[2] and interest groups.[3] While the reviewers' appreciation has been rather generous,[4] we would like to use this opportunity to engage with the few instances of criticism.

One reviewer has accurately noted the absence of any theoretical framework in our book.[5] This has been a deliberate decision on our part. 'Showing instead of telling is what movies are supposed to do',[6] and in that sense the largely descriptive and meditative nature of Solzhenitsyn's *One Day in the Life of Ivan Denisovich*, coupled with its lack of spectacular action and love interest, does not readily lend itself to screen adaptation. Filming the unfilmable successfully is nothing short of a miracle. Can one really develop a theory of something as exceptional as this?

And what exactly is a success, when it comes to film adaptations? Another reviewer alleges that we have presented 'Wrede's *One Day* as a success due simply to its fidelity to the literary source'.[7] If this is how it looks, it is primarily because Wrede himself had opted to make faithfulness to Solzhenitsyn's

---

[1] See Elena Namli, 'Snön och kylan imponerade inte på Solzjenitsyn', *Svenska Dagbladet*, 22 February 2011.
[2] See, for example, *Historical Journal of Film, Radio and Television*, 31:4 (2011), pp. 598-600 (Alexis Klimoff); and *Slavic & East European Journal*, 56 (2), 2012, pp. 319-320 (Olga Klimova).
[3] See *Society for Co-operation in Russian and Soviet Studies: Information Digest*, Autumn 2010, pp. 14-15 (John Riley); and *The Scotland-Russia Forum Review*, December 2010, p. 9 (Claire Knight).
[4] Cf.: 'Hellman and Rogachevskii's book can be a valuable resource for scholars who study either Wrede's films or Solzhenitsyn's literary works' (*Slavic & East European Journal*, 56 (2), 2012, p. 320); the co-authors 'use just about every scrap of evidence, including Wrede's extensive private archive' to 'closely follow the film's production – at some points even turning detective, using Wrede's airline tickets to pursue him across Europe. <...> <The> book is a valuable reminder and hopefully will encourage more interest' (*Society for Co-operation in Russian and Soviet Studies: Information Digest*, Autumn 2010, pp. 14-15).
[5] See *Slavic & East European Journal*, 56 (2), 2012, p. 320.
[6] Terrence Rafferty, 'Henry James Goes to the Movies', *International Herald Tribune*, 26 April 2013.
[7] *The Scotland-Russia Forum Review*, December 2010, p. 9.

book an integral part of his adaptation strategy. It is probably true that, although used all too frequently by film critics, filmgoers and filmmakers alike, 'fidelity to its source text <...> is a hopelessly fallacious measure of a given adaptation's value because it is unattainable, undesirable and theoretically possible only in a trivial sense'.[8] On the occasion, however, it would be unfair not to judge Wrede by his own criteria. As for our own general standpoint on the matter, we are inclined to share Walter Kendrick's view: 'it seems self-evident that to film a book is to interpret it, comment on it, violate it perhaps, but not <necessarily> to capture it' and 'in the rendering of literature into movies, too much respect is worse than too little'.[9]

This quote may serve as our response to the reviewer who has expressed his preference for 'a clear<er> authorial position'.[10] It has to be pointed out, though, that the same reviewer happens to cite from David Robinson's analysis of Wrede's *One Day*, published in *The Financial Times* of 14 January 1972. It is precisely this analysis that comes closest to our own perception of the film's strengths and weaknesses (in particular, the section on Solzhenitsyn's and Wrede's use of understatement that yields different results and makes *One Day* powerful more as a book than as a film[11]). We do hope that other readers have also deducted where our sympathies lie, without much need for us to state it in so many words in a patronisingly obvious way.

On a related issue, another reviewer has wished we would deal more 'with the failure of the film to connect emotionally with numerous critics'.[12] What is termed here a 'failure' may well be rooted in Solzhenitsyn's original: his fan mail contains both complimentary and reproachful mentions of *One Day*'s dispassionate manner.[13] Similarly, Wrede's 'style of directing was not flam-

---

8   Thomas Leitch, 'Twelve Fallacies in Contemporary Adaptation Theory', *Criticism*, vol. 45, no. 2 (Spring 2003), p. 161.
9   Walter Kendrick, 'The Unfilmable', *Salmagundi*, no. 121/122 (Winter-Spring 1999), pp. 50, 60.
10 *Historical Journal of Film, Radio and Television*, 31:4 (2011), p. 600.
11 See pp. 105-06 of the present publication.
12 *The Scotland-Russia Forum Review*, December 2010, p. 9.
13 E.g. the book encapsulates 'the essence of prison life <...> without pathos and embellishment' (the ex-convict Nadezhda Politova in a letter dated winter 1962-63; and 'more anger (*zlost'*) and agitation (*vzvolnovannost'*) would be desirable' (the ex-convict Samuil Lipshits in a letter of 2 December 1962; in G. A. Tiurina (ed.), *Dorogoi*

boyant... so what you saw was pretty unadorned when you saw it... [He] wanted the audience to receive what the <film or> play was about, straight'.[14] Could it be, then, that in the case of *One Day*'s adaptation, Wrede's reserve proved to be somewhat less efficient than Solzhenitsyn's because cinema (as well as theatre) – in contrast to the printed word *per se* – is fundamentally more about the need to arouse concentrated and strong-felt emotions (if only because the spectators have to be kept in their seats for a relatively short period of time, while books are rarely read in one sitting)? Besides, manipulating emotions was not what Wrede had in mind for his version of *One Day*. According to its star, Sir Tom Courtenay, the director 'wanted the film to be otherworldly, which it is'.[15] Going for estrangement in preference to empathy may have been Wrede's way of allowing for the 'basic – perhaps unbridgeable – gap of understanding'[16] (i.e. the inability of the free world to comprehend, and relate to, the suffering under totalitarianism).

The same reviewer observes that we mention 'the documentary-like feel of the film <...>, but without any exploration of the significance, origin, or even intent of this effect'.[17] Once again, the documentariness originates from Solzhenitsyn's book. The author was understandably keen to make the GULAG experience a matter of public record. *One Day*'s first readers, many erstwhile GULAG prisoners among them, called it 'a truthful document' and 'a felicitous snapshot of life in a labour camp', and challenged anyone to find as much as 'a modicum of fancy' in it.[18] It is not therefore too surprising to discover that in

---

Ivan Denisovich!..: Pis'ma chitatelei, 1962-64. Moscow: Russkii put', 2012, pp. 208, 155).

14 Braham Murray, an artistic director of the Royal Exchange Theatre in Manchester and Wrede's long-term collaborator, interviewed by Andrei Rogachevskii on 11 March 2011.
15 Tony Earnshaw, 'Bradford Marks 50 Years of *Billy Liar*', *Yorkshire Post*, 12 April 2013.
16 *Historical Journal of Film, Radio and Television*, 31:4 (2011), p. 599.
17 *The Scotland-Russia Forum Review*, December 2010, p. 9.
18 G. A. Tiurina (ed.), *Dorogoi Ivan Denisovich!..: Pis'ma chitatelei, 1962-64*. Moscow: Russkii put', 2012, pp. 197, 187, 217. Incidentally, documentariness is not always the same as verisimilitude. Solzhenitsyn came under fire from some GULAG inmates, such as V. T. Shalamov, V. G. Iodko and A. V. Movsesian, for misrepresenting various aspects of the camp life (see ibid., pp. 135, 141, 210-11). Despite his intention to look authentic, Wrede is guilty of the same: in the sick bay scene, when Ivan Deniso-

the transition from page to screen Wrede retained Solzhenitsyn's documentary-like approach, just like he tried to keep everything else the book had. Knowing full well that an event has a better chance of surviving in the memory of future generations if it is properly recorded, Wrede presciently did all he could to preserve *One Day* for the visual age.

Let us return, however, to the issue of a film adaptation's success. The box office takings aside, it can be claimed that an adaptation is successful if it works as a film, quite irrespective of its relationship to its literary source. Yet one man's trash is another man's treasure, and it is not always possible to establish beyond any doubt whether or not a film actually works. An example is *Den Første Kreds / The First Circle* (1973) by Aleksander Ford, a Danish/Swedish co-production based on another famous book by Solzhenitsyn and released shortly after Wrede's *One Day*.

The Polish-Jewish director Aleksander Ford held what might be called a competitive advantage in turning Solzhenitsyn's *The First Circle* into a successful film. A forty year long carrier in the film industry had given him the necessary professional skills. As a card-carrying Communist and head of the Polish film production during the first years of Soviet Poland, he had gained quite an insight into the nature of Stalinism. However, in 1968-69, this influential film director and member of the intellectual elite was dismissed from the Polish Filmmakers' Union, expelled from the Communist Party and forced to leave his country as a victim of an anti-Semitic campaign. His films ended up on the list of prohibited works and his name was wiped out from the history of Polish filmmaking. Outside the Eastern Bloc, he managed to resume his work as a film director, with *The First Circle*, shot in Denmark, being his most ambitious project, restricted only by financial considerations.

The film's critical reception upon the 1973 premiere makes a strange reading.[19] An extremely harsh, not to say insulting, tone of many reviews is rather

---

vich's temperature gets measured, Courtney takes the thermometer in his mouth, while the Russian custom dictates putting it under one's armpit.

19 Twelve American film reviews are quoted in *Filmfacts* (Vol. XVI, No. 1, 1973, pp. 26-28), three of them – from *New York Times*, *Newsweek* and *Time* – in extenso, and those from *New York*, *Cue*, *Los Angeles Times*, *Newsday*, *N.Y. Daily News*, *Village Voice*, *San Francisco Chronicle*, *New Yorker* and *Washington Post* in abridgement.

striking. The film is called 'fairly unforgivable' (*New York Times*), 'a complete shambles' deserving 'to be laughed off the screen' (*The New York Daily News*), 'a crime against literature' (*Newsday*), a 'barbarous adaption of the novel' (*Time*), 'an atrocity' and even 'crap' (the *New York* magazine). It looks as if some critics, anticipating Solzhenitsyn's negative attitude, took the task of defending the honour of a respected writer, persecuted in his own country and unable to speak up against the attempts by profit-hungry producers in the West to create sensation and make money off his work. Turning a large novel with its many themes and characters into a 100-minute long film was considered a task even more difficult than Wrede's endeavour. It was *a priori* doomed to fail both as a work of art and an illustration of Solzhenitsyn's novel. Consequently, all aspects of the film were seen as disastrous by the distrustful critics.

In their reviews, Ford was accused of turning the book into a flat, static film, lacking in passion and immediacy. The filmmakers' wish to cover the novel in its entirety resulted in very little of it being left. Solzhenitsyn's criticism of the Communist system became reductive and his anger nullified. The novel's characters were moved to a timeless, abstract unreality, with all their features simplified. The descriptive parts of the novel were rendered through pale and lifeless visual devices. Ford also came under attack for filming in colour, instead of black and white. His choice of a multinational cast produced an 'international mess' with a tastelessly dubbed dialogue. As a result, spectators watched *The First Circle* without any emotional engagement.

Nevertheless, there were alternative voices, cautiously ready to accept Ford's film on its own terms. It packs 'a considerable punch', declared *Newsweek*. The agony was there: it was a passionate *cri de coeur* against the tyranny of our times. And *The New Yorker* found *The First Circle* to be a thoughtful film, forcing cinema audiences to face the same issues that the book had raised. It was 'an intelligent condensation of the novel', true to the spirit of Solzhenitsyn's work, declared *Washington Post*. The power of accusation was still

---

Also, *Films in Review* (No. 24, 1973, p. 183), the Swedish newspaper *Dagens Nyheter* (13 November 1973) and the Swedish film journal *Chaplin* (No 127, 1973, p. 290) have been consulted.

there (*Dagens Nyheter*) and Solzhenitsyn's anti-totalitarian message did come through (*Chaplin*). Even the cast was praised as talented and apt.

It seems as if *The First Circle* – in fact, a decent, sombre and respectable film – gains in credit as Solzhenitsyn's struggle against Communism recedes into history and the audiences no longer seek primarily to compare the book and the film and to judge the latter, first and foremost, by its truthfulness to every aspect of the novel. Phil Berardelli, an enthusiastic cineaste, includes *The First Circle* among his five hundred favourites, calling Ford's film 'a compelling work', 'a small movie, but beautifully written and crafted – and making as a point of wisdom that a man who has nothing to lose also has nothing to fear'.[20] And the influential Finnish cinema critic Antti Alanen, who watched the film in 2012 on its Finnish premiere, has found the structure of the screenplay to be successful in its own right. According to him, the film did justice to Solzhenitsyn's main themes and wit, and its atmosphere rang true, as if personally felt. 'It's a memorable movie',[21] concluded Alanen.

The First Circle can easily serve as an example of how fatally misunderstood some films are. It seems every now and then that all a film needs is a bit of luck. We do hope that, sooner or later, Wrede's *One Day* will have its lucky break.

BH, AR

---

20 Phil Berardelli, *Phil's Favorite 500: Loves of a Moviegoing Lifetime,* Mountain Lake Press, 2011. The e-book version we have used lacks page numbering.
21 Antti Alanen, *Film Diary,* http://anttialanenfilmdiary.blogspot.no/2012/08/den-frste-kreds-first-circle.html (consulted on 8 December 2013).

INTRODUCTION

When the Nobel-Prize-winning Russian author Aleksandr Solzhenitsyn died of heart failure on 3 August 2008, at the age of 89, his legacy was summed up as railing 'against all forms of what he saw as spiritual darkness',[1] although his stance could frequently be characterised as 'conservative moralising'[2] and was sometimes perceived to be 'domineering and self-righteous'.[3] Yet all observers unanimously praised Solzhenitsyn for the role he had played in revealing to the world the nature of the Soviet penitentiary system and the Soviet regime in general. Such revelations had begun long before Solzhenitsyn,[4] but only the appearance of his story *One Day in the Life of Ivan Denisovich*, printed in 1962 by special permission of the Soviet leader Nikita Khrushchev as part of his policy of de-Stalinisation, managed to capture the attention of a broad cross-section of readers across the globe. The story has been labelled a 'sensation' by *The Times*, *The Guardian* and *The New York Times*,[5] and one reader called it 'a *Day* that shook the world'.[6] In December 1963, as a sign of its wide recognition in Solzhenitsyn's native country, the journal *Novyi mir* and the Central State Archive for Literature and Art (TsGALI) nominated *One Day* for a Lenin Prize, one of the Soviet Union's most prestigious annual awards. However, with the deposition of Khrushchev in 1964 and a moderate re-Stalinisation under his successor, Leonid Brezhnev, the 'hard-liners, who feared that Solzhenitsyn had opened a Pan-

---

1 The unsigned obituary 'Aleksandr Solzhenitsyn: Indomitable Russian Writer' in *The Times* of 5 August 2008.
2 Ibid.
3 The unsigned obituary 'Alexander Solzhenitsyn, Voice of the Gulag' in *The Daily Telegraph* of 4 August 2008.
4 See, for example, Libushe Zorin, *Soviet Prisons and Concentration Camps: An Annotated Bibliography, 1917-1980*, Newtonville, Mass.: Oriental Research Partners, 1980, pp. 7-84.
5 See the unsigned obituary 'Aleksandr Solzhenitsyn: Indomitable Russian Writer' in *The Times* of 5 August 2008; Damien Francis, 'Solzhenitsyn, Soviet Dissident Writer, Dies at 89', *The Guardian*, 4 August 2008; and Michael T. Kaufman, 'Solzhenitsyn, Literary Giant Who Defied Soviets, Dies at 89', *The New York Times*, 4 August 2008.
6 N. Reshetovskaia, *Solzhenitsyn i chitaiushchaia Rossiia*, Moscow: Sovetskaia Rossiia, 1990, p. 98.

dora's box from which the evils of the Soviet system would escape and sweep the regime away',[7] did everything within their power to block the author's further publications in his homeland. Solzhenitsyn's two major novels, *The First Circle* (1968) and *Cancer Ward* (1968-69), came out in the West without the required permission of the Soviet authorities. In November 1969, he was expelled from the Soviet Writers' Union, and in February 1974, after the publication in Paris in December 1973 of the first volume of his non-fictional *Gulag Archipelago* – called by the American statesman George F. Keenan 'the greatest and most powerful single indictment of a political regime ever to be levelled in modern times'[8] – he was expelled from the Soviet Union 'for the systematic execution of actions incompatible with Soviet citizenship and harmful to the USSR',[9] to return only in 1994.

In all these and subsequent years, even *The Gulag Archipelago*, Solzhenitsyn's three-volume magnum opus on political repression in Soviet Russia in 1918-1956, could not fully surpass *One Day in the Life of Ivan Denisovich* in importance, possibly because the latter, a slender book in an easily accessible fictional form, seems to contain in a nutshell most of what the average reader needs to know about life in Stalin's labour camps and, at the same time, generates a universal appeal by serving as an 'affirmation of man's will for survival and his capability of achieving and maintaining dignity under almost unbelievably inhuman conditions'.[10] *One Day*'s lasting significance was re-emphasised by the decision of the BBC Russian Service to mark the twentieth anniversary of the book's publication by broadcasting its entire text, read by the author, to listeners in the Soviet Union, on a short wave frequency. In his interview with the journalist Barry Holland that accompanied the broadcast in November 1982, Solzhenitsyn compared the publication of *One Day* in the Soviet Union, which had occurred thanks to a collaboration of several outstanding personalities and a combination of improbable circumstances, to a

---

7   Carol J. Williams, 'Solzhenitsyn, Chronicler of Russia under Communism, Dies at 89', *The Los Angeles Times*, 4 August 2008.
8   J. Y. Smith, 'Nobel Winner Chronicled Tyranny of Soviet Union', *The Washington Post*, 4 August 2008.
9   Michael Scammell, *Solzhenitsyn: A Biography*, London: Hutchinson, 1985, p. 840.
10 Richard Luplow, 'Narrative Style and Structure in *One Day in the Life of Ivan Denisovich*', *Russian Literature Triquarterly*, No. 1 (1971), p. 399.

situation when objects start rising from the ground, or cold stones become red-hot, for no apparent reason, defying the laws of physics.[11] In his later memoirs, recalling how he recorded *One Day* for this broadcast, Solzhenitsyn talked, perhaps immodestly but not inappropriately, of sensing the story's timeless nature.[12] A recent Swiss article reaffirms this sensation, well familiar not only to *One Day*'s author but to many other people, by quoting the Soviet literary critic Vladimir Lakshin, who claimed in 1964 that the story is 'destined to have a long life'.[13]

One Day in the Life of Ivan Denisovich was written in 1959, revised and submitted for publication in 1961, first published in the November 1962 issue of the literary journal *Novyi mir*[14] and then appeared in a separate edition in the *Roman-gazeta* series (no. 1, 1963) and under the imprint of the Sovetskii pisatel' publishers (also in 1963). Ten years later, its full, uncensored version – known as the 'canonical' one[15] – was issued in book form in Paris by YMCA-Press. By 1973, *One Day* had been translated into more than thirty languages, including Afrikaans, Albanian, Bengali, Chinese, Hebrew, Icelandic, Malayalam and Slovene (with at least two different translations available in Czech, Italian, Korean, Portuguese, Swedish and Turkish; at least three, in

---

11   See A. I. Solzhenitsyn, *Publitsistika v trekh tomakh*, Iaroslavl': Verkhniaia Volga, 1997, vol. 3, p. 25.
12   A. I. Solzhenitsyn, 'Ugodilo zernyshko promezh dvukh zhernovov', *Novyi mir*, no. 9 (2000), p. 180.
13   V. Lakshin, 'Ivan Denisovich, ego druz'ia i nedrugi', *Novyi mir*, no. 1 (1964), p. 245.
14   For more on the magazine, see, for instance, Linda Aldwinckle, *The Politics of Novyi mir, 1950-1970*, PhD thesis, London School of Economics and Political Science, 1977; Edith Rogovin Frankel, *Novy mir: A Case Study in the Politics of Literature, 1952-1958*, Cambridge: Cambridge University Press, 1981; and Dina R. Spechler, *Permitted Dissent in the USSR: Novy mir and the Soviet Regime*, New York: Praeger, 1982.
15   Gary Kern, 'Solženicyn's Self-Censorship: The Canonical Text of *Odin den' Ivana Denisoviča*', *The Slavic and East European Journal*, vol. 20, no. 4 (1976), p. 429. However, in the third volume of Solzhenitsyn's *Collected Works* published in Russian in Vermont in 1978, *One Day* 'appeared with a small number of further emendations. <…> It follows that only <this> text <…> can be regarded as canonical' (Alexis Klimoff, 'The Sober Eye: Ivan Denisovich and the Peasant Perspective', in Alexis Klimoff (ed.), *One Day in the Life of Ivan Denisovich: A Critical Companion*, Evanston, IL: Northwestern University Press, 1997, p. 23). To avoid complicating matters unnecessarily, in our study the term 'canonical' refers to the first uncensored publication of 1973 only.

German; at least four, in Greek; and at least five, in English, Japanese and Spanish).[16]

Solzhenitsyn's story describes one day in a high-security labour camp, where convicts are required to wear identification numbers on their clothes, in Kazakhstan in January 1951. The main character is a peasant prisoner called Ivan Denisovich Shukhov, who had received a ten-year sentence for allegedly spying for the Germans, as he had been held by them for several days on the North-Western front in early 1942, and had then escaped and rejoined the Russian troops (ostensibly to carry out the instructions of Nazi intelligence). Shukhov's day in the camp, from getting up at 5am to lights out at 10pm, includes both routine actions (such as having his three daily meals and marching to work and back) and exceptional features (such as being ordered to wash the floor in a guards' room as a punishment for getting up late, unsuccessfully trying to obtain exemption from work on medical grounds, deceiving the cook into parting with two extra bowls of gruel at lunchtime and erecting a brick wall at a power station construction site).

A number of inmates from Ivan Denisovich's team (known as Team 104) are also focused upon. These include the Baptist Alyoshka, convicted for his religious beliefs; the naval captain Buinovsky, falsely accused of spying for the British; the Latvian Kilgas,[17] two Estonians (one of whom is called Eino, while the other's name is not given) and two Ukrainians (Gopchik and Pavlo), arrested in the aftermath of Stalin's takeover of the Baltic States and Western Ukraine; Senka Klevshin, a former prisoner of Buchenwald, now serving time in a labour camp back home; Fetyukov, a former high-ranking official, now reduced to cadging cigarette butts and licking out other people's bowls; Tsesar Markovich, a former film director, now holding a cushy job as a norm checker's assistant at the construction site office; and the team leader Andrei Prokofievich Tyurin, the son of a *kulak*.

---

16 Donald M. Fiene, *Alexander Solzhenitsyn: An International Bibliography of Writings by and about Him*, Ann Arbor: Ardis, 1973; Werner Martin (Hrsgb.), *Aleksander Solschenizyn: Eine Bibliographie seiner Werke*, Hildesheim: Olms, 1977.
17 In the canonical text of the story, the name of this character has been changed to Kildigs.

The book's world-wide popularity (by the mid-1960s, its composite print run, including translations, had reached a million copies[18]) made it natural to expect that it would be considered for film adaptation. Soon after *One Day*'s publication, Solzhenitsyn received several offers to turn it into a film in the Soviet Union, but he declined them all, because, according to his first wife Natalya Reshetovskaia, at that point in time he was against making a film version of the book as a matter of principle, believing that every work of art could have only one optimal form of expression.[19] The post-1964 political changes, unfavourable to Solzhenitsyn, put paid to further attempts to adapt his works for the Soviet screen (although the Lenfilm studios briefly entertained the possibility of filming his short story 'Sluchai na stantsii Kochetovka' <An Incident at Kochetovka Station> and even talked about signing a contract to that effect).[20] As for the film industries in the West, from their point of view, *One Day*

> lacked, to say the least, a certain glamorous appeal. Presumably, the motion picture studios' reports on the subject would have contained a resume as follows: 'Set in Siberia, in Soviet prison camp. Lots of snow. Lots of long Russian names. No women. No escapes. No violence. <...> CONCLUSION: Depressing. Dismal locale. RECOMMENDATION: Not for us'.[21]

It took the resolve and determination of one person, the British-trained theatre and television director Casper Wrede, and the commitment of those he had inspired to assist him, to make the idea of adapting *One Day* for the screen a reality. To fill a gap in Solzhenitsyn studies,[22] this study discusses little-known

---

18   See Reshetovskaia, op. cit., p. 178.
19   Ibid., pp. 70, 94.
20   See Reshetovskaia, op. cit., p. 122. In the first publication of the story (*Novyi mir*, no. 1, 1963), the name of the station was changed to Krechetovka, to avoid displeasure of the author Vsevolod Kochetov (1912-73), editor-in-chief of the *Oktiabr'* magazine (*Novyi mir*'s main literary rival at the time).
21   Ronald Harwood, 'Introduction', *The Making of One Day in the Life of Ivan Denisovich* <by> *Alexander Solzhenitsyn*, transl. by Gillon Aitken, Introduction and Screenplay by Ronald Harwood, New York: Ballantine Books, 1971, p. 3 (hereafter referred to as *The Making*).
22   To the best of our knowledge, Wrede's film has never been analysed in press by Solzhenitsyn scholars, except for a brief mention praising it as an antidote to 'some-

facts, partly drawn from archival sources, about the film's pre-production and production history, compares the film to the book and analyses the film's reception and impact, especially in some Scandinavian countries, Britain and the US, against the background of Solzhenitsyn's complex relationship with the art of film making.

---

    times ludicrous travesties which were perpetrated when some of <Solzhenitsyn's> works were transferred to screen or stage. Honourable exceptions to this would include the film of *Ivan Denisovich* starring Tom Courtenay' (Robert Porter, *Solzhenitsyn's One Day in the Life of Ivan Denisovich*, London: Bristol Classical Press, 1997). An otherwise authoritative source on *One Day* the book mistakenly names one of the companies involved in the film's production as 'Leontief', instead of 'Leontes' (see Klimoff (ed.), op. cit., p. 128). There does not seem to be much beyond that.

1 A FILM IN THE CAREER OF CASPER WREDE

According to Casper Wrede's documents, issued by his Helsinki parish before he enrolled as a student at the University of Helsinki, he was born on 8 February 1929 in Lappee, Eastern Karelia (near the town of Lappeenranta), into a wealthy aristocratic Swedish family.[23] Soon the family moved to the neighbouring city of Viipuri, Finland (now Vyborg, Russia).[24] As a result of the Winter War of 1939-40, Viipuri came under Soviet jurisdiction. Shortly before that, the Wredes had fled the city, first to their relatives in Norway, and then, on the eve of the German occupation of Norway, to Sweden. In autumn 1940, the Wredes returned to Finland and settled in Helsinki. Casper was accepted into the third year at Tölö Svenska Samskola, a Swedish gymnasium in Helsinki. It has been suggested that in 1944, at the age of fifteen, he served, apparently as a volunteer, in an anti-aircraft defence unit in Helsinki, but there are no documents to verify this.[25] In 1946, he graduated from Tölö Svenska Samskola with the highest mark (*laudatur*). His favourite subject was history,[26] but his school certificate reveals that he was also good at languages, arts and sport. In autumn 1946, Casper Wrede enrolled as a student at the Faculty of Arts, University of Helsinki, but did not sit exams for any courses. On 22 April 1947, he enrolled as a Faculty of Arts student at the University of Gothenburg for the Spring semester of 1947 (matriculation number 1746/4988) but did not pay his fees and did not re-enrol in the autumn.[27] Afterwards he worked as a freelance journalist in Norway, where he met his mentor Amund Hønningstad (1908-72) – a translator of Fromm and Nietzsche

---

23 For the Wrede coat of arms, see Appendix IV, pic. 1.
24 Wrede's son David, however, asserts that Casper had always referred to Viipuri as his birthplace.
25 Wrede mentioned more than once that he had a 'short experience of army life during the war' (see Erkki Arni, 'Nobel-kirjailijan filmaus vaatii näyttelijältä sisua: Suomalainen rakensi Stalinin vankileirin', *Helsingin Sanomat*, 13 December 1970), serving as a 'schoolboy soldier' (Jack Allen, '*Ivan Denisovich* Film Culmination of Dream', *The Buffalo Courier-Express*, 27 September 1971), but would not give any details.
26 Marie-Louise Fock, '"Casper" – teater i England', *Astra* (Helsinki), no. 1, 1955, p. 4.
27 This information has been kindly supplied by Lars Kristensen who did research at the Gothenburg University Archives on our behalf.

into Norwegian and the editor of the *Samfunnsliv* (Society Life) journal. Hønningstad

> saw our civilisation as being at the end of a 2,000-year cycle spiritually; <...> that the power of Christianity was now declining. That its hold as the spiritual regulator was weakening. That we were living in a time which would become increasingly degenerate as we lost all sense of that wise voice within which told us how to live. <...> He believed that as one spiritual impulse declined, another was being born: degeneration was always followed by regeneration. A Martian visiting Britain in February would see a grey, barren land. If you told him that within three months <...> everything would be transformed he would ask, 'But where is all this going to come from?' The answer would be that it is already happening, under the earth. <...> in February, the activity under the ground is phenomenal, preparing for spring. Then when it comes to fruition it does so suddenly and dramatically. <...> Amund taught that this was where we now stood. We could not see what was to come but we could be sure that it would come. Our job was to hold on to all that remained powerful and positive from the declining civilisation, to keep the ground fertile for the new impulse when it came. <...> What Casper wanted to know was what he should do, what anyone could do, to further this end <ie regeneration>. Amund's reply was astonishing. The power to change things lies <...> rarely in so-called leaders in the political world. Politicians follow what is actually taking place, they maintain power by gauging what the *Zeitgeist* demands. The people who have always led have been the artists. They have been the visionaries, and, through their art, have directly influenced the hearts and minds of civilisations. In our time one art form was more important than any other: the theatre. With the decline of religion, theatre was the only place where people came together in a community and experienced the mysteries. <...> The two men, who knew nothing of the theatrical world, did their research. England was the centre of world drama. Casper must go and study theatre in England.[28]

---

28 Braham Murray, *The Worst It Can Be Is a Disaster: The Life Story of Braham Murray and the Royal Exchange Theatre*, London: Methuen Drama, 2007, pp. 65-66. Hønningstad continued to exert some creative influence on Wrede at a later stage too. The

While in Norway, Wrede made contact with theatre circles, started publishing on theatrical topics and was even asked to direct a play for the Oslo Student Theatre. As he did not have any professional training or experience, he declined the offer. Nevertheless, his interest in theatre had been awoken. The fact that his aunt, Gerda Wrede, was an actress and a director at the Swedish Theatre in Helsinki, also helped. In 1950, Wrede entered the Old Vic School in London, having been told that this was 'the best thing in the world of its kind. If you want to learn about the theatre, go there'.[29] Among his tutors were the French actor and drama theorist Michel Saint-Denis (1897-1971) who had revolutionised English theatre in the 1930s; the influential theatre manager and teacher George Devine (1910-66); and the school's director Glen Byam Shaw (1904-86), one of Britain's greatest Shakespeare experts.

> Many more candidates had applied for entry to this prestigious new theatre school than could be accommodated, and what chance had a Finn with no theatrical experience at all? But Glen Byam Shaw was interested in military matters, and in artillery in particular, and on Wrede's mentioning that he had served in the artillery <...>, Byam Shaw questioned him closely for half an hour on the subject and then told him that he was accepted.[30]

At the Old Vic school, where Wrede studied directing, he met his future wife, the actress Dilys Hamlett (1928-2002),[31] as well as James Maxwell (1929-95) who played the Captain in *Ivan Denisovich*, and the designer Richard Negri (1927-99) who later turned the derelict Cotton Exchange building in Manchester into the Royal Exchange Theatre – home of one of Wrede's companies –

---

two collaborated on the 1967 adaptation of Gogol's *Diary of a Madman* for the Norwegian television, and on the 1968 production of Gogol's *Government Inspector* for the National Theatre in Oslo.

29   The unsigned article 'What Are the Prospects for Theatrical Adventure?' in *The Times* of 3 April 1959.
30   Michael Meyer, *Not Prince Hamlet: A Life in Literary and Theatrical London*, Oxford: Oxford University Press, 1990, p. 126. For Wrede's description of the school, see his 'Old Vics Teaterskola', *Handels- och Sjöfarts-Tidning*, 20 August 1951.
31   In 1951, Wrede 'and a group of fellow students returned very late to their afternoon class with the excuse that he had been delayed by his marriage to Dilys Hamlett' (Trevor Peacock, 'Casper Wrede', *The Independent*, 30 September 1998). For an appreciation of Dilys Hamlett's life, see *The Times* of 9 November 2002.

'the most distinguished and acclaimed theatre outside London, some would say superior to any in London, including the National'.[32] When after one year, four of the new students were selected to continue their studies, Wrede was one of them. At the end of every year the students were obliged to direct a play with other students engaged as actors. Wrede's first work was a production of Shakespeare's *All's Well That Ends Well*.

Upon leaving the school in 1952, Wrede directed various productions at the Edinburgh Festival and for the Oxford University Dramatic Society (OUDS), including Strindberg's *Miss Julie*, Marlowe's *Edward II* and Euripides's *Hippolytus*.[33] In 1955 and 1956 respectively, Wrede directed Shakespeare's *Twelfth Night* and Lope de Vega's *Fuente Ovejuna* for a festival in Varberg, Sweden. In June 1956, at the Victoria Palace in London, Wrede co-directed (with George Hall) a musical comedy called *Jubilee Girl* by Alexander Kevin (music) and Robin Fordyce and David Rogers (lyrics), about a country girl who arrives in London to become one of the first female secretaries.

Together with Michael Elliott (1931-84), whom he had met at Oxford and who acted as assistant director on some of Wrede's productions, he became a trainee TV director at the BBC.[34] January 1957 saw Wrede's and Elliott's first co-production for television theatre, at that time a fairly new cultural medium. It was Anton Chekhov's *Uncle Vanya*. Wrede had taken an interest in Chekhov's plays while still at the Old Vic School, analyzing *Uncle Vanya* and producing *Three Sisters*. In this TV version of *Uncle Vanya*, Wrede strove to stress the humorous side of the play at the expense of its tragic elements. Although the London *Times* found the production 'as taut as an overstrained violin string; speeches were rattled smartly off, tea was gulped down with indecent haste, close-up followed close-up in unselective profusion',[35] the result led to more TV assignments for both Wrede and Elliott. Shakespeare's

---

32 Meyer, op. cit., p. 195.
33 Wrede's production of *Edward II* deserved special praise for his handling of the mass scenes and the lighting, see Marie-Louise Fock, 'Casper Wrede retrospektivt', *Hufvudstadsbladet*, 5 April 1957.
34 Afterwards, Wrede described this career turn as being '"hauled" into <working in> a medium which he'd hardly ever seen' (Cameron Dewar, 'Life in a Siberian Labor Camp', *The Boston Herald-Traveler*, the Show Guide supplement, 3 October 1971).
35 The unsigned note 'BBC Television: "Uncle Vanya"' in *The Times* of 21 January 1957.

Twelfth Night, again co-produced by Wrede and Elliott, was broadcast by the BBC in March of the same year. In May 1957, Wrede and Elliott co-directed for TV *The Survivors* by Irwin Shaw and Peter Viertel, a drama set in the period shortly after the American Civil War. The following year saw Elliott's and Wrede's television adaptation of Euripides's *Women of Troy* (January), followed by Laurence Olivier's debut in TV theatre in Wrede's production of *John Gabriel Borkman* by Ibsen (November).

Wrede preferred to 'work for television on a free-lance basis, thus enabling himself to have ample time to prepare for his productions. He took three months to prepare for *John Gabriel Borkman*',[36] whereas a producer or director under contract may have had to do all his/her work on a play in a month or so and then be limited to only a couple of days in the studio because of the shortage of studios and camera crews.

One of Wrede's responsibilities as a producer was directing the actors.[37] He swiftly earned the reputation of being 'probably the best producer of television drama whose work has been seen in this country'.[38] He mainly worked with a classical repertoire showing little interest for the modern theatre of the absurd exemplified by Ionesco, Beckett and Pinter. Wrede used to say: 'I don't like anti-theatre, where the subject is exhausted in advance and the dramatic power is missing. What there is left to be acted out, that is tedium and emptiness, is not enough'.[39]

In 1959, Wrede co-founded the 59 Theatre Company, characterised by a 'fixed determination to give the public not what it is supposed to want but what it ought to want'.[40] The enterprise was bankrolled by James H. Lawrie, a vice-president of the British Bankers' Association and a managing director of

---

36 Michael Wall, 'Directing for the Actor', *The Manchester Guardian*, 7 May 1959.
37 See Ossian Trilling, 'Trettondagsafton i BBC i regi av Casper Wrede', *Nya Pressen* (Helsinki), 27 March 1957.
38 The review of the BBC production of *John Gabriel Borkman* in *The Manchester Guardian* of 21 November 1958.
39 Meta, 'Åbostoff till story för film om Sibelius', *Åbo Underrättelser* (Turku), 31 October 1964.
40 The unsigned review 'A Magnificent Performance: Ibsen's *Brand* Seen Clearly' in *The Times* of 9 April 1959.

the National Film Finance Corporation.[41] For six months, the company presented *Danton's Death* by Büchner, *Brand* by Ibsen, *The Cheats of Scapin* by Molière (in Thomas Otway's seventeenth-century adaptation), *The Creditors* by Strindberg and *The Rough and Ready Lot* by Alun Owen at the Lyric Theatre in Hammersmith and attracted national attention (the company's versions of *Danton's Death* and *Brand* were even televised in May and August of the same year). For a small part in Ibsen's *Brand*, Wrede hired a South African actor and playwright, Ronald Harwood (b. 1934), the husband of the 59 Theatre Company's stage manager Natasha Richie. Thus began Wrede's collaboration with Harwood (now a renowned screenwriter, who has been awarded an Oscar for the script of Roman Polanski's *The Pianist*, and a CBE).[42] In April 1961, Wrede directed a television version of Harwood's play, *Private Potter* (a year later turned into a film for an MGM release by very much the same creative team), about a soldier whose behaviour, on a mission to apprehend a leader of the Cypriot insurrection during the Cyprus Emergency, leads to the leader's escape and the death of a fellow soldier. The offender, charged with disrupting the operation by screaming, claims that he screamed because he saw God. The regiment's priest believes the claim to be genuine, while the military psychiatrist suspects that the soldier is either psychotic or has been hallucinating. Either way, the soldier has to face a court martial and a possible fifteen years in jail, as his case makes it clear that there is little room for religious faith not only in the Army but in the modern society at large.[43] For the title role, a recent graduate of the Royal Academy of Dramatic Art (RADA) Tom Courtenay (b. 1937) was chosen.[44] This

---

41 See the unsigned article 'What Are the Prospects for Theatrical Adventure?' in *The Times* of 3 April 1959.
42 By Harwood's own admission, made in 1990, Wrede gave him 'a sense of myself both as a person and as an artist <...> explained the importance of art in general and insisted that before embarking on an enterprise, whether it be writing or directing a play, or <...> building a theatre, one had to make sure to the best of one's abilities that the central motive and all the components that attach to it were in harmony' (Braham Murray, 'Wrede Defined', *Plays and Players*, March 1990, p. 18).
43 For the film's novelization, see John Burke, *Private Potter: Based on the Screenplay by Ronald Harwood and Casper Wrede* (London: Pan Books, 1962).
44 At the suggestion of Wrede's and Courtenay's mutual friend James Maxwell, Wrede first saw Courtenay's performance in Caryl Brahms's and Ned Sherrin's musical *Shut Up and Sing*, directed by Michael Ashton and performed by RADA students at the Vanbrugh theatre in February 1960, during Courtenay's fifth term at RADA. Courtenay played the part of Bernie, the leader of an East End gang of 'teddy boys' (a

was his screen debut.[45] Both Harwood and Courtenay were to make significant contributions to the film adaptation of *One Day* – arguably the biggest creative effort and achievement of Wrede's entire career, certainly as far as film and television are concerned.[46]

Oddly enough, by Wrede's own admission, he never though he would get into films:

> The power structure is too overwhelming. Yet I always loved movies. As a boy in Finland during the war one of the things that sustained me were all those wonderful American movies, the musicals, gangster stories and Westerns from the late 1930s and early 1940s. One night I remember I went to see movies in three different theatres. <...> Life was so grim and

---

1950s teenage group, thus nicknamed for wearing clothes reminiscent of King Edward VII's reign, Teddy being short for Edward). After the musical's opening, 'the "C" pigeonhole was filled with letters from all the leading agencies wanting to sign me up. <...> I have always thought of that little musical at RADA as the greatest success I have ever had' (Tom Courtenay, *Dear Tom: Letters from Home*, London: Black Swan, 2001, p. 280). Several months later Wrede invited Courtenay to a meeting with Harwood at the prestigious Savile Club to discuss his possible appearance in *Private Potter*. Courtenay recalls that 'the combination of the teeth <he underwent a major dental operation shortly beforehand; for details, see footnote 117 – BH, AR> and a gentleman's club proved too much for me and I felt horribly shy. Ronnie told me many years later that after my departure he had said to Casper, with some firmness, "That boy is not an actor. I don't want him in my play". And Casper had said, "Fine, but in that case I don't want to direct your play"' (ibid., p. 337).

45 'It was recorded on a Sunday and <...> aired in the spring of 1961. It had a wonderful cast: Leo McKern, Brewster Mason, Ralph Michael <...>, James Maxwell and Eric Thompson <Tsesar in *Ivan Denisovich*. – BH, AR> <...>. It was inspiring to work with all these wonderful men. <...> It was much more effective on television than when it was later filmed for the big screen' (Courtenay, op. cit., p. 337). For a review of the film version, see *The Guardian* of 2 February 1963.

46 Wrede's collaboration with Harwood also involved a TV and a film adaptation of Harwood's play *The Barber of Stamford Hill* (1962), about one Mr Figg, a middle-aged Jewish barber who dreams of having a family but eventually has to accept life as a bachelor with the dumb Dober as his sole friend (for a review of the film version, see *The Guardian* of 9 February 1963). Wrede himself preferred the television version to the film: 'I knew a lot about TV, but too little about film, and the film version became too reminiscent of the TV version. It is much more difficult to handle the tempo and the rhythm in a regular film' (Bez, 'En betydelsefull dag i Casper Wredes liv', *Hufvudstadsbladet*, 5 January 1970). As for Courtenay, Wrede directed him in *Hamlet* for the 1968 Edinburgh Festival (launching the Manchester-based 69 Theatre Company, which was financed by grants from the Arts Council of Great Britain, the North West Arts Association and a number of private contributions; later it became famous as the Royal Exchange Theatre).

dark that <...> American pictures were the only bright spot in a boy's life.⁴⁷

Yet Wrede's own films could not be further from the notions of escapism and light entertainment. When asked if he would like to direct films in the US, he replied:

> <'>Yes, <...> but not in Hollywood style<'>. Besides, <Wrede> explained, he'd have to come and live <in America> in order to absorb the feel and the history of the country. <And> he expressed concern about being coerced into doing something with which he did not agree. 'If you have a very difficult digestive system as I have for my work, you have to pick and choose very carefully, otherwise you lose what little you have', he said. 'A film must relate to me in every way I can think and feel'. In other words, he is not a man who feels he can do everything. He waits for specialized work. ⁴⁸

Wrede read *One Day* in 1964, or thereabouts, in the 1963 English translation by Ralph Parker,⁴⁹ and

---

47   George McKinnon, '*Ivan Denisovich* 8 Years in Planning', *The Boston Globe*, 3 October 1971.
48   Dewar, 'Life in a Siberian Labor Camp'.
49   On more than one occasion, Solzhenitsyn criticised this translation in his communications with the Mezhdunarodnaia kniga agency, which initially represented his interests outside the Soviet Union (see Reshetovskaia, op. cit., p. 114). His attitude was echoed in a review of *One Day* by Leonard Schapiro, a leading British Sovietologist. Schapiro compared two 1963 English translations of the book, by Parker (released by the Gollancz publishers in London) and by Max Hayward and Ronald Hingley (released by the Praeger publishers in New York): 'The trouble with Mr Parker's version is twofold. First, he has apparently found the camp slang too difficult, and has made a number of plain mistakes. <...> These mistakes might not matter much if the translation were otherwise good. It is not. It is stilted, inelegant and pedestrian, interlarded with slang terms dragged in from everywhere. <...> Nothing of the original style is preserved. Messrs Hayward and Hingley are far more successful' (Leonard Schapiro, 'Bent Backs', *New Statesman*, 1 February 1963, p. 158). As the Hayward and Hingley translation was not available in the UK, Schapiro advised those who were interested in literature, not in politics, to read the New York version, 'even if they have to swim the Atlantic' (ibid.).

thought it would make a wonderful movie <...> I was attracted by the theme of confinement, of survival and of man's indomitable will to win through against all the odds <...> But more than anything else, it is the universality of the theme that attracted me. It is not a particular story. The author makes his stand and sticks to it. There is hope for the future implicit in everything the prisoners do'.[50]

Although Wrede was instinctively dissatisfied with the quality of Parker's translation[51] (in his adaptation, he used the 1963 Finnish translation by Markku Lahtela, and later even commissioned, for USD480.00, a new English translation of the book from Gillon Aitken, whose renditions of Pushkin's prose he admired), he did manage, on its basis, to get Harwood interested in writing a screen version, and Courtenay, in starring in it.

For Wrede, *One Day* must have resonated well with Hønningstad's ideas about intense spiritual activity below the visibility level in barren land, of which Solzhenitsyn himself was a prime example, having sprung up suddenly, as if out of nowhere, when Khrushchev's Thaw came to replace the Stalinist freeze.[52] In a 1971 interview, Wrede said:

---

50   McKinnon, op. cit.
51   Wrede did not know Russian but was fluent in Finnish, Swedish and English, as well as Norwegian. Michael Meyer recalls how demanding Wrede could be when it came to translation. Before co-directing, with Michael Elliott, Ibsen's *Lady from the Sea* (aired by the BBC in August 1958), Wrede 'asked me to come and go through with him the translation which I had, as I thought, completed two years earlier. I imagined that this might take an evening; in the event it filled three of the most traumatic and educative weeks of my life. <...> He sat with Ibsen's original text on his knee while I read out my version. Line by line he destroyed what I had written. "You've used twelve words where Ibsen used seven." "Yes, but –" <...> "You've put the key word in the wrong place... This line should be evasive, you've translated it too directly... You've put in an image that isn't there, Ibsen's spareness is better... This line would get a laugh in the Norwegian, yours won't... Ibsen repeats a word that appeared three lines earlier, you've missed that." By the time we had finished, barely a line of my original version remained' (Meyer, op. cit., p. 159). Wrede's input in Meyer's this and other translations from the Norwegian (Ibsen's *Ghosts, Little Eyolf, The Master Builder* and *John Gabriel Borkman*), as well as from the Swedish (Strindberg's *Creditors*), was sufficient enough to merit a third of the royalties for translation sales and stage and radio productions (see Meyer's letters to Wrede of 28 September and 14, 25 and 27 October 1972, kept in David Wrede's private archive).
52   Curiously, Solzhenitsyn too believed that 'new historical configurations form long in advance of coming into action. And it takes a great deal of time for people to discover

> I knew it was a film I must make. It was a turning point for me. I have felt that we are in a state of transition from something towards something. But I feel we are in danger of leaving something valuable behind. We have not arrived yet and there is no certainty. But I feel that the book was one of those milestones that made you aware that you were on the way.[53]

Those less attuned to Hønningstad's teaching doubted *One Day*'s suitability for a film version. In a later interview, Courtenay admitted that he had had serious misgivings about the project:

> I thought it was a great book, a universal book – the prison camp is an image of life, of what we all have to do both morally and physically to survive – but I didn't see how it could work as a film. In the end I did it for Casper. He's very much a sort of guru to me. I've known him since I was virtually a little baby, well, since I was at RADA anyway, and I've always had enormous respect for him.[54]

For his part, Casper Wrede, who had been fascinated with neighbouring Russia ever since his childhood years, recalled in his previously unpublished 1993 autobiographical essay 'Russia on My Mind', preserved in David Wrede's private archive, why Solzhenitsyn's book became such a magnet for Wrede himself and for many of those who became involved in its screen adaptation:

> Nothing remains in my memory of the time when I first read Solzhenitsyn but the experience is with me still. It was a kind of homecoming <...> It was not only myself I met in meeting Ivan Denisovich. For the first time I met ordinary Russians of my own generation. For the first time I was

---

and understand them' (Solzhenitsyn, 'Ugodilo zernyshko promezh dvukh zhernovov', *Novyi mir*, no. 9 (2000), p. 136).
53 McKinnon, op. cit.
54 Barry Norman, 'Tom Courtenay in *Ivan Denisovich* – a film with legs', *The Times* of 6 Nov 1971. Courtenay elaborates on this point in his memoirs. In his opinion, Wrede 'was the deepest person I had ever met. He could see right through me and out the other side. His little nod of approval was more of a compliment than any of the extravagant things that were said to me at that time' (Courtenay, op. cit., p. 336).

shown – without bitterness or recrimination – life backstage at the great Soviet show. And I knew with the whole of my being that what I was shown was the truth. My guide did not only possess the necessary experience; he had the genius to convey it in the simplest and most accessible form. I only regret that the political implications of the story have obscured its universal lesson: that we are what we do; that it is not what we do but how we do it that makes us what we are. This little book created the first living bond between the Russia of the future and the people in the world outside who chose to believe in forces stronger than violence and murder. I never knew when it was that it chose me to put it into pictures. The process was remarkable: before I knew it I had been joined by all those who were needed to realise the project and the assured impossibility of the task dissolved before us and was overcome at every stage.[55]

---

[55] See Appendix I (section '1961-70').

2   COSTINGS AND FUNDING

In 1968, Wrede, whose enthusiasm about the project was 'infectious',[56] convinced Erik Borge, head of Norsk Film AS, to co-finance the adaptation and offer a studio and technical facilities, to the tune of USD100,000 (the other financial backer was Group W, the film division of the US Westinghouse Broadcasting Corporation, which provided USD325,000;[57] the third partner was a company called Leontes Productions Ltd, founded by Tom Courtenay to 'engage in production of significant films he personally wants to make'.[58]) Wrede had worked as a director in Norway in the past, making a TV version of Gogol's *Diary of a Madman* in 1967 and staging his *Government Inspector* at the National Theatre in Oslo the following year (incidentally, Hønningstad also contributed to both adaptations). Some of the Norwegian actors Wrede had directed were cast in *One Day*. Thus, Espen Skjønberg (b. 1924) played the part of Tyurin, and Frimann Falck Clausen (1921-83), that of Senka Klevshin. They spoke accented English, which turned out to be quite appropriate, because it conveyed the international atmosphere in the labour camps, whose population was composed of people from different ethnic backgrounds. Norway was also convenient for snow scenes.

On 1 February 1969, a formal agreement was signed between Leontes Productions Ltd and Wrede, putting him in charge of the film adaptation of Solzhenitsyn's *One Day in the Life of Ivan Denisovich* as the director and producer, for a sum total of USD25,000, of which USD10,000 was paid upon signing the agreement; a further USD7,500, at the start of the shooting; and a final USD7,500, on completion. Additionally, Leontes Productions Ltd undertook to reimburse Wrede's work-related expenses and pay him half of the net profits of the film.

---

56 *The Making*, p. 7.
57 Among other films produced by Group W were the thrillers *The Violent Enemy* (1967) and *A Taste of Excitement* (1969), directed by Don Sharp; the comedy *Squeeze a Flower* (Marc Daniels, 1970); and the historical drama *Eagle in a Cage* (Fielder Cook, 1972), about Napoleon's days on St Helena.
58 Group W's press release of 30 September 1969.

According to the rough cost estimates, sent from London to Wrede c/o Hønningstad at Klingenberggatte 7 in Oslo, by Peter S. Katz of Group W Films on 24 March 1969, the overall film budget was expected to be USD410,000,[59] of which the pre-production expenses amounted to USD5,000; the production staff – including the cameraman, the art director, the dubbing editor, the make-up artist, the seamstresses, the wardrobe mistress, the animal trainer and various assistants – were to be paid USD65,000 (including Norwegian insurance and Swedish pension contributions); Tom Courtenay, USD15,000; and the rest of the cast, USD40,000 (double the amount to be spent on the extras, on the one hand, and on the local technical staff and equipment, on the other). The film stock would cost USD17,500. The construction of the camp and the working site would set the producers back USD50,000; the crew's travel and living expenses, USD30,000; the soundtrack, USD2,500; and the post-production, USD8,500.

On 1 April 1969, a contract was drawn up between Leontes Production Ltd and Harwood, engaging his services as scriptwriter for a screenplay based on Aitken's translation of *One Day in the Life of Ivan Denisovich*, to be delivered by 1 July 1969, for USD12,500 (plus expenses if any), the first half of which was to be paid on the day when the contract was signed; and the second, in two equal instalments, on 19 September 1969 and no later than 1 November 1969 respectively.[60] The screenplay had to be approved (or otherwise) within fourteen days of its submission.

On 17 April of the same year, in his letter to Erik Borge, Peter Rawley of the London-based Creative Management Association (Wrede's agents)[61] outlined the financial guarantees of Norsk Film's involvement in the project. In return for their investment, Norsk Film was to have all the income from the film's release in the Scandinavian territories. Furthermore, up to 75% of the Norsk in-

---

59 It is curious that the film's budget was reported in the press as USD750,000 (see the unsigned note 'Group W Films to Make "Denisovitch" with Tom Courtenay, Norsk Films' in *Variety* of 1 October 1969), although it did not in fact exceed USD500,000.
60 By Ronald Harwood's later admission, 'we did it for very little... Certainly in comparison with what Tom could earn, it was a great labour of love' (Hugh Hebert, 'The Next Media Man', *The Guardian*, 17 April 1970).
61 Peter Rawley also produced Wrede's film *Ransom* (a.k.a. *The Terrorists*, 1975), starring Sean Connery.

vestment would be covered out of Westinghouse's takings received in the first year of the film's release in the Eastern hemisphere. The remaining 25% of the Norsk investment would be recovered, if necessary, from the additional fees Tom Courtenay was entitled to in the event of Westinghouse making 2.5 times more than their investment after the film's world-wide release. Also, Norsk Film would receive 10% of the entire profit made out of the Eastern hemisphere release. According to Wrede's handwritten notes on an undated piece of paper with the Norsk Film letter heading, for his part, Borge requested the guaranteed recoupment, from the Eastern hemisphere receipts obtained in the first year of the film's release, of the entire sum Norsk was going to contribute, because of the uncertainty of the Scandinavian market.[62] From the documents at our disposal, it is not clear how the issue was resolved, but a solution was undoubtedly found, because the project went ahead, with Norsk Film underwriting just over a quarter of the budget (which totalled USD443,640) and a quarter of the contingency (estimated at USD20,000), and Group W shouldering the rest.[63] On 25 June 1969, Peter S. Katz (Group W's London representative, appointed the production executive on the Solzhenitsyn adaptation) wrote to Wrede with a suggestion to register the titles *One Day*, *One Day in the Life* and/or *One Day in the Life of Ivan Denisovich* with the Film Production Association of Great Britain.

---

62 The *One Day* film proposal did not qualify for a subsidy from the Norwegian Ministry of Education and Religious Affairs, which could cover up to 45% of its costs (see a letter to Wrede of 1 July 1969, kept in David Wrede's private archive and written by Sverre Gran, an actor and a Norsk Film producer).
63 See a copy of the financial statement drawn in Oslo on 26 November 1970, which survives in David Wrede's private archive. Sverre Gran's letter to Wrede of 1 July 1969 reveals that Norsk Film A/S refused to accept liability for any budget overspills beyond the sum agreed in the contract.

3   PRE-PRODUCTION

The Russian author Mikhail Demin (1926-84; real name Georgii Evgen'evich Trifonov), who had spent eight years in the Gulag as a criminal, not as a political prisoner, and had defected to Paris in 1968,[64] provided Wrede with drawings that proved invaluable in making sets, props and clothes, for a scenic consultant fee of USD1,800.00.

In the first part of his autobiographical trilogy, *Blatnoi* (Thief, 1981), Demin states that in the late 1930s – early 1940s he studied at the Repin Art School in Moscow and took private lessons from the famous poster artist Dmitry Moor (real name Orlov; 1883-1946). Shortly after World War Two, Moor reportedly helped Demin to get a job as a designer at the Stalin (now Likhachev) car plant's advertising agency. At the same time, Demin attended graphic design and watercolour painting classes at the art courses run under the auspices of the All-Union Central Council of Trade Unions (Tsentral'naia studiia izobrazitel'nykh iskusstv VTsSPS), whose members of staff included well-known artists, such as Petr Aliakrinskii (1892-1961), Georgii Riazhskii (1895-1952) and Konstantin Iuon (1875-1958).[65] In 1954, Demin was employed as an illustrator and page layout designer by the *Sovetskaia Khakassiia* newspaper in Abakan.[66] This explains the professionalism of Demin's drawings.[67]

---

[64] See the unsigned news item 'Asylum Sought by Russian Poet' in *The Times* of 15 August 1968. Demin was the son of the poet and revolutionary Evgenii Andreevich Trifonov (pseudonym Brazhnev; 1885-1937) and the cousin of the novelist Iurii Valentinovich Trifonov (1925-81). For more on Demin, see E. Karmazin, 'Pamiati Mikhaila Demina', *Russkaia mysl'*, 12 April 1984, p. 15; and Stanislav Kuniaev, *Poeziia. Sud'ba. Rossiia*, Moscow: Nash sovremennik, 2001, vol. 1, pp. 337-38, 341-42.

[65] See M. Demin, *Blatnoi*, New York: Russica Publishers, 1981, pp. 75-76, 103-04. Demin's *Taezhnyi brodiaga* (1986) and *Ryzhii d'iavol* (1987), published by Russica posthumously, form the second and third parts of the trilogy.

[66] See M. Demin, *Ryzhii d'iavol*, New York: Russica Publishers, 1987, p. 91.

[67] See Appendix III.

Demin came to London from Paris to see Wrede in mid-June 1969. David Wrede's private archive contains Demin's undated handwritten note stating that his agent, Marie Schébéko of Bureau Littéraire D. Clairouin in Paris,[68] had sent Peter Rawley an invoice for his travel expenses, and a verbal agreement has been reached that on his arrival in Britain Demin would be given cash to the tune of GBP20 for his living expenses. Undoubtedly related to this note are a letter of 13 June 1969, from Alicia B. Orr of Group W Films, informing Wrede that a money order for GBP15 can be cashed by him at Barnes Post Office, and a receipt from F J Wards Art Shop of 124 and 130 King's Road, Chelsea, for £1.5s.11d for 'pencils etc.' – presumably, for Demin's drawing utensils – dated 14 June 1969.

In his autobiographical essay 'Russia on my Mind', Wrede describes his meeting with Demin:

> Sunday afternoon in Hyde Park. I am lounging in the grass with a successful Russian writer and former Gulag inmate who had defected from Moscow only a couple of weeks earlier.[69] He is taking great delight in trying to identify the ethnic origins of all the people picnicking and strolling by. His years as an orphan in Soviet institutions and later in the Gulag archipelago have given him a vast knowledge of types and he is very observant. He gets tired of this game and becomes thoughtful. "It's a good thing that the people of the Soviet Union do not know about this place", he says, "and that having been told about it they would not believe it exists". Why is it a good thing? "Because if they would believe it, you would have 200,000,000 people in Hyde Park".[70]

Demin took the Ivan Denisovich project very much to heart, as soon as he became convinced that Wrede saw it in a similar light. Once the terms and conditions of Demin's contract had been agreed upon (by which time he had already returned to Paris), he dictated to Marie Schébéko a letter to Wrede,

---

68 Among other things, Bureau Littéraire Clairouin is famous for helping Vladimir Nabokov in 1955 to find a French publisher for his novel *Lolita*.
69 In fact, Demin defected a year before.
70 See Appendix I (section '1968').

dated 25 June 1969. Schébéko translated the letter into English and forwarded it to the addressee, on the D. Clairouin headed paper indicating her contact details (66, Rue de Miromesnil, Paris VIII, telephone Laborde 18-06):

Dear Wrede,

I believe it is clear to you, after our conversations, that it will give me great pleasure to be working with you. I feel our approach to the project is on similar lines and in the same spirit, so let us hope that in spite of those financiers' stinginess it will be brought off satisfactorily and successfully.

As my agent tells me that Rawley is sending out the agreement concerning my job on the (ungenerous) terms the financiers have finally agreed to, I am leaving for the South of France the day after tomorrow to get started on it immediately.

It seems to me that it is essential for me to send you first and just as soon as possible a detailed plan of the camp, indicating the general layout with the disposition, size, nature of the buildings, etc. from which I suggest you have a dummy (or rather a model) made upon receipt. Such a model will be of key importance throughout and will help to solve any number of problems.

Next, I will follow the book page by page and give you drawings with explanatory notes, whenever necessary, of every object described.

In order to save time, I shall be sending you direct from Menton (or wherever I land in the South) the drawings in small lots as they are completed.

If you have any recommendations, queries or whatnot for me, would you please phone them or send them in writing to Marie Schébéko, who will pass them on to me in Russian, as I cannot be sure to have a competent translator to hand. She can be reached at the above address and telephone at almost any time, but more certainly in the mornings (that includes weekends if she is in town).

Again my warmest thanks for your hospitality and the many kindnesses which made my first glimpse of England a very pleasant one.

With kind regards to you and Mrs Wrede,
Yours sincerely,
Mikhail Demin

Demin had to prepare a full set of drawings by 31 July of the same year. In an accompanying note, also dated 25 June, Schébéko suggested that Wrede should send Demin regular reminders at frequent intervals to make sure the deadline was met, because, as she put it, 'like most Russian intellectuals, he has little sense of immediate timing and also may be too much of a perfectionist by nature who will therefore start a drawing or sketch from scratch half a dozen times before he is satisfied with it, whereas the first one would give you all the indications you want'. It is not clear if Wrede followed this advice, but a large batch of drawings was sent to Oslo[71] even slightly ahead of schedule, as a letter to Wrede from his solicitors Harbottle and Lewis of 31 July 1969 confirms.

Upon Wrede's return to London in mid-August, he sent Demin additional questions. According to Marie Schébéko's note to Harbottle and Lewis of 21 August 1969, Demin responded to Wrede's queries with a twenty-page letter (which apparently has not survived) and some extra drawings. After that, Wrede came back with more questions and asked for further drawings. Meanwhile, a model version of the camp was made, and in her letter to Wrede of 29 August, dispatched to Oslo c/o Norsk Film at Kirkeveien 59, Schébéko communicated Demin's request to send him without delay photo-

---

71   Wrede went to Oslo on 14-18 July and 4-10 August for business meetings at the Norsk Film (including those with the art director Per Schwab, who had already been Wrede's set and costume designer on the Norwegian National Theatre's 1968 production of Gogol's *Government Inspector*), in between squeezing in a week-long holiday and a visit to the mining town of Røros, which was to become the film's shooting location. The dates of Wrede's visits to Oslo and Røros have been established thanks to his expenses claims and work schedule, approved by Alicia Orr on behalf of Peter S. Katz of Group W Films in August 1969.

graphs of the model, taken from different angles, so that he could verify if everything was correct, and make comments and suggestions if necessary.[72] In the same letter, Schébéko urged Wrede to exert his influence with the 'money-bag holders' (her own expression), to expedite the payment of the remainder of Demin's fee. Its first istalment, USD600.00, was transferred to Demin on 8 August, and the rest, according to his contract, had to be paid no later than 1 September. However, it took yet another reminder from Schébéko to Harbottle and Lewis of 1 October 1969, stating that Demin had interrupted his usual work for over a month and had delayed the submission of one of his manuscripts to his publishers to do the drawings for *Ivan Denisovich*, before the money was paid in full. As she said about Demin in her letter to Wrede of the same date, 'We are not giving the poor man a happy image of the ways of the Western world! My thanks for whatever you can do to improve it'.

Twenty-eight of Demin's drawings, some of them numbered and with inscriptions in Russian (mostly translated into Norwegian), have survived in David Wrede's archive, either as originals or as photocopies. The first drawing is a general layout of the labour camp (with an average length of 100-120 meters and an average width of 80-85 meters), explaining the respective location of various buildings, such as the staff hut, the guardroom, the prison block, the storeroom, the sick bay, the bathhouse, the mess hall, the kitchen, the bread store, the culture and education section, the parcels office and prisoners' huts (with Ivan Denisovich's hut clearly marked). The location of the gates, the watchtowers, the wells and the thermometer is also indicated. The second drawing is a general ground view of the entrance to the labour camp consisting of a watchtower, a guardroom, the small (inner) and large (outer) wooden gates, reinforced with metal plating along the edges, and the parade ground delineated by barriers. The third is a ground view of the watchtower and the barbed-wire fence from the front and the back, indicating the height of the barbed-wire posts with mounted searchlights (six meters), the distance between the posts (five-six meters) and the width of the harrowed strip of bare earth, known as the 'control strip', running between two rows of such posts (two meters). A separate picture of a wooden watchtower, equipped with a

---

72   For one such photograph, see Appendix IV, pic. 5.

telephone, a searchlight and a machine gun, is drawn on the same sheet, indicating the tower's height (seven-eight meters) and the area it occupies (from three square meters at the bottom to two square meters at the sentry's level). The fourth drawing is a layout of the mess hall, which looks like a rather spacious hut with a porch and no bars on the windows (except for the window in the bread store, which is barred). The mess hall can house 18-20 wooden tables for 12-14 people each, with an appropriate number of long wooden benches. Prisoners get their food and return the used bowls through the hatches opening into the kitchen section, where the stove, the dishwashing area and the staff entrance are. The drawings of a typical tin bowl (four to five centimetres in height and about 18 centimetres in diameter) and a typical wooden or aluminium spoon can be seen on the same sheet, as well as the illustrations to two scenes from the book – prisoner U-81 at his evening meal and an orderly called Khromoi beating up unruly prisoners who are trying to enter the mess hall[73] – are also included. The fifth drawing is a ground view of the exterior of a prisoners' hut, built from wooden planks or small logs, with either brick or tin round chimneys, small barred windows and a roof covered with wood chips or tarred felt. The sixth is a general layout of a typical prisoners' hut (four meters high, nine meters wide and 25-30 meters long) consisting of two identical sections, linked by a shared common area with a WC (containing wash stands and wooden latrine barrels) and a five meter wide passage that leads both from one section to another and to an outside entrance. Every section contains either a round iron or a square brick stove, several drinking water tanks and a number of bunk beds (two meters high and 150 centimetres wide) to accommodate four people each. The average distance between the beds is half a meter. The beds are made of wood, although sometimes metal pipes are used for supports. Number 1 on the picture marks Ivan Denisovich's bed. The seventh drawing explains what a latrine barrel looks like. It is an eighty litre barrel with two metal rings on each side, to put a pole through and lift it for slopping out. The water tanks look very much the same, only somewhat smaller. At the bottom left of the same drawing, there is a picture of a square brick stove with an iron chimney and a metal or asbestos sheet under the oven door. On the stove, prisoners' felt

---

[73] See *The Making*, pp. 138-42, 146-47.

boots are drying. On the right-hand side, in the 'Evening in a Hut' section, a bunk bed is drawn, with two prisoners lying on top, one prisoner sitting on the lower bed, and another standing next to one of the supports. The standing prisoner is fully clothed, wearing a coat over his quilted jacket and trousers. Explanatory comments indicate that prisoners' coarse woolen blankets are either grey or black, while their mattresses and pillow-cases are filled, as a rule, with wood chips. At the bottom right of the same sheet, there is a picture of a prisoner's drawer (75 centimetres high and 45 centimetres wide, with either three shelves or four compartments inside).[74]

Several drawings belong to a storyboard variety, such as the one picturing Ivan Denisovich entering the guardroom with a bucket of water to wash the floor there; another featuring prisoners on their march to the worksite, accompanied by guards and guard dogs; and yet another, showing how Pavlo is mixing the mortar, Fetyukov and the Captain are carrying the hods and Ivan Denisovich is laying the bricks at the power station.[75] A few more pictures are, in fact, imaginary portraits of important characters: the chief disciplinary officer Lieutenant Volkovoi, the team leader Tyurin, Fetyukov, Tsesar talking to the Captain, and Ivan Denisovich smoking and feeling content before going to sleep.[76] It is obvious that some of these pictures, especially the first three and the last, directly influenced the film's mise en scène.

Yet another drawing that clearly affected *One Day*'s visual presentation shows the respective location of the camp guards, the escort guards and the teams leaving the camp for work during the morning parade (B2). A team of prisoners moving towards the open inner gates is schematically represented by a shaded square just below the picture's centre. The camp guards in front of the shaded square are waiting to search the prisoners. The shaded square is flanked by more camp guards on its left and right sides. To the left of the picture's centre, there is a guardroom with a porch leading inside the camp and a door on the opposite side leading to 'freedom', as the explanatory notes put it. Next to the porch, several human figures represent the camp's

---

74 See Appendix III, pics 1-7.
75 See Appendix III, pics 8, 10, 16.
76 See Appendix III, pics 12-15, 18.

administrators, a production planner, a camp artist and so on. On the right-hand side, a watchtower and a 'control strip' can be seen. At the top of the picture, beyond the outer gates, the escort guards – in the same formation as the camp guards – are waiting for the prisoners to come out.[77]

The remaining drawings depict the interior and exterior of other important labour camp building structures, such as the staff hut, the sick bay, the worksite office, the prison block and the well; the labour camp's standard procedures, such as the work parade in the morning; and various items of guards' and prisoners' clothing and other kinds of paraphernalia (such as kitchen appliances and working tools). Drawing No. 9 contains a general layout of the staff hut, including the premises used by the security officer and the chief disciplinary officer, with special focus on the guardroom where Ivan Denisovich washes the floor (the location of the bucket is indicated in the room's top right corner). In the centre of the guardroom, there is a table at which guards play chess, and some stools. Next to the table, there is a stove. Along the walls, there is a wardrobe and two benches, one of which is occupied by a sleeping guard. The staff hut's windows do not have any bars on them. On the same sheet, there are also pictures and descriptions of the guards' garments worn in the summer and in heated rooms (such as a field shirt, a pair of riding breeches, a pair of high boots, a service cap and a trench coat), and in winter time (a pair of quilted trousers, a pair of felt top boots, a half-length sheepskin coat and a full-length sheepskin coat with a goat fur lining, to wear on the watchtower). Drawing No. 11 is devoted to what prisoners wear. On it, there is a front and a back view of a quilted jacket, as well as a pair of quilted trousers with a knee pocket. A picture of a coat, worn over the quilted jacket, is drawn nearby. The accompanying notes explain that the coat is longer than the jacket and, although padded with cotton, is smooth on the outside, not quilted. Solzhenitsyn also mentions a coat made of a trench coat, which, according to the notes, is done by cutting off the trench coat's flaps. The colour of the jacket and trousers is usually either grey or dirty green, whereas the coat's colour is either khaki or black. Underneath, there is an en face and a profile view of a prisoner's winter hat, which demonstrates how to pull down

---

77   See Appendix III, pic. 21.

the hat's peak in frosty weather. The positions of prisoners' numbers on the jacket, the trousers, the coat and the hat are clearly shown. Further on the same sheet, there are pictures of prisoners' padded mittens with fabric or tarpaulin sewn over them, prisoners' felt boots (which lack the foppish tops that the guards' felt boots have) and a piece of cloth that is wrapped around a prisoner's face to protect it from the cold. Two unnumbered drawings reveal what the labour camp underwear was like (an undershirt and a pair of long johns made of off-white flannel), in one case, and the exact look of the shawl-like collar of the guards' full-length sheepskin coat, in another. Drawing A1 completes the visual representation of the labour camp's couture with the garments of the paramedic Kolya Vdovushkin: a white surgical coat with a waistband tied at the back, and a white nurse's hat. On the same sheet, there is also a general layout of the sick bay, which normally occupies less than a third of a standard prisoners' hut turned into a hospital. The scheme indicates the respective location of the stove and the paramedic's desk (to the left and to the bottom of the room's centre), with a coat rack, a wardrobe and several benches along the room's walls. Also on the same sheet, drawing A2 explains what a serving hatch in a mess hall looks like, with an open shutter and a shelf to put the bowls onto. The top section of drawing A5 presents a general layout of the office which Tsesar works at. This is a nine-to-ten meter long and a ten-meter wide building divided into two equal parts, one being the work superintendent's office, and the other, the room for Tsesar and the bookkeepers. Their desks, as well as a bench and a stove, can be seen on the scheme. The bottom section of drawing A5 shows how prisoners fry their bread on a round iron stove. Drawing B3 is a ground view of a low-height rectangular well made of logs. At its top, there is a hand-operated windlass with a rope, which is attached to a bucket by a hook. This small picture – which, however, observes all the right proportions – shows how a prisoner pulls the bucket out of the well. An unnumbered drawing concludes the sequence of the camp's typical exteriors and interiors with a front ground view of the concrete felt-roofed building (four meters high, nine-to-ten meters wide and fifteen meters long), housing the isolation cells. It is separated from the rest of the camp by a three-meter tall wooden fence with barbed wire on its top.[78]

---

[78] See Appendix III, pics 9, 11, 19-20, 22, 25-27.

Drawing No. 17C depicts Ivan Denisovich's tools: a mason's hammer, a trowel, a set square and a plumb on a piece of string. Drawing C7 gives an approximate idea of the external appearance of an electrical hoist (a conveyor-belt for transporting bricks from one level to another). Demin did not remember it well but stated in the explanatory notes that this should not be much of a problem, as in Solzhenitsyn's book the hoist was broken and covered with snow. At any rate, concluded Demin, an expert in building construction should be able to offer further assistance in the matter. The sheet with drawings C10, C15, C17 and C19 pictures more building appliances and guards' and prisoners' personal effects: a one-and-a-half meter long crowbar, a pickaxe, a tobacco pouch (with a piece of string running through its opening to hold it together, just like an elastic band in underpants), a tin kettle with a two-litre capacity and a wooden slate for managerial notes.[79]

The last drawing gives examples of typical slogans and placards adorning guardroom and hut walls and the entrance to the mess hall, where everyone can see them (the so-called 'visual propaganda'): 'In the USSR, labour is a matter of honour, valour and heroism (Joseph Stalin)', 'He who does not work does not eat', 'The United States of America will be caught up with and overtaken' and 'The prisoner's meekness makes the prison beautiful'. Such slogans would be painted in red on sheets of plywood and wide planks.[80]

This is the only feature that was not used in the film, for unknown reasons. Otherwise, the whole camp site was built according to Demin's drawings and radiated 'grim authenticity',[81] especially to those who had never seen a real Soviet labour camp. One such person described the film set on location as follows:

> Tiny beads of snow and ice glisten on the strands of barbed wire and, in a curious way, it is rather beautiful. Then, as you approach the huge gates, you get a depressing impression overall of stark, bleak emptiness.

---

79 See Appendix III, pics 17, 23-24.
80 See Appendix III, pic. 28.
81 *The Making*, p. 22.

As you go inside, you feel that this is a place from which there is no escape, and <where> mere survival <is> the only concern.[82]

The set constructors and props manufacturers made a very good job of paying attention to every little detail. Even small objects, such as kitchen utensils, looked so genuine, that none other than Solzhenitsyn himself thought they must have been smuggled out of a camp,[83] although his familiarity with catering in confinement went far beyond the famous 'Glorious Food' scene in the Dickens-based 1968 musical *Oliver!* (director Carol Reed), when gruel is served in a Victorian workhouse to orphans, whose identical monochrome garb and cheap metal bowls, as they appear on screen, are not unlike those of the inmates in *One Day in the Life of Ivan Denisovich*.

The London-based court, theatrical and film costumiers L & H Nathan Ltd. lent the *One Day* production team fourteen guards uniforms and holsters for a hire charge of '15 guineas per uniform, plus carriage', the Other Ranks uniforms being insured 'at £50 each and the Officers' at £100 each' (John W. Nathan's letter to Wrede of 12 November 1969). In this letter to Wrede, John W. Nathan also described in some detail what the uniforms looked like: 'they all have bright blue tabs and the O<ther> R<ank>s have red piping around the tabs, and the Officers gold piping around the tabs'. L & H Nathan Ltd. volunteered to take part in the project, having read in the press about Wrede's plans to make a film version of *One Day*. The company had already worked in Norway before, for instance, on *Song of Norway*, a 1970 musical biopic of Edvard Grieg, directed by Andrew L. Stone (see John W. Nathan's letter to Wrede of 7 October 1969).

---

82 Richard Pack, 'Where Is It Colder Than a Sponsor's Heart?: Filmmaking in Røros, Norway', *Variety*, 11 February 1970. Cf.: Wrede's 'labour camp <is> twinkling under an icy moon like some evil jewel set in snow' (Paul D. Zimmerman, 'Prisoner's Base', *Newsweek*, 24 May 1971, p. 46).
83 See Sven Nykvist, *Vördnad för ljuset: Om film och människor i samtal med Bengt Forslund*, Bonnier: Uddevalla, 1997, s. 119.

4 FILMING

After considering 'every alternative from plastic snow to Alaska',[84] it was decided that the shooting would take place near the mining town of Røros (population 3,200), some 185 miles north of Oslo 'and about 100 miles south of Hell',[85] where 'the topography, light condition and bitter climate closely resemble those of Siberia'.[86] Needless to say, going to Siberia proper was impossible for political reasons. Røros was also selected because of logistical convenience (a tourist destination, it had its own airport) and because of the local community's previous experience with assisting film and television crews. The Swedish-West German television series, based on Astrid Lindgren's children's books about *Pippi Långstrump* (1969), was shot there by the director Olle Hellborn, while Norsk Film chose Røros to make *An-Magritt* (director Arne Skouen, 1969), an adaptation of Johan Falkberget's 1940 novel, set in a seventeenth-century mountain village, with Liv Ullmann in the title role.[87] Røros was even referred to humorously as Norway's Hollywood.[88] 'A local sports club could provide and marshal the extras needed to play Beria's henchmen – the camp guards – and zeks, or prisoners. And an extra's minimal per diem pay of 75 Norwegian crowns (about $10) was crucial for the <…> budget, <…> shoestring-sized'[89] by the industry's standards at the time. In addition to 'some men, who were simply down and out' and others 'off the street <…>, there were also some distinguished judges and pro-

---

84 The unsigned article 'Hollywood North', *Scandinavian Times*, no. 2, May 1970, p. 42.
85 Pack, op. cit.
86 The unsigned article 'Simulating Siberia', *Time*, 2 March 1970, p. 55. In Wrede's own words, 'We searched all the Scandinavian countries from the Polar Circle down to Copenhagen before deciding on Røros which is the coldest and driest, but most even tempered area we could find. We have exactly the same climate as described in <*One Day in the Life of Ivan Denisovich*>' (Pack, op. cit.).
87 The author and Labour politician Johan Falkberget (real name Lillebakken, 1879-1967) was born on a farm near Røros and is buried in a Røros churchyard.
88 See the unsigned illustrated report 'Full fart på Røros – Norges Hollywood', *Verdens Gang*, 27 January 1970, p. 31. Røros is still used as a motion picture location from time to time. Thus, the Dutch film *Siberia* (Robert Jan Westdijk, 1998) and the Swedish-Norwegian-Danish co-production *Magnetisörens femte vinter* (The Magnetist's Fifth Winter, 1999; director Morten Henriksen) were shot there too.
89 'Hollywood North', p. 42.

fessors who were friends of friends, and interested in the project. In a few days, I could not tell them apart', Wrede recalled.[90] Courtenay reminisced warmly about 'great extras from among the townspeople', adding: 'The extras in London are such bored, tired, familiar people'.[91]

Sundays were the only days when the local extras, employed in the mining industry and elsewhere, could participate in the mass scenes. Therefore, Mondays had to be designated as the film crew's days off. A disused Storwartz copper mine was rented eight miles away from Røros. The place also allowed the possibility of studio work in case of snowstorms. For the first month of production, most of the filming had to be done outdoors and at night.

Keeping the mine in operation necessitated stripping bare 'hundreds of acres around it <so> that not the smallest sapling remains. It offered Wrede what he calls the "quintessential Siberia" – a totally barren but gently rolling expanse; Siberia without being dull'.[92] Courtenay shared Wrede's enthusiasm about the location:

> I don't think this kind of picture could have been made anywhere else. <...> The surroundings are perfect for the actors. I find that I don't have to try and imagine the kind of environment this story calls for, I am in it. I've never been this far north before, and I get a strange feeling of isolation which is, of course, just right for this film.[93]

---

90 P<aine> K<nickerbocker>, 'A Young Director's Struggle to Make Denisovich', *The San Francisco Chronicle*, 1 October 1971.
91 Jerry Tallmer, 'Tom Courtenay: No More Anti-Heroes, Please', *The New York Post*, 5 June 1971.
92 'Hollywood North', p. 42. Strictly speaking, Røros could stand in for Ivan Denisovich's camp only in the absence of better alternatives, as 'the camp described in the story is, judging by the tree-less steppes around it, located in Kazakhstan – it is, indeed, modelled on Ekibastuz where Solzhenitsyn himself served the last years of his sentence. The climate in this district is better than in the Arctic regions where millions of <...> prisoners <...> found their deaths' (L. Toker, 'On Some Aspects of the Narrative Method in *One Day in the Life of Ivan Denisovich*', in W. Moskovich (ed.), *Russian Philology and History: In Honour of Professor Victor Levin*, Jerusalem: PRAEDICTA, 1992, p. 270).
93 Pack, op. cit.

The principal cast (Team 104) was assembled from British and Norwegian actors, many of whom had already worked with Wrede before. By his own admission, Wrede 'searched for a cast that would not overact as Russian actors frequently do. He wanted his actors simple, basic and magnificently capable – and he found them'.[94] In addition to being offered the part of Fetyukov, the Norwegian Alf Malland (1917-97) was appointed Wrede's assistant with authority to approach various actors in Norway and sound them out about roles in *One Day*, without promising anything for certain.[95] Wrede's notes show that he considered Maxwell Shaw (1929-85) for the part of Tsesar; Fulton Mackay (1922-87) and Tim Preece (b. 1938), for the part of Alyoshka the Baptist; and Trevor Peacock (b. 1931) as Kilgas.[96] These parts subsequently went to Eric Thompson, Alfred Burke and Matthew Guinness (the son of Sir Alec Guinness). On the Norwegian side, the biggest name Wrede tried to secure for the part of the team leader Tyurin was Espen Skjønberg, a leading actor at the Norwegian National Theatre. This proved to be difficult. Although Skjønberg was very interested in the role (in his letter to Wrede of 24 February 1969, sent from Oslo, he asks what the English title of the book is, because he would like to read it before signing the contract,[97] and also enquires if he would have to speak English without an accent), he was engaged in the Norwegian National Theatre's production of Christopher Marlowe's *Edward II*, directed by Kazimierz Dejmek (1924-2002). The rehearsal and performance dates for the play, which opened on 11 February 1970, partially coincided with *One Day*'s anticipated filming schedule. In his letter to Skjønberg of 7 August 1969, copied to Wrede, the artistic director of the Norwegian National Theatre, Arild Brinchmann (1922-86), initially denied Skjønberg permission to take part in Wrede's film, because it would not be easy for the theatre to find a replacement for him. Brinchmann promised, however, to

---

94   Ann M. Beierfield, '*Denisovich* Important Work', *The Record-American*, 2 October 1971.
95   See Malland's letter to Casper Wrede of 16 May 1969, kept in David Wrede's private archive.
96   In his letter to Wrede of 16 May 1969, Alf Malland suggested that the part of Kilgas would suit the RADA-trained Norwegian Ivar Nørve (b. 1941), who had spent two years at the Goodman Memorial Theatre in Chicago.
97   The Norwegian translation by N. Fredriksen, *En dag i Ivan Denisovitsjs liv*, published in 1963 in Oslo by Tiden Norsk Forlag, must have gone out of print by 1969, because it was reissued by Den Norsk bokklubben in 1970.

speak to Dejmek about the problem in an attempt to find a mutually acceptable solution. Eventually, Skjønberg was allowed to join the cast of *One Day*. His name does not appear on *Edward II*'s cast list.[98]

The shooting began on 5 January 1970, 'at a time when no sane person would film in Scandinavia'.[99] (Røros is among the coldest places in Norway, and even the test shooting was carried out in a temperature of minus 20 degrees centigrade. During the seven weeks of filming, the temperatures fluctuated between minus 20 and minus 30, accompanied by cold winds.[100]) An eye-witness described the conditions as follows:

> You shiver despite your ski pants, heavy trousers, three pairs of socks, long woollen underwear, two sweaters, sheepskin-lined coat, two sets of mittens, two woollen caps and thick felt boots. The only warming fact is that, thankfully, you are only a transient observer and not one of the actors who have to bear eight freezing hours a day.[101]

The filming would normally start at four in the afternoon, 'after a Norwegian cold table lunch',[102] and last until eleven at night or even later. 'At eight o'clock a hot snack consisting of steaming soup, sandwiches and coffee was delivered to the location and, a little later, a hot drink – red currant juice perhaps – would be served'.[103] This kind of diet was absolutely vital on a set exposed to the Arctic winter. According to one report from the location, 'the only protection from the cold and wind are small unpretentious heated trailers, where the cast can take shelter when they're not on camera. They play chess, Scrabble and just plain sit and enjoy the warmth before the next scene'.[104]

---

98 We are grateful to Ingrid E. Handeland of the Norwegian National Theatre for helping us to clarify this point.
99 *The Making*, p. 19.
100 Nykvist, op. cit., p. 119. 'The sound man has been forced to wrap his microphone in a woman's stocking to soften the noise of the wind that howls across the snow' ('Simulating Siberia').
101 Pack, op. cit.
102 *The Making*, p. 19.
103 *The Making*, p. 19.
104 Pack, op. cit.

Although undeniably very demanding, filming in natural weather conditions was deemed absolutely necessary for authenticity's sake. It also helped the actors with their performance. Tom Courtenay explained:

> It's important to be out there a good while before the shot is done. The cold changes the face; it becomes pinched, and we behave more intensely and dramatically. The costumes are drab, the scenery is muted; all you have after a few minutes is the face. There is nothing to detract from it.[105]

Still, the actors' highest professionalism could not make them impervious to cold. A journalist reported from the film set: 'In one scene that required going without gloves, Tom Courtenay, who stars as Ivan (and uses no stand-in) had to call a halt because he became much too numb to continue'.[106] The situation was exacerbated by a ban on feet stamping and arm slapping when filming, because, 'Mr Wrede said, to do those things only releases energy and the man eventually is colder',[107] and prisoners would know that from experience and would behave accordingly. The Scandinavians, more used to sub-zero temperatures, were better placed to withstand harsh weather, but the British were trying to put on a brave face too. According to one account, the Norwegian Alf Malland

> watched carefully one particularly bitter evening. He saw that John Cording (Pavlo) had just about sapped his stamina. Intuitively, Malland asked: 'Are you giving up?' – 'Of course not', replied Cording, strengthened by the question. 'I'm Welsh'.[108]

Although provisions were made for the clothes that the actors 'could wear when not participating in a scene: great full-length maxi-coats, fur-lined jackets and caps, bulky felt boots',[109] some crew members, including Courtenay,

---

105 'Hollywood North', p. 42.
106 'Simulating Siberia'.
107 Nora E. Taylor, 'Denisovich: Wrede's Eight-year Saga', *The Christian Science Monitor*, 29 September 1971.
108 'Hollywood North', p. 43.
109 *The Making*, p. 19.

suffered frostbite. Even the local extras had to resort to time-tested precautions. The production manager Jac Hald admitted that 'the older ones <...> drank to keep warm. Late at night we had some problems – you know. They would turn right when they were supposed to turn left'.[110] Yet the director pressed on undeterred. A journalist described his conduct on the set:

> Wrede still shouts 'Come out and get cold!' to his actors when they linger overlong in dressing-room trailers. He delights in close-ups that capture the frost etched on a ten-day growth of stubble, or the gleam of a runny nose. 'The rule in actual prison camps was to suspend work if it reached 40 below', he says. 'My rule is 39 below, not to be worse than Stalin'.[111]

There were days when members of the cast would refuse to speak to the director 'because of his insistence that shooting continue in spite of <...> the agonizing temperature. "We knew we couldn't have 'performances' in this film; to be successful we had to achieve feeling <...>. That's why I had to work them under such conditions"', Wrede explained once.[112] As he put it on another occasion, 'there were spots where I could have spared the actors <...> but they would have felt betrayed'.[113] (Perhaps, a certain self-irony can be detected in the fact that Wrede cast himself as the paramedic Kolya Vdovushkin refusing Ivan Denisovich a place in the sick bay and sending him out to work in the frost.)

The cast's uncommon dedication frequently matched Wrede's high expectations.[114] Sometimes the actors went to extraordinary lengths to get under their

---

110 'Hollywood North', p. 43.
111 'Simulating Siberia'.
112 Fred Dickey, 'Siberian Prison Movie Has Cold Message', *San Jose Mercury-News* of 24 October 1971.
113 'Hollywood North', p. 42.
114 Trevor Peacock noted once that 'Wrede's method as a director was quite unique. He could somehow make you "find" your performance without "pushing" you, as the following story illustrates. In the 1968 Hamlet I was attempting Horatio. With 10 days to go to opening night, I nervously approached Wrede and explained that the essential core of the role seemed to be eluding me. A twinkle came into his eye as he explained in his high-pitched Scandinavian tones: "Yes, well, you see, my dear, it is not so much this" – and he held his right hand at right angles to his left – "it is rather more this" – and he switched hands. "You know – yes, yes – you know". I didn't exactly

characters' skins. Tom Courtenay modestly pointed out in an interview that Ivan Denisovich 'was not a showy part but there was a lot of work to be done, quietly'.[115] In fact, in preparation for the role, the rather slim Courtenay had to go to a health farm to shed an additional half a stone.[116] To acquire the authentic Ivan Denisovich look, he also had his head shaved and the caps from two of his front teeth removed.[117]

As if going on a strict diet in advance of the trip to Røros was not enough, Courtenay voluntarily did not eat anything at all for a day when on location too, before acting in one scene in which Ivan eats, so that he could 'concentrate on-camera as if it really were my only food for a long time'.[118] Clearly, Courtenay did not believe that the so-called 'Kuleshov effect' would suffice to evoke the sensation of hunger on screen merely from juxtaposing a frame with the actor's expressionless look and a frame featuring a bowl of gruel.[119] Having visited the set, a journalist observed that, as a result of these semi-voluntary privations, 'a certain prisoner psychology is taking hold. One cast member recently denounced a hot meal served on location as "proper swill".

---

know, but from then on, his apparent confidence in my efforts meant that I began to enjoy the search. <...> He was too wise a man to tell actors how to act. He could draw from a cast a harmonised performance as if by magic' (Peacock, op. cit.). Courtenay had something different to say about Wrede's manner as a director: 'From the first, he told me how to do things, and he was right. The others all used to say, "Do what you like", or, "Be more quick or more slow", and they were all much more famous than Casper, but they were also much more vague. He has vision. <...> But he can also be extremely tactless and has been with people like Olivier and that hasn't helped him get ahead' (Joseph N. Bell, 'Courtenay's Missionary Zeal for Ivan Denisovich', *Los Angeles Times*, 7 November 1971). It is possible that Wrede's directing varied depending on the actor. His philosophy of acting performance has been summarised in his 'Letter to a Young Actor' (see Appendix I).

115 Norman, op. cit.
116 'One looks at him and wonders where in heaven's name he lost it', remarked a critic upon hearing this (see Bell, op. cit.).
117 Courtenay had already used dental surgery in the name of art before. Two of his front teeth had been removed, two reduced in size and two more twisted to secure the part of Constantin in Chekhov's *Seagull*, Courtenay's professional debut with the Old Vic company at the Edinburgh Festival in 1960 (see Courtenay, op. cit., pp. 306-08).
118 'Simulating Siberia'.
119 In the film director and theoretician Lev Kuleshov's 1918 experiments with the montage technique, it was a shot of the actor Ivan Mozzhukhin's face followed by a shot of a plate of soup.

Another says darkly: "We're even beginning to fight over extra bowls and hide away pieces of stale cake"'.[120]

The thirty-man film crew stayed in the town's Turisthotell that had 'a sort of elementary ski-lodge comfort'.[121] Harwood recalled:

> When filming finished for the night, it was back to the hotel for a full three-course dinner, more often than not with a nourishing stew as centrepiece. On occasions, at the moment of the return to the hotel and before the hot dinner was eaten, the director, the cameraman and several of the actors would thaw out in the hotel sauna bath.[122]

A typical pastime under the hotel's roof after a day's work included

> a foursome of movie-makers itching to get to the ping pong table off the recreation room, where salesmen were pondering the milking-machine market; a wardrobe mistress nonchalantly sitting in the lobby mending an ostensibly hopeless pair of drab trousers; <and> Casper Wrede, à la Professor Higgins, crying 'He's got it!' when a Norwegian actor came up with the proper intonation in a line.[123]

There was little to do at the Turisthotell in the middle of the Norwegian winter. The cast occasionally spent their free time 'devising new ways of getting six or eight layers of clothing beneath the tattered costumes for the next day's shooting'.[124] On 11 January 1970, Eric Thompson sent the following letter to the editor of the London *Times*:

> Sir, – Have you ever considered the insulation qualities of your newspaper? I am filming "A Day in the Life of Ivan Denisovitch" here in Norway,

---

[120] 'Simulating Siberia'.
[121] 'Simulating Siberia'. For a hotel's advertising leaflet, see Appendix IV, pic. 4.
[122] *The Making*, p. 19.
[123] 'Hollywood North', p. 42. Professor Higgins is a leading character in George Bernard Shaw's 1913 comedy *Pygmalion*, who teaches a Cockney flower girl how to speak with an upper class accent.
[124] 'Simulating Siberia'.

and I find *The Times*, well crinkled and pushed into the sole of a boot, can help keep out up to 40deg. of frost.[125]

Some crew members turned their attention to local women ('"If her father answers", a young actor explains to the hotel operator, "he does not speak any English, so would you please ask him if she's in?"'[126]), while others entertained their friends and relatives who were keen to join studio executives and numerous inquisitive journalists from different countries (reporters from *Life* magazine, *The New York Times* and *The Daily Telegraph* among them) and use an opportunity to visit their nearest and dearest at such an exotic location. As Dilys Hamlett put it in her letter to Wrede of 15 January 1970, written in London, 'I think Røros has become the Mecca of the North'. She elaborated on the topic in her letter of 16 February 1970 to the same addressee, also written in London:

> Tonight Barbara Burke came for supper and we compared notes on Røros – the actors seem to be having a rare experience and Alfie's letters are very funny.[127] As in the concentration camp, every small experience is noted, analysed and discussed. We thought of you always being

---

125 Eric Thompson, 'Frostproof Edition', *The Times*, 15 January 1970. This letter unexpectedly struck a cord with a number of the paper's readers by bringing back a few memories of similar nature. Spike Milligan, of all people, felt compelled to write to the editor shortly afterwards: 'Sir, – Eric Thompson claims a crinkled copy of *The Times* inside his boot resisted 40 degrees of frost. I have done better. World War II scene, winter in Italy, conditions freezing, the mail arrives, with it three copies of *The Times*. After reading I removed my battledress, then page by page wrapped the three editions around my body, before re-donning my uniform. From them on, for the next three weeks, I never felt the cold. We were withdrawn from the line to do a refit, I removed all the pages from around my person, reassembled them and they were still all readable' (Spike Milligan, 'Frostproof Edition', *The Times*, 19 January 1970). Brigadier E. J. Todhunter could not remain indifferent either and contributed a military tale of his own, which appeared several days later: 'Sir, – Mr Eric Thompson <...> is not unique in discovering that *The Times* has other uses, apart from the crossword. Many years ago when the British Army reckoned (perhaps rightly) that spit and polish was the basis of all training and discipline, a limber gunner in my battery found that *The Times* had unique properties as a burnisher to produce the much prized blue sheen on steelwork. As I was lucky enough to have one or two reasonably intelligent officers, who read *The Times* as well as the *Sporting Life*, the battery was almost unbeatable in turn-out competitions' (E. J. Todhunter, 'Using *The Times*', *The Times*, 21 January 1970).
126 'Simulating Siberia'.
127 The actor Alfred Burke played the part of Alyoshka the Baptist.

in the cold & marvelled at your resilience – Ronnie <Harwood> + Michael <Elliott> say you have never seemed nor looked better – but how exhausting must be the pressure + the conditions <!>

One Røros guest stated that the director and the leading cameraman

challenge the visiting press and other observers to see if they can stay the whole course, which is to remain outside on location for an entire evening of filming. Few can do it. A *Life* reporter, who used to be with their Moscow bureau, did, but admitted Moscow weather wasn't quite as bad. Group W films exec veepee Howard G. Barnes shivered, but said he thought the 110-degree heat he suffered in the Australian outback while scouting a location there last year was far worse to bear.[128]

As for Harwood, when in Røros, he had to fall back on the skills that he had acquired in his acting days, when a bit actor fell ill and Wrede asked the dramatist to step in and 'play the part of a camp sergeant, including a few lines. It was the first time Harwood had ever appeared in the film'.[129]

One of the leading cinematographers in the world, Sven Nykvist, 'an expert at communicating mood on the screen',[130] famous for his work with Ingmar Bergman, was responsible for the photography. Wrede was keen to use the camera as if it was 'one of the prisoners – a newcomer in the camp, who sees everything for the first time and puts two and two together'.[131] Style-wise, Wrede was 'very wary of pretty pictures, those Zhivago-style long wide shots',[132] and Nykvist, 'whose austere lens could seek out the gloom in a

---

[128] Pack, op. cit.
[129] Ibid. According to one account, Harwood 'leapt at the chance of acting again. They cut his hair and rigged him up with a Russian uniform and checked his union credentials, and turned him out to shoot the scene in 15 degrees below. Afterwards, <the cameraman> <...> nudged him and said: "You have done this before". Harwood the professional was pleased about that; very pleased indeed' (Hebert, op. cit.).
[130] Nora E. Taylor, op. cit.
[131] Nils-Erik Ekstrand, 'Ryskt fångläger filmas i Norge', *Dagens Nyheter*, 13 January 1970.
[132] 'Simulating Siberia'. Boris Pasternak's novel *Doctor Zhivago* was adapted for Metro-Goldwyn-Mayer by the director David Lean in 1965. Courtenay played the part of Antipov-Strel'nikov in it. To quote from a contemporary review, 'Successful <...> beyond

travel poster',[133] suited Wrede's intentions ideally. Moreover, Nykvist had already filmed in Røros, when he had been the principal cameraman on *An-Magritt*. According to one testimony, 'Unlike his Hollywood or London colleagues, Nykvist prefers to operate his own camera, even when it comes to lugging a 50-pound 35mm Arriflex on his shoulders for some vital hand-held shooting'.[134] Under the supervision of Hans Nord (1919-2005), Norsk Film's chief cameraman, who had been 'rebuilding the equipment for the expected conditions',[135] this camera was fitted 'with arctic oil and a special heating element beneath the motor, neither of which keeps the film from going brittle and breaking periodically'.[136] Wrede took great interest in the light conditions – night scenes, the cold light surrounding the camp and the warm light within the barracks – and did not accept any film-making trickery. The effect was one that no studio work could have accomplished. According to some reports, 'the English technicians marvelled at the way <...> Nykvist could muster every available ray of light.[137] There were, in fact, barely three shades of colour: black, grey and white. The actors' ashen faces registered powerful col-

---

question is the physical production of this film – the brilliant visual realization. <...> <Lean> has got very good performances from Rod Steiger and Tom Courtenay – the former as the bourgeois opportunist <Komarovsky> who first seduces and later plagues <the leading female character> Lara, and the latter as the thin-lipped revolutionary who is strangely and briefly loved by her. <...> But all these people and others are but characters in a sad romance that seems almost as far away from Russia as the surging revolution seems from them. They are as fustian and sentimental as the music of Maurice Jarre that has a nostalgic balalaika tinkle. They are closer to Hollywood than to the steppes' (Bosley Crowther, 'Doctor Zhivago', *The New York Times*, 23 December 1965). It is curious that after *One Day*'s release, it was favourably compared to *Doctor Zhivago* by one critic, who applauded the fact that the former 'avoids a sweep-of-history Dr Zhivago trial-and-tribulation approach; the camera catches sombre visual starkness rather than flashy lushness and there is little sensationalism in the film's depiction of brutality. No frills, no thrills, no plaintive balalaikas playing in the background' (Peter Eglick, 'A Study in "Absolute Insecurity"', *34th Street: The Magazine of The Daily Pennsylvanian*, 30 September 1971).
133 'Simulating Siberia'.
134 Pack, op. cit.
135 *The Making*, p. 19.
136 'Simulating Siberia'.
137 Thus, on the last day of the shooting in Røros, Wrede reportedly 'required one more setup to complete the location schedule. Nykvist, light meter in hand, took a reading. "We can't do anything in this", he said. Wrede replied that it was to be the last shot. "Right", said Nykvist and photographed the scene; it appears in the film' (*The Making*, p. 23).

ours, though'.[138] This is how a journalist characterised Nykvist's palette in *One Day*:

> Despite the overwhelming drabness of Ivan Denisovich's life, the colours that surround him are often spectacular. The dark blue of dawn gives way to a smokey purple-orange-hazy grey of the early day. The guards' khaki and red uniforms stand out with stark, ascetic beauty against their luxurious sheepskin coats. The only colour missing from the world is green. The basic colour of life is altogether missing from Ivan Denisovich's world.[139]

Courtenay recalled: 'Sven Nykvist <...> told me once that Casper had pulled off some shots that Bergman would not even try'.[140] The result was so good that in his memoirs Nykvist claimed that it was one of his most successful films.[141] As one critic put it, 'Nykvist can achieve a tactile sense of dread; <in *One Day*>, his expanses of snow are more than weather: they seem vast pages upon which no one dares to write'.[142]

The mood on the set was described as a 'genuine feeling of involvement. Perhaps the incredible cold made brothers of us all, for certainly the whole operation was endowed with an extraordinary community feeling'.[143] There was also a palpable sense of something like supernatural intervention. Summing up the atmosphere in Røros at the time, Wrede wrote in 'Russia on My Mind':

---

138 'Hollywood North', pp. 42-43.
139 John Weisman, 'Jail in Siberia: A Smoothly Running, Never Ending Example of Man's Inhumanity to Man', *Rolling Stone*, 11 November 1971, p. 66.
140 Norman, op. cit.
141 Nykvist, op. cit., p. 120. Whenever possible, Wrede championed filming in natural light conditions. His *Private Potter* (1962) was even criticised for the night time photography, which was so dark that it became difficult to see what was going on (see http://www.imdb.com/title/tt0056376/). *Private Potter*'s principal cinematographer was Arthur Lavis, who also worked with Wrede as a cameraman on the film version of *The Barber of Stamford Hill*.
142 S<tefan> K<anfer>, 'Witness', *Time*, 31 May 1971, p. 41.
143 *The Making*, p. 22.

I began to feel the presence and the power of the host of those who had died in the camps working with us in the dark and the snow: for the first shot on the first day of filming the thermometer nailed to the wooden post in front of the guards' hut showed precisely 27 degrees centigrade below zero as prescribed by Alexander Solzhenitsyn; when our cameraman, after hours of preparation in the pitch dark, shouted 'the moon, we've forgotten the moon',[144] I could raise my hand and point to the full moon rising from the hills at exactly the required spot; after weeks of work in the open air one of the actors was asked by a newcomer what the weather would be like the next day, the actor turned to me and asked in turn, 'what weather do you want tomorrow?' I told him. He turned back to the newcomer and said, 'there you are, that is tomorrow's weather'. <...> The locals and the mountain farmers who were helping, threatened us day after day with the inevitable week-long mid-winter snowstorms – and they were snowed in right enough by terrible blizzards and cut off for a week as soon as we had gone. These were the most spectacular instances of a sequence of most unlikely events that only come once in a lifetime.[145]

It is hardly surprising that on the set 'even the least superstitious <...> wondered if the word "co-production" had special meaning for Wrede'.[146]

When work on the outdoor scenes was over, the cast and crew moved to the Norsk Film studios in Oslo. Put together by the production manager Jac Hald, the working schedule of 6 March 1970, which survived among Wrede's papers in Norwegian, makes it easy to imagine what a typical morning at work in Oslo was like. On that day, a scene at the mess hall was filmed, and eleven regular and thirty additional extras were to join the entire principal cast (except for Eric Thompson, whose character was supposed to have his meal brought for him to his office). The production secretary Eric Hurum was asked to meet the eleven regular extras at the Gyldenløwe hotel at 7.15am and take

---

[144] To illustrate a discussion of the moon in a conversation between Ivan Denisovich and the Captain. – BH, AR.
[145] See Appendix I (section '1961-70').
[146] *The Making*, p. 23.

them to the studios. The production assistant Per Gran had to do the same for Courtenay, Maxwell, Burke, Cording, Guinness and the sound mixer Paul LeMare at the Continental hotel at 7.45am. Malland's regular responsibility was picking up Wrede and Nykvist. While the British cast were on their way to the studio, the local actors, who had obviously been expected to arrive there on their own, were already either waiting, or queuing for, their appointments with the chief make-up artist Nurven Bredangen. Frimann Falck Clausen was to see Nurven at 7.50am, followed by Malland at 8am, Cording at 8.05am, Maxwell at 8.10am and Courtenay at 8.20am. At the same time, the make-up assistant Kari Hermansen was dealing with the second group of actors: Jo Skønberg (Gopchik) was scheduled for 8am, Torstein Rustdal (playing the part of the Estonian prisoner Väino[147]) for 8.05am, Odd Jan Sandsdalen (playing the part of the Estonian prisoner Eino) for 8.10am, Guinness for 8.15am and Burke for 8.20am. Meanwhile, all the extras, including the additional ones, had to be made up from 7.30am onwards.

Hidden behind these dry organisational details was the fact that during the filming in Røros the production went over budget, and savings had to be made. According to Harwood,

> In the calmest of atmospheres, without a distributor or an executive producer breathing down his neck, Wrede made his decision in private: a five-week stay in the studios had been planned; Wrede drove the unit with unrelenting pressure and finished in four, just before Easter. Even this hard-driven phase caused no display of temperament or resentment.[148]

---

147 This character remains nameless in Solzhenitsyn's book.
148 *The Making*, p. 24. Despite Wrede's cost-saving efforts, the production went over budget. According to a financial statement, prepared in Oslo on 26 November 1970, i.e. after the film's completion, *One Day*'s budget was meant to be USD443,640 (excluding contingency) but amounted to USD499,680. The balance sheets in Norwegian currency, attached to the statement (in 1969-70, one US dollar equalled 7.14 Norwegian crowns), demonstrate that the over-expenditure was incurred in almost every category, from a smallish overspend under the 'Story and Script' heading (NOK969) to significant ones under the 'Production Unit Salaries' and the 'Laboratory' headings (NOK96,132 and 97,821, respectively). The only areas where savings were made overall, were costumes and make-up (NOK3,790 under budget), studio hire (NOK12,443 under budget), insurance (NOK14,012 under budget) and props

It was at this time that Richard Pack's son Bob visited the *One Day* crew to get a taste of film studio work. In his letter to Wrede of 26 March 1970, Richard Pack records his son's reaction expressed on his return to the United States as 'brimming over with enthusiasm for you, Sven <Nykvist>, the film itself and just about everyone connected with the production. He had an exciting time, but more importantly, he learned a great deal'.

Arguably there was something to learn not only about the day-to-day business of a film production unit, but also about the way Solzhenitsyn's book had been transformed into a script, truly remarkable for 'a fidelity rarely seen in screen translations',[149] considering that 'film versions of bestselling novels often end up as cinematic bastards, complete with extraneous intercourse and a plot that appears to have been written by the same bunch that condenses classics for comic books'.[150]

(NOK19,505 under budget). There have been suggestions in the press that *One Day*'s demanding location had 'one pleasant advantage <…>, <namely> the money it saved the film company. "The crew wanted out of there so badly that we finished well ahead of schedule", Wrede remembers' (Dickey, op. cit.). However, the same balance sheets reveal that, although the main cast and the actors in bit parts did indeed receive NOK27, 532 less than had been budgeted for, the extras had to be overpaid by as much as NOK69,054, which ultimately resulted in an overspend of NOK31,174 in the 'Artists' category. All in all, the contingency, initially estimated at USD20,000, was exceeded by USD36,040 (about 8% of the budget).

149 P<aul> D. Z<immerman>, 'A Last Look at 1971's Movies', *Newsweek*, 3 January 1972, p. 33. One might find symbolic the fact that a still from *One Day* featuring Maxwell and Courtenay adorns p. 8 of the 'canonical' version of the book published in 1973 in Paris.

150 Eglick, op. cit.

5 THE BOOK – THE SCRIPT – THE FILM: A COMPARISON

Harsh weather conditions were not the only thing to grapple with when adapting *One Day* for the screen. Perhaps the toughest nut to crack was the book itself, which contained little dramatic action in the Hollywood sense of the term, and for that reason was virtually unfilmable. Harwood recalls how he and Wrede tried to solve this particular problem:

> Armed with Aitken's translation, we read and reread the novel and made a breakdown of the action. We studied the book in the severest detail, a painful, unceasing process. Each made his own notes. My method was to make detailed lists of every action culled from Solzhenitsyn's descriptions; Wrede's method was to underline the key words in the text. I ended up with *One Day* rewritten in telegram form, and Wrede ended up with every word in the book underlined. The conclusion was inescapable: everything contained in the novel was of importance.[151]

Only the third draft of the film script was deemed successful. Some scenes, such as the prisoners collecting firewood at the worksite to bring to the labour camp to keep themselves warm, only to be told by the guards to drop half of what they had gathered, were inevitably sacrificed.[152] The initial idea of flashbacks interspersing the linear narrative, to elucidate the inmates' past,[153] was rejected in favour of the narrator's voiceover, which 'seems stilted at first – but is necessary in a film that relies so heavily on the pantomime of gesture

---

151 *The Making*, p. 9.
152 See *The Making*, pp. 117-18, 127, 246. The firewood scene had been present in the very first draft of the script, written in April-May 1969.
153 Wrede reportedly believed that the Soviet Union was 'planning its own picture from the book <...> <involving> the families of Ivan and the other characters. That sort of verisimilitude was not possible' for Wrede who had not been to the Soviet Union, and the plan to visualise Ivan Denisovich's reminiscences was dropped (Nora E. Taylor, op. cit.).

and facial expression to convey an aura of irony and composure'.[154] Also, the voiceover would work best in a situation when the Soviet labour camp set-up, unfamiliar to Western audiences, had to be explained and commented upon.[155]

Curiously, in Solzhenitsyn's book,

> there are two distinct narrative voices <...>: the voice of a <...> narrator, which is the controlling voice of the novel, and the voice of Ivan Denisovich Shukhov, represented through quasi-direct discourse.[156] <...> The <...> narrator's voice is clearly meant to represent the generalised voice of the camp prisoners. <...> Very often these two voices <...> blend together to such an extent that in many passages they cannot be told apart with certainty. Thus, the <...> narrator's voice comes to represent the generalised voice of the prisoners in such a way that it includes Shukhov's voice as the dominant one within the general blending or mixture. This blending of voices gives a strong sense of the unity or wholeness of the camp experience being portrayed. <...> However, the presence of a narrator's voice distinct from Shukhov makes it possible for him, and therefore for the reader, to step out of Shukhov's subjective consciousness and view him more objectively in some scenes.[157]

The authors of the film adaptation strove to preserve this complex narrative structure as best they could. In the screen version, the narrator's voiceover is read by the same actor who plays the part of Ivan Denisovich (Courtenay), thus at times converging the narrator's point of view with that of the protago-

---

154 Eglick, op. cit.
155 Cf.: *One Day in the Life of Ivan Denisovich* 'is written in an extremely compressed form with the data on the camp scattered throughout the narration. The camp rations, the rules for work and punishment, the number of packages a zek <prisoner. – BH, AR> receives, his privileges, his number, his name, the type of work he does – all of these data construct the severe regime of the camp <...>. One must read the work more than once and add up the data with mathematical precision in order to draw the full implications' (Kern, 'Solženicyn's Self-Censorship', p. 424).
156 The quasi-direct discourse (*nesobstvenno-priamaia rech'*) takes place when a character is referred to in the third person singular but his/her thoughts and feelings are expressed in the way the character himself/herself would have done it.
157 Luplow, op. cit., pp. 401, 406.

nist.[158] This device, unusual in cinema, was duly noticed and interpreted correctly by at least one critic: 'Ivan's voice is on the sound track, talking about himself in the third person. <...> The technical angularity is a risk but successful <sic! – BH, AR>, obviously chanced so as to keep as much as possible of Solzhenitsyn's own voice there, too'.[159]

For variety's sake, and perhaps quite predictably so, some of the lines that belong to the book's third-person narrative were distributed among the characters in the film. The Captain proved especially useful in this respect. A newcomer to the camp, he could plausibly question his fellow prisoners about various aspects of life in the camp, and their answers would be beneficial not only to him but also to the viewer. When a member of Team 104, an inmate called Panteleyev, remains in the camp because he is ostensibly indisposed, Fetyukov, Tsesar and Ivan Denisovich tell the Captain that Panteleyev is in fact an informer, who will be questioned by the camp's security officers in the other prisoners' absence, once the teams leave for the worksite.[160] In another scene, when Kilgas expresses his regret that there have not been any snow-

---

158 In the version of the film released in Scandinavia, the narrator speaks Norwegian (Espen Skjønberg's voice was used; see Arvid Andersen, 'Det fineste og mest profesjonelle film-*miljø* jeg har opplevd! Espen Skjønberg: Solsjenitsyns nøkterne fangehverdag var alltid vår rettesnor', *Dagbladet*, 26 November 1970). This has been seen by some as a drawback, because it creates a larger distance between the narrator and the characters (who speak English) than there is in the book, and undermines the illusion of reality that the film is seeking to create (for details, see the opinions of students No. 5 and No. 7 in Appendix II, containing student feedback after the viewing of *One Day in the Life of Ivan Denisovich* at the Department of Slavonic and Baltic Languages and Literatures, University of Helsinki, on 15 November 2007).
159 Penelope Gilliatt, 'Worlds Away', *The New Yorker*, 22 May 1971, p. 71. Solzhenitsyn's own point of view was deliberately dissolved in that of the prisoner-narrator. According to one observation, in the book 'we cannot separate any authorial point of view that would differ from the narrator's; they are one and the same' (Vladimir J. Rus, '*One Day in the Life of Ivan Denisovich*: A Point of View Analysis', *Canadian Slavonic Papers*, vol. 13 (1973), p. 173; see also L. Rzhevskii, 'Obraz rasskazchika v povesti Solzhenitsyna "Odin den' Ivana Denisovicha"', in Robert Magidoff, George Y. Shevelov, J. S. G. Simmons and Kiril Taranovski (eds), *Studies in Slavic Linguistics and Poetics in Honor of Boris O. Unbegaun*, New York and London: New York University Press; University of London Press, 1968, p. 174). From time to time, Shukhov's invisible presence continues to be felt in Solzhenitsyn's narrative even in *The Gulag Archipelago*, *The Oak and the Calf* and *The Red Wheel* (see Mariia Shneerson, 'Golos Shukhova v proizvedeniiakh Solzhenitsyna', *Grani*, no. 146 (1987), pp. 106-33).
160 Compare and contrast the relevant bits in the book and the script (see *The Making*, pp. 47 and 191).

storms in the winter, he and Gopchik explain to the Captain that blizzards give prisoners a chance to get time off work and even to escape.[161] The need to describe how the parcels office was run and what Ivan Denisovich heard and thought about while he was queuing in it, led to the invention of several characters, such as prisoner R-936 (whose jam is poured by the guard directly into a sack because prisoners are not allowed to keep tins and jars from parcels) and prisoners F-689 and D-301 (discussing the Muscovites and the rumour that the prisoners would have to go to work on Sunday).[162] As if in compensation, some characters mentioned by Solzhenitsyn (e.g. Shkuropatenko and Yermolaev) did not make it to the script. Neither did the second reference to Panteleyev (who comes to the mess hall to eat his dinner, thus confirming the suspicion that there is nothing wrong with him).[163] All in all, however, both the prisoners and the guards remain conspicuously numerous in the film. 160 extras and actors for bit parts were hired to show how overcrowded the labour camp population was, and to create an impression that those occupying the film's foreground (most notably, Team 104) were merely a small part of a gigantic nameless mass.[164]

We are fortunate to be able to gain a further insight into the meticulous and painstaking process of adapting Solzhenitsyn's book for the screen by comparing a typewritten version of Harwood's shooting script (distributed by Scripts Limited of 8 Gerrard Street, London W1), with Casper Wrede's handwritten alterations, which survive in David Wrede's private archive; its printed version, published in *The Making of One Day in the Life of Ivan Denisovich* (New York: Ballantine Books, 1971, pp. 169-271); and the film itself which differs both from the typewritten and the printed versions.[165] The typewritten edi-

---

161 Cf. *The Making*, pp. 65-66 and 200-01.
162 Cf. *The Making*, pp. 133-36 and 249-51.
163 See *The Making*, pp. 70, 90-91, 143-44.
164 Wrede's notes reveal that he had envisaged using from 10 to 20 regular extras, and from 50 up to 1000 additional extras, in some of the film's scenes, but the numbers had to be scaled down.
165 As any film director worth his salt, Wrede would readily deviate from the script for the sake of an impressive shot. Thus, the script has Ivan Denisovich in the sick bay 'putting the thermometer under his armpit' (*The Making*, p. 187; cf.: 'Ivan is given a thermometer (probably under his arm)' in Gary Kern, 'Ivan the Worker', *Modern Fiction Studies*, vol. 23, no. 1 (1977), p. 19). In the film, Ivan Denisovich is shown in profile, with the thermometer sticking out of his mouth.

tion (hereafter referred to as Typescript) is clearly an earlier version of the printed one. Nevertheless, the printed one (hereafter referred to as Print) does not incorporate some of the changes, which were presumably introduced during the production stage and remain in the film but not in the published screenplay.

The typewritten version consists of 224 scenes, while the printed one has only 219. However, it was not merely a matter of cutting five scenes out. In the editing and rewriting process, some scenes were either deleted (such as Typescript 137, 138 and 139, focusing on the details of building the power station's brick wall) or split into shorter ones (such as Typescript 108 and 109, covering most of the team leader's personal story and replaced in the printed version by scenes 110, 111 and 112), while others were reshuffled (e.g. the Captain and Ivan Denisovich's argument in Typescript 152 – about what happens to the moon when it becomes invisible – is moved from before the recount scene to after it, to become Print 154), with some lines added, altered, reassigned[166] and omitted, as and when necessary. Also, when the typewritten script was checked over for publication, some revised scenes in it received new numbers (e.g., Typescript 25 and 25A became Print 25 and 26, whereas Typescript 222 and 222A became Print 216 and 217).[167]

There are only seven scenes that were dropped altogether, all of them involving various stages of Team 104's bricklaying assignment. Scenes 112, 114, 115 and 116 dealt with resuming work after the lunch break and were placed between Print 114 and Print 115:

112
IVAN DENISOVICH *getting to his feet, with a sigh.*

---

[166] Thus, the sentence 'You can't expect me to remember all those damned numbers, can you?', pronounced by the team leader in the book, was given to his deputy Pavlo in the film (see *The Making*, pp. 156, 261), while Alyoshka's phrase 'If we have to work faster, then let's work faster' was changed to 'We'll have to keep up with them; won't we?' and given to the Captain (see Typescript, pp. 57-58; and *The Making*, p. 228).
[167] During the production, the renumbering is normally avoided to prevent confusion, and any new scene is allocated the previous scene's number, with letters A, B, C etc. attached as appropriate.

IVAN DENISOVICH: I'll go and hack off the ice.
From the pile of tools he begins to take a small hatchet, a brush, a mason's hammer, a levelling rod, a plumb and a length of string. <…>

114
RESUME IVAN DENISOVICH
By now he has collected his tools and makes his way to the door. Others have risen, too.
KILGAS (O<ff> s<creen>): Hey, Ivan Denisovich – wait for me! I am coming too.
IVAN DENISOVICH *stops as* KILGAS *joins him.*
IVAN DENISOVICH: Come on then, fat-face. If you were working for yourself you'd have been out there before me.
KILGAS *laughs as they go.* SENKA *follows.*

115
EXT<erior shot>. THE SECOND STOREY – DAY
IVAN DENISOVICH *appears and looks out.*

116
THE SITE (IVAN DENISOVICH'S p<oint> o<f> v<iew>)
Sun gleaming on snow; the dark watch towers. Then a distant belch of smoke blackens the sky; an engine wheezes and begins to hoot. PRISONERS *slowly emerge from the warm places and begin to tramp across the snow to their working sites.*[168]

Scenes 137, 138, 139 – placed between Print 132 and Print 133 – described the erection of the brick wall as follows:

---

[168] Typescript, pp. 53-54. Scene 113 of the typewritten version involved Pavlo and Tyurin. Pavlo's lines 'Sure there are enough for the block laying, team leader? Shouldn't we send up somebody else? Or won't there be enough mortar?', as well as Tyurin's 'You work here on the mortar. We'll put six on the job. See there's a steady flow. Not a moment's break' (ibid., p. 53), were excised, while Tyurin's phrase 'I'll make the fourth block-layer myself' and Pavlo's response 'If you're going to lay blocks I'll mix the mortar for you myself. We'll see who's working faster! Hey, where's the longest shovel?' were altered a little and moved to Print 116 (see *The Making*, p. 225).

137
THE SECOND STOREY
THE MASONS *racing as the walls are near to meeting in a corner.*

138
IVAN DENISOVICH, SENKA AND PAVLO *working.* IVAN DENISOVICH *gazes along the wall, making sure of its straightness. He pushes* SENKA *aside and takes over the laying of the blocks towards the corner. Then –*
IVAN DENISOVICH: Stop!
He shoves PAVLO *away from a block and gets it into line himself. He turns to see that* SENKA's *section is going out of line. He hurries over and straightens it out with two blocks.*

139
ANOTHER ANGLE
THE CAPTAIN *totters up with his barrow. He is exhausted and can barely speak.*
CAPTAIN: Just two more barrows.
As he goes, IVAN DENISOVICH *and* KILGAS *dip into the same barrow for mortar.*
IVAN DENISOVICH: Had a horse like him once. Willing. Worked itself to death.
KILGAS. Look.
He points <at the sight of other teams finishing work and getting ready to leave the construction area>.[169]

Although all seven scenes were based directly on Solzhenitsyn's text,[170] they presumably had to go because they slowed the action down even further in a film that could hardly be called fast-paced in the first place. After all, not every prospective viewer could be expected to feel as deeply involved with the bricklaying craft as Ivan Denisovich and his team mates. Besides, scene 139 presented a problem with continuity: in an earlier episode, it was made clear that there were four mortar carriers in the team, 'two to each barrow of ce-

---
169 Typescript, pp. 64-65.
170 See *The Making*, pp. 97-98, 110-11.

ment'[171] (the electrical hoist was broken and could not be repaired). The Captain's appearance on his own, without a partner, might have created an impression that the mortar was delivered to the power station's second floor in wheelbarrows, not in hods, although special care was taken to explain that even if the prisoners had wheelbarrows (they did not), they would not have been able to use them anyway. During an altercation with the foreman Der, the team leader says: 'What d'you think we are – donkeys? Carrying blocks up to the second storey by hand?' The foreman replies: 'They'll give you double rates for taking them up'. The team builder continues: 'Yes, the wheelbarrow rates. You try pushing a wheelbarrow up here. We want triple rates for carrying 'em up by hand'.[172]

Other *omissions* mostly include lines which either state the obvious (e.g. Ivan Denisovich's opinion of Alyoshka, 'What a treasure a meek man is to a team'[173]), or dwell on superfluous details (e.g. Ivan Denisovich's protest against an attempt to move his boots away from the stove, addressed to an inmate 'with red hair'[174]), or do not add anything new to a particular scene, thus making it longer than necessary (e.g. the team leader's story about his encounter with a girl at a train station: 'a large kettle she had. <…> What was she supposed to do with <loaves of bread>? She wasn't worried about the kettle' in Typescript 109; the escort sergeant's exclamations 'Recount! Recount!' in Typescript 151; the Captain's unfinished sentence in Typescript 157 on what would happen if the rotten fish in the prisoners' rations were replaced with rotten meat, 'I bet we'd…'; D 301's opinion of the Muscovites who jabber so fast, 'they might as well not be talking Russian. More like bloody Rumanians'; and the anonymous prisoners' catcalls 'Serve you right!' and 'Being clever, eh?', directed at their idle fellow inmates, who are being thrown out by force from Hut 9 during the evening recount in Typescript 214[175]). A special category of omissions includes geographical locations that were presumably

---

171 See *The Making*, p. 226.
172 Typescript, p. 61. This wording has been used in the film almost exactly (with 'bringing' instead of 'taking'). For the original one that remained in the script's printed version, see *The Making*, p. 231.
173 Typescript, p. 58.
174 Typescript, p. 99.
175 Typescript, pp. 51, 69, 74, 84, 98.

perceived as either too obscure (such as a reference to the Kyrgyz city of 'Frunze' – now Bishkek – in the team leader's personal story in Typescript 111[176]), or excessive (for instance, a reference to the 'Siberian' frost in Ivan Denisovich's line in Typescript 213 and Print 207[177]), or simply inappropriate (for example, a mention of Jerusalem in Alyoshka's quote from Acts 21:13, 'I am ready not to be bound only but to die for in Jerusalem in the name of the Lord Jesus', because he speaks of the labour camp, not Jerusalem, and the symbolic parallel between the two, passable in the book, seems quite out of place in the film that tends to shun symbolism in favour of matter-of-factness[178]).

There is a general trend to keep the dialogue to a minimum, which becomes even more obvious once the script is transferred onto the screen. The film successfully crossbreeds the art of British understatement (augmented by the comprehensible lack of desire to open one's mouth in sub-zero temperatures, well familiar even to chatty Russians) with the Finnish preference for a silent mode of communication (in the words of Berthold Brecht, Finns are 'silent in two languages'[179]), thus producing an overall 'less is more' effect. For example, the prisoners' march from the labour camp to the worksite is performed in complete silence, uninterrupted by the guards' shouts 'U 48, hands behind back! B 502, keep up!' that are provided in both the typewritten and the printed versions of the screenplay.[180] This three-and-a-half minute walk, ac-

---

176 Typescript, p. 52. It was removed both from the printed version of the script (see *The Making*, p. 224) and from the film.
177 It did not make it to the film version.
178 The reference to Jerusalem can be found both in Typescript 217 and Print 211 (see Typescript, p. 102; and *The Making*, p. 267) but was excluded from the film version.
179 In his poem 'Finnische Landschaft' (1940): 'ein Volk, das in zwei Sprachen schweigt' (implying Finnish and Swedish, the language of the largest minority). Michael Meyer, whose play *The Ortolan* was directed by Wrede in February 1954 for OUDS, recalls that Wrede has taught him 'that one of the most important and least publicised roles of a director, where new plays are concerned, is to sit down with the author and persuade him to correct his play's faults, to cut, add and rewrite. <...> I remember there was one long speech of which I was especially proud. Wrede somehow persuaded me that it would be far more effective if the character simply said "No"' (Meyer, op. cit, p. 127).
180 Typescript, p. 23; and *The Making*, p. 197. In the very first draft of the script, dated April-May 1969, the marching scene was accompanied by a voiceover explaining how important a good team leader was for his labour camp gang. This first draft is marked by many more instances of the voiceover intervention (talking, for example, about

companied only by Arne Nordheim's atmospheric music and beautifully filmed in transition from darkness into sunrise by alternating long- and middle-distance shots of the prisoner's column with close-ups of their dour faces, mesmerizes the viewer by its solemn and bleak determination. Words would only undermine the impact of the scene.

Whenever there is a chance, characters are consistently deprived of their lines. Kilgas, for instance, loses two sentences revealing his reaction to Der's appearance at the power station: 'I don't usually deal with big shots. But if he slips off the ramp – call me'.[181] The Captain loses half a sentence, 'such a luxury',[182] at the very beginning of his story about something that happened to him in Archangel. For his part, the guard, who came to escort the Captain to the cell block, loses the end of his phrase, 'well enough'.[183] Even the omniscient Voice of the narrator, whose remarks are indispensable when it comes to the labour camp's internal regulations and Ivan Denisovich's private feelings and thoughts, is cut short in mid-sentence while elucidating the prisoners' reluctance to do any work: 'We'll do nothing during the day and the night is our own' (the last nine words are excluded from the film).[184]

This excision, however, is fully recompensed in advance by the voiceover lines that can be heard when the prisoners arrive at the construction site, i.e. some twenty scenes before. The Voice says: 'Only when the towers were manned were the prisoners allowed to enter the worksite. Here, from sunrise to sunset, they worked and then were marched back to the camp again after darkness had fallen'. These words, missing from both the typewritten and the printed versions of the script, were obviously deemed necessary to describe

---

Ivan Denisovich's leather boots, as well as prisoners' identification numbers) and of prisoners' and guards' dialogues (e.g. two orderlies arguing whose turn it is to get hot water and two guards comparing millet to rice), in contrast with the typewritten and printed final versions. There had also been Ivan Denisovich's mutterings to himself (e.g. after Der's demand to use more mortar when laying bricks) which were later discarded too.
181 Typescript, p. 59; and *The Making*, p. 229.
182 Typescript, p. 94; and *The Making*, p. 260.
183 Typescript, p. 96; and *The Making*, p. 262.
184 Typescript, p. 34; and *The Making*, p. 208.

the otherwise insufficiently clear arrangements of this particular aspect of life in the labour camp.[185]

Another exception is the scene when Ivan Denisovich visits a Latvian in a nearby hut to buy some tobacco from him (Typescript 201, Print 195). Here the terse small talk before the transaction ('Evening...' – 'Evening...')[186] is expanded as follows:

> <IVAN DENISOVICH:> Well, how's life?
> <THE LATVIAN:> Not bad.
> <IVAN DENISOVICH:> Cold today.
> <THE LATVIAN:> Yes.[187]

Presumably, these lines, entered by hand in the typewritten version of the screenplay and further modified in the film (to make Ivan Denisovich say 'Had a good day?' and 'Cold...'), were required to lay an emphasis on the prisoners' reticence in going about their business in conditions when an ill-considered utterance might cost them dear.[188]

Otherwise, there is only a handful of <u>additions</u>, mostly made to clarify the situation, such as the team leader's phrase 'and wait till I know where we have to work today', attached to his request to Team 104 to go to the repairs shop. It was inserted by hand in Typescript 52 and later transferred (with minor variations) to the corresponding Print 53 scene.[189] Similarly, Kilgas's words 'it was lying about. I put it here after the snow fell. Still there!', explain-

---

185 For a similar reason, scene 17 of the printed version – as well as the film – include two explanatory comments from the Voice on the nature of the prisoners' diet, which are missing from Typescript 17 depicting Ivan Denisovich in the mess hall at breakfast (cf. Typescript, pp. 10-11; and *The Making*, pp. 185-86).
186 Typescript, pp. 89-90; and *The Making*, p. 256.
187 Typescript, p. 90.
188 The additional exchange between Ivan Denisovich and the Latvian, as per Typescript 201, was copied verbatim from the narration in Solzhenitsyn's book (see *The Making*, p. 148). This is how the book's author explains the characters' reluctance to proceed immediately to the discussion of the matter that interests them both: 'It was a small room, and everyone was keeping his ears open – who is this fellow? Why has he come? They both realised that, which was why Shukhov sat there talking about nothing special' (ibid.).
189 Cf. Typescript, p. 25; and *The Making*, p. 199.

ing the provenance of a roll of tarred felt, were also added by hand to Typescript 58 and kept (in a slightly modified form) in the corresponding Print 60 scene.[190] Curiously, Ivan Denisovich's line 'I signed', concluding his story about his forced (and false) confession about spying for the Germans and added by hand to Typescript 80, survived in the film but did not make it to the printed version of the screenplay.[191] Conversely, a guard's order, 'Open the gates!', given before the prisoners are marched out of the construction area, is missing from the typewritten version of the script but can be found in both its printed version and the film.[192] However, Tsesar's words 'of the cinema' (attached to his 'Eisenstein was a genius', to make allowances for those in the audience who might not have heard of Eisenstein) were included in the printed version,[193] as well as the film, and so were the following handwritten additions to the team leader's monologue in Typescript 108 (with the exception of the first four sentences and the second half of the fifth):

> So I said to this regimental commander – I was shaking in my boots – 'I serve the working people'. He went white. 'You are not a peasant', he screamed at me. 'You're the son of a farmer, a land-owning pig. You've betrayed Soviet power. You've been hiding in the army for years'. I was discharged the same day. It was <in> the middle of November.[194]

One of the most significant of these additions is scene 56A in the typewritten version of the script, which was meant to help the viewers understand why Kilgas and Ivan Denisovich had to go and search for some tarred felt:

> EXT<erior shot>. BEFORE THE POWER HOUSE
> KILGAS *crouching*, I<VAN> D<ENISOVICH> *standing*.
> TYURIN: Now, boys, after we've eaten, we'll be working on the second storey laying blocks. We'll use the generator room for mixing the mortar.
> KILGAS: And for keeping warm.

---

190 Cf. Typescript, p. 29; and *The Making*, p. 203.
191 Cf. Typescript, p. 39; and *The Making*, p. 212.
192 Cf. Typescript, p. 75; and *The Making*, p. 242.
193 Cf. Typescript, p. 48; and *The Making*, p. 106.
194 Cf. Typescript, pp. 49 (reverse), 50; and *The Making*, pp. 222-23.

> T<YURIN>: Right. If we are to live through the next few weeks, we must keep out the cold, so find something to cover those windows.
> T<YURIN> *goes – called*!
> KILGAS: Any ideas… Find something to…
> *Thinks.*[195]

It became scene 58 of the printed version, with the action being moved to the repair shop and the shot changed to an interior one. Tyurin's departure and Kilgas's last lines were dropped, and minor stylistic alterations were made.[196]

Another important addition was made by hand to scene 210 in the typewritten version of the script, when Tsesar asks Ivan Denisovich to lend him a knife nicknamed 'ten days' (because of the length of time to be spent in the cell block if the guards discover it). According to the addition, Ivan Denisovich produces not only the knife but also a piece of hacksaw blade:

> *He shows the blade to Tsesar.*
> I<VAN> D<ENISOVICH>: I found this today. If you want to buy a knife I can make it for you.
> TSESAR: No thanks.[197]

We do not find this in the corresponding scene in the printed version of the script,[198] but it was included in the film, in a slightly altered form, because it would have remained unclear without it why Ivan Denisovich picked the blade from the snow at the worksite and decided to bring it into the camp despite the risks involved.

One particular addition did not originate from the book, which was very rare for this adaptation. In Print 161, the Captain says to Tsesar: 'No, no, they're very strict about such things. If you are in command of a ship but with a lower rank they call you captain only as a courtesy', and Tsesar replies: 'Is that

---
195 Cf. Typescript, a separate folded handwritten sheet of paper, inserted between pp. 27 and 28.
196 See *The Making*, p. 202.
197 Typescript, p. 93.
198 See *The Making*, p. 259.

so?'[199] In the book, the conversation begins with the next phrase in the film script's dialogue: 'And how do you come to know so much about life in the British Navy?'[200] The addition was apparently deemed necessary to give the viewer an illustration of the Captain's inside knowledge of British naval traditions. Another scene that was not in the book – the one showing the Captain's desperate attempts to fight off cold in his cell (Typescript 222A, Print 217)[201] – was undoubtedly added to demonstrate the way conditions in the cell block were worse than in the huts and on the worksite. Finally, the high angle shots of the camp, fading in and out in the opening and closing scenes of the film ('from a distance the camp looks like a solitary star in the cosmos: it glows a sickly yellow; its circles of light are no more than a luminous blur'[202]), were included in the narrative at the suggestion of Wrede, who 'had had the first and the last shot in mind for some time'.[203]

Replacements of one bit of text with another, which occur throughout, were mostly introduced either to improve the writing style or to enhance clarity. Thus, 'hooter' in Typescript 111 was changed to 'whistle' in the corresponding Print 114; 'midshipman' in Typescript 122, to 'sailor' in Print 120; 'lorry' in Typescript 124, to 'truck' in Print 122; and 'blocks' in Typescript 131, to 'mortar' in Print 129.[204] In the film, the word 'wilderness' was swapped for 'turmoil', to express the thought better in Alyoshka's line 'In freedom what little faith you have left will be lost in the wilderness'.[205] There was an obvious tendency to tone down the expletives, which resulted in a replacement of the expression 'screw you' in Typescript 192 with 'you wait', and the use of 'to hell with the bookkeeper' instead of 'screw the bookkeeper' in Typescript 129. The adjective 'bloody' was changed to 'damned' in Typescript 111, and to 'lousy' in Typescript 189, as well as deleted on at least one occasion (Typescript 80). The word 'shit' was deleted twice (Typescript 141 and 158).[206] This must have been done to make the film accessible to the widest audiences possible (on

---

199 *The Making*, pp. 243-44 (cf. Typescript 167 in Typescript, p. 76).
200 Cf. *The Making*, pp. 123 and 244.
201 See Typescript, p. 105; *The Making*, p. 269.
202 *The Making*, p. 177; cf. ibid., pp. 270-71.
203 *The Making*, p. 13.
204 See Typescript, pp. 53, 57-58, 63; and *The Making*, pp. 225, 228, 232.
205 Cf. Typescript, p. 102; and *The Making*, pp. 266-67.
206 See Typescript, pp. 86, 61, 52, 84, 39, 65, 74; and *The Making*, pp. 212, 224, 234.

its release in Norway, it was given certificate 12, for those aged twelve and above; in the UK, certificate A, for those aged five and over; and in the US, certificate G, suitable for all ages). It is worthy of note that some of the expletives, edited out or softened in the film, were restored in the published version of the script (see scenes 127, 151, 186).[207]

Other replacements also demonstrate concern about the audience, albeit from a different point of view. In Solzhenitsyn's book, Ivan Denisovich is ironically referred to by Kilgas as 'Stakhanovite',[208] a member of a Soviet movement to increase productivity, named after the miner Aleksei Stakhanov (1906-77) who set an example by over-fulfilling his daily quota by fourteen times in August 1935. Although Stakhanov became an international celebrity (in December 1935, his portrait even appeared on the front cover of *Time* magazine), in the late 1960s he remained a household name only in the Soviet bloc. This is why 'Stakhanovite' was changed to 'Hero of the Soviet Union' in the script and the film.[209] Another area where insufficient understanding could impair the film's reception was pointed out to Casper Wrede and Ronald Harwood by Richard M. Pack, the president of Group W in New York, its vice-president Howard Barnes and its London representative Peter S. Katz. When discussing the script, they 'expressed a wish to change some English words that would not be understood by Americans (vest and undershirt, for example, caused much confusion)'.[210] In Typescript 33, the guard's line 'flannel vest, sir' was duly changed by hand to 'flannel undershirt'.[211] However, the original version of the line was reinstated both in the printed version of the script[212] and in the film, for reasons that remain unclear.

---

207 See *The Making*, pp. 231, 239, 253. The very first draft of the script, written in April-May 1969, contained many more swear words, in keeping with the atmosphere in the camp as described in Solzhenitsyn's book, where 'everyone curses and is cursed: the curses create an environment of brutalisation' (Kern, 'Ivan the Worker', p. 11). Thus, in that first draft Prisoner X-123 called Eisenstein 'an arse-licker' (cf. 'an opportunist' in the script's final version and 'a toady' in Aitken's translation; see *The Making*, pp. 91 and 221).
208 See *The Making*, p. 99.
209 See Typescript, p. 54; and *The Making*, p. 225.
210 See *The Making*, p. 16.
211 Typescript, p. 20.
212 See *The Making*, p. 194.

Some replacements were apparently introduced in the film as a partial compensation for the reduction of either the number of scenes or the number of lines in a scene (undertaken to speed up the action), so that there would be no overall loss to the meaning. Such compensations could appear either within the scene that was affected by reductions, or elsewhere. For instance, Ivan Denisovich's lines 'Hey, boys, put the blocks straight on to the walls for me. Heave 'em up here', and Alyoshka's response 'All right, Ivan Denisovich. Show me where to put 'em', followed by the off-screen clanging of the rail 'adding a wild urgency to the work' (Typescript 132), were deleted and replaced by Ivan Denisovich's exclamation 'Don't let me down, brothers!', which was moved from Typescript 134 to form the first part of what became Print 130.[213] Thus, the atmosphere of urgency remained preserved but was communicated by fewer lines than previously.

As a result of another similar alteration, the way Ivan Denisovich gets hold of Tsesar's evening bread ration was changed slightly. In the book and in both versions of the script, Ivan Denisovich gets to eat Tsesar's supper for saving a place for him in a queue to the parcels office. The supper includes a bowl of gruel and two hundred grams of bread. However, since the bread, being more filling and nutritious than the gruel, played a more important role in the prisoners' diet, Ivan Denisovich, having eaten Tsesar's gruel at the mess hall, brings Tsesar's bread for him to the hut. Only when Tsesar expressly allows Ivan Denisovich to eat that bread too, he is contemplating doing so in the course of the next twenty-four hours. This additional permission is described in scenes 206 and 207 of the typewritten version and in scenes 200 and 201 of the printed version of the screenplay:

> IVAN DENISOVICH (o<ff> s<creen>): Your bread, Tsesar Markovich.
> <...>
> TSESAR: You keep it, Ivan Denisovich.[214]

This brief exchange is not in the film, though. Instead, one line has been added to scene 191 of the printed version (scene 197 of the typewritten ver-

---
213 Typescript, p. 63; and *The Making*, p. 233.
214 Typescript, p. 92; and *The Making*, p. 258.

sion), which depicts Pavlo distributing chunks of bread to the Team 104 members. Ivan Denisovich says to Pavlo: 'Tsesar Markovich's ration'. Thus the film shows that Ivan Denisovich receives not only Tsesar's gruel but also his bread, and leaves the viewer with an assumption that he is automatically entitled to, and will undoubtedly make use of, both. As Ivan Denisovich does eat both eventually, the fine distinction between the bread and the gruel was apparently deemed negligible by the film-makers and discarded to save several seconds of valuable screen time.

Sometimes replacements do not involve any changes, but their place within the script is altered, usually to increase the dramatic tension. The most remarkable replacement in this respect is the team leader's reaction to the news that the regimental commander and the commissar, who both drove him out of the army for being the son of a *kulak*, had been shot in the 1937 purges: '"So You *do* exist", I said to myself. "You are patient, but when You strike, You strike hard!"'.[215] In the book, these lines can be found in the first half (closer to the middle) of the team leader's personal story.[216] In the typewritten version of the story (scene 108), they serve as its very beginning.[217] In the printed version of the script (scene 114) and in the film they provide the story's moralistic conclusion about grave sinners being inevitably punished by God's wrath, sooner or later. In our opinion, the ultimate position of these lines in the film makes them sound even more powerful than in Solzhenitsyn's original.

Other examples of a similar kind include scenes 154-157 of the typewritten version of the screenplay, which became scenes 147-150 in the printed version. In Typescript, scene 154 describes the team leader counting his men and reporting to the Escort Sergeant: '104th all present and correct'. In the next scene, Tsesar and the Captain enjoy some small talk of the 'how was your day' variety, and voices are heard saying that a man is missing in Team 32. The missing person is identified as prisoner K-460. In scene 156, a dialogue between Ivan Denisovich, Kilgas and Fetyukov establishes that this

---

215 *The Making*, p. 224.
216 See *The Making*, p. 94.
217 See Typescript, p. 50.

prisoner was sentenced for spying for Rumania (and doing so genuinely, not like many other prisoners, who were arrested on trumped-up charges). Scene 157 contains a dialogue between Tsesar and the Captain about the strong points and the shortcomings of Eisenstein's film *The Battleship Potemkin* (1925).[218] In the printed version of the screenplay, scene 156 is moved to the end of the sequence, to become scene 150, and is followed by K-460's appearance before a crowd of angry guards and prisoners who shout abuse at him for being late. Scenes 155 and 157 are merged and become scene 148, the second in the sequence, with the team leader's report to the Escort Sergeant also moved here from the previous scene and providing a *sui generis* demarcation line between Tsesar's and the Captain's small talk, on the one hand, and their discussion of *The Battleship Potemkin*, on the other.[219] The typewritten version of the script presents the scenes in the same order as they appear in the book.[220] The new order of the scenes in the printed version and in the film makes them easier to follow for the viewer, because his/her attention does not have to jump back and forth from Tsesar and the Captain to K-460, then to Tsesar and the Captain again, and finally to K-460 again. The team leader's interpolation also enhances the viewer's interest by separating small talk from meaningful conversation.

There were some changes that the adaptation could have done without. In the film, the identification number (a combination of Cyrillic letters and Arabic numerals) that Ivan Denisovich has to wear, just like any other prisoner in the camp, appears as С-854, although it should have been Щ-854. This is a result of a backward translation, from English into Russian, of 'S-854' (a simplified transliteration adopted by Aitken – instead of 'SHCH-854' that would have been prescribed under the Library of Congress transliteration system – to limit it to one easily pronounced consonant in preference to the conventionally required four which make quite a mouthful[221]). The replacement of

---

218 See Typescript, pp. 72-74.
219 See *The Making*, pp. 238-39.
220 See *The Making*, pp. 118-21.
221 Aitken was neither the first nor the only translator to choose the 'S' over the 'SHCH'. Hayward and Hingley, Parker and Bela von Block (New York: Lancer Books, 1963) in their respective translations of *One Day* had opted for the 'S'. Thomas P. Whitney, however, had decided on a 'Shch' (in his 1963 translation, published in New York by

Ivan Denisovich's 'Щ' with a 'C' demonstrates to anyone familiar with Solzhenitsyn's original that the film crew lacked Russian language expertise. For some speakers of Russian, this could undermine the film's credibility, especially because Ivan Denisovich's individual number, imposed on him by the inhuman authorities, is an integral part of his identity as an inmate and was even used by Solzhenitsyn in the initial version of the story's title.[222]

Other gaffes are of less importance. For example, the team leader's response to Pavlo's suggestion to melt snow instead of bringing water in buckets when mixing mortar was changed from 'Right' to 'No' in Typescript 69 and remained like that in Print 71[223] and in the film. The change, however, makes little sense, as members of Team 104 are said to have been 'melting snow in a large can over the potbellied stove'[224] several scenes later.[225] Also, scenes 108-109 in the printed version (as well as Typescript 106-107), depicting how Ivan Denisovich retrieves his personal trowel from where it has been hidden, cannot be found in the film, which makes it difficult to understand why, under

---

the Fawcett World Library). For a comparative analysis of all translations of *One Day* into English (except for the one by H. T. Willetts, which appeared only in 1990, remains the only one based on the 'canonical' Russian version and uses a 'Shcha', indicating the way many Russians would pronounce the consonant if used on its own), see Lauren G. Leighton, 'On Translation: *One Day in the Life of Ivan Denisovič*', *The Russian Language Journal*, vol. 32, no. 111 (1978), pp. 117-30. Incidentally, Leighton notes that 'many of Aitken's equivalents coincide with those of Hayward and Hingley, Parker, and Whitney. Aitken did well to use the best of his predecessors' works to attempt an improved translation' (ibid., p. 129). Willetts's translation, against the background of the other five, is examined briefly in Barry P. Scherr, 'Aleksandr Solzhenitsyn', *Encyclopedia of Literary Translation into English*, ed. by Olive Classe, London-Chicago: Fitzroy Dearborn, 2000, p. 1301; and compared in more detail to the translations by Hayward/Hingley, Parker, Whitney and Aitken in Rachel May, *The Translator in the Text: On Reading Russian Literature in English*, Evanston, IL: Northwestern University Press, 1994, pp. 48, 73-75, 79-81, 92-93, 123-27, 133.

222 See A. Solzhenitsyn, *Bodalsia telenok s dubom: Ocherki literaturnoi zhizni*, Paris: YMCA-Press, 1975, p. 31. 'Щ' is the twenty seventh letter of the Russian alphabet, which, in conjunction with a rather high number of 854, is meant to show how populous Ivan Denisovich's labour camp was.
223 See Typescript, p. 33; and *The Making*, p. 207.
224 *The Making*, p. 209.
225 In the book, there is no dialogue between Pavlo and the team leader about the advantages of melting the snow. The third-person narration merely relates that Pavlo made the decision on his own because the water was freezing in the buckets on the way and it was pointless to keep carrying it like that (see *The Making*, p. 73).

the threat of punishment for being late at the count,[226] he takes such great care in hiding the trowel in the generator room in scene 141 of the printed version (Typescript 148) – which *has* survived in the film.[227] Finally, it is a pity that the team leader's expression of regret over not joining 'a gang of drifters, thieves, pickpockets'[228] when he had a chance (Typescript 111), was dropped from both the corresponding Print 114 scene and the film, although it could have given an additional insight into the prisoners' predicament, indicating that even some of the wrongly convicted ones were reduced to envying real criminals on the run from the law.

Still, as a rule, Harwood's and Wrede's (very minor) deviations from the letter of Solzhenitsyn's book only brought the adaptation closer to its spirit. Thus, a prisoner's off-screen remark, 'You think that old bastard in Moscow with the moustache will take pity on you? Uncle Joe? He doesn't trust his own brother' is present in Typescript 203 and Print 197[229] but is missing from the film – as if the authors of the adaptation knew that Solzhenitsyn's oblique reference to Stalin ('Do you think that old bastard with a moustache is going to have any mercy on you? He wouldn't lift a finger for his own brother, let alone you, you creep!'[230]), paraphrased in the screenplay, had been inserted under pressure from Khrushchev's assistant, Vladimir Lebedev, as a pre-condition for the work's publication.[231]

---

226 To specify what the punishment could be, Senka Klevshin, Ivan Denisovich's workmate, was made to exclaim: 'I won't survive ten days in the cells!' (Print 138), instead of 'Let's hop it!' (Typescript 145); see Typescript, p. 67; and *The Making*, p. 235.
227 See Typescript, pp. 49 and 68; and *The Making*, pp. 222 and 236. In the book, Solzhenitsyn comments that 'a trowel means a lot to a mason if it fits his hand and is light. However, wherever you worked, there was a rule: every night you had to hand back any tool you had been given that morning. It was a sheer tossup what sort of tool you got the following day. Shukhov had once managed to pull the wool over the eyes of the man in the tool shop and got hold of the best trowel. Now he had to hide it in a different place every evening, and recover it every morning he learned he was going to be laying blocks' (*The Making*, p. 68).
228 *The Making*, p. 224 (originally, 'some roadworkers', see Typescript, p. 52; in the book, it is a gang of crooks warming themselves up around a cauldron with boiling asphalt (see *The Making*, p. 97), hence the confusion between the workmen and the criminals).
229 See Typescript, p. 91; and *The Making*, p. 257.
230 *The Making*, p. 150.
231 See Solzhenitsyn, *Bodalsia telenok*, pp. 47-48. Solzhenitsyn deliberately sought to avoid mentioning Stalin in *One Day*, partly because naming him in such a context

Another aspect of Solzhenitsyn's work that becomes enhanced in the film is the homage it pays to Christian faith. A perceptible religious undercurrent runs throughout the book which carefully records the instances when the inmates cross themselves, pray, read from the hand-written Holy Gospel which they hide from the guards, and discuss God as the Creator of the Universe (cf. the dialogue between Ivan Denisovich and the Captain during the count before Team 104 leaves the worksite), as well as other things spiritual, e.g. the kind of prayer God is most likely to answer and blessing imprisonment as an opportunity to do some soul-searching (cf. the dialogue between Ivan Denisovich and Alyoshka shortly before the last recount). Even when the labour camp's artist freshens up prisoner's numbers on their caps, the act is compared to 'being anointed on your brow by a priest'.[232] All these scenes have been kept in both the typewritten and the printed version of the screenplay.[233] However, there is a clear tendency to give the character of Alyoshka more prominence and significance in the adaptation than he is afforded in the book itself.[234] The camera is briefly fixed on him getting off his bunk and going through his morning prayers as early as scene 7 (although there is a cor-

---

could be perceived as blaming him for the Soviet miscarriages of justice, and this, in turn, would be too simplistic an explanation of what exactly went wrong in Communist Russia. Another reason for the absence of explicit references to Stalin in the initial version of *One Day* might be that, possibly inspired by Eisenstein's concept of montage, 'Solzhenitsyn wanted to evoke, not state, an image of Stalin because he realised that an image the readers themselves had generated would stay with them longer' (James M. Curtis, *Solzhenitsyn's Traditional Imagination*, Athens, Georgia: The University of Georgia Press, 1984, p. 153). The film, however, does not ignore Stalin completely but replaces a verbal reference to him with a visual one, when the camera shows his portrait adorning a wall in the guardroom where Ivan Denisovich washes the floor. The portrait's presence seems to have been suggested by one of Mikhail Demin's drawings, see Appendix III, pic. 8.

232 *The Making*, p. 48.
233 See Typescript, 10, 14-15, 17, 46, 50, 70, 80, 100-02; and *The Making*, pp. 185, 189-90, 192, 218, 224, 242, 247, 265-67.
234 Cf., however: 'Alyosha is perhaps the most important single figure in *One Day* apart from Ivan, and it is obviously no coincidence that he is a Baptist. According to the magazine *Time* <of 27 January 1975>, Soviet civil rights leaders have reported that more than one third of the known political prisoners in the Soviet Union during the past two decades were made up of Baptists' (David Pike, 'A Camp Through the Eyes of a Peasant: Solzhenitsyn's *One Day in the Life of Ivan Denisovich*', *California Slavic Studies*, vol. X (1977), p. 217).

responding half-sentence to that effect in the story).[235] In Print 48 (Typescript 47), the prisoners' arrival at the worksite is described as follows: 'They turn their backs against the wind, stamping their feet. Only ALYOSHKA, the Baptist, is smiling sweetly, *mumbling a prayer* <the emphasis is ours. – BH, AR>, his face glowing the faintest red from the first rays of the sun',[236] while Solzhenitsyn merely says: 'Alyoshka, standing beside Shukhov, looked at the sun and rejoiced, a smile on his lips'.[237] In the next scene, the camera looks at the sunrise from Alyoshka's point of view. Furthermore, in Print 101 (Typescript 109), depicting lunch at the worksite, Alyoshka is portrayed as 'finishing his bowl and then muttering a prayer of thanksgiving'.[238] The entire shot is pure invention, because Alyoshka is not mentioned at all in the corresponding episode in the book. At the same time, other characters' potential screen presence is sometimes reduced. For example, in the second half of Typescript 52 there is Der, 'the works superintendent, but also a prisoner (number B 731), a pig of a man', who says to Tsesar: 'Where the hell d'you think you're going?'. Tsesar replies: 'I'm assistant to the quota-checker. I work in the office' – 'Reluctantly, DER allows him to pass, then goes off to snoop somewhere else'.[239] However, Der has been edited out of the corresponding Print 53 scene (as well as the film), which has ended up containing Tsesar's request: 'Will you bring my lunch to the office, Ivan Denisovich?'[240] In Typescript 58, Der is mentioned in a conversation between Ivan Denisovich and Kilgas. They are discussing how to carry the roll of tarred felt to the generator room without being seen. Kilgas says: 'Yes, that pig Der. He's supposed to be in charge of all this. He'll spot us sure as sure'.[241] The corresponding Print 60 scene merely has Kilgas say 'Yeah, they are sure to spot us'.[242]

It looks as if Alyoshka has been given a certain preference over other characters, because in the book Ivan Denisovich, a practical man who professes his

---

235 Cf. Typescript, p. 3; and *The Making*, pp. 30 ('while the Baptist was whispering his prayers...') and 179.
236 See Typescript, p. 24; and *The Making*, p. 198.
237 *The Making*, p. 59.
238 Typescript, p. 46; and *The Making*, p. 219.
239 Typescript, p. 25.
240 *The Making*, p. 199.
241 Typescript, p. 29.
242 *The Making*, p. 203.

faith in God but refuses to believe in the existence of heaven and hell,[243] symbolically occupies a middle position between his closest bunk bed neighbours, the Captain and Alyoshka,[244] both representing two mutually exclusive ideologies and models of behaviour.[245] The Captain, an ex-Communist with a flair for scientific explanations of natural phenomena, who bravely but inconsiderately protests against the unnecessary extremes of the labour camp regime, was treated by some Soviet officials and literary critics as the story's positive hero.[246] It would be natural to expect a Western interpretation of *One Day* to reserve more sympathy for his opposite number Alyoshka, a modern day Christian martyr who accepts the militant atheist persecution with gratitude and relishes the prospect of achieving grace through suffering. It is noteworthy that Ivan Denisovich's story about a rich and corrupt priest in his home parish, told in the course of his conversation with Alyoshka to illustrate Ivan Denisovich's scepticism in the matters of faith,[247] has been omitted from the screenplay and the film, thus purifying the adaptation's subliminal religious message, expressed through the figure of Alyoshka.[248] It is also important that in the film the bunk directly underneath Ivan Denisovich is occupied not by the Captain but by Tsesar,[249] who is conspicuously surrounded by things material, such as real Moscow bread, sausage, butter and smoked fish, which he receives in the parcels sent from

---

243 *The Making*, p. 164.
244 Cf.: 'Two of his neighbours started to get up at the same time – parallel to him, the Baptist Alyoshka, and below, the ex-naval captain Buinovsky' (*The Making*, p. 29). In Solzhenitsyn's original, the word 'naverkhu' (above) is used instead of 'parallel', see A. Solzhenitsyn, *Odin den' Ivana Denisovicha* (Paris: YMCA Press, 1987, p. 9).
245 Cf.: 'the spiritual scale would seem to apply to the bunks' (Kern, 'Ivan the Worker', p. 15).
246 See Solzhenitsyn, *Bodalsia telenok*, p. 47.
247 See *The Making*, p. 164.
248 Curiously, the adaptation alters Alyoshka's readings from the New Testament, making them more relevant to the circumstances. In the book, he quotes from the First Epistle of Peter (4:15): 'But let no one of you suffer as a murderer, or as a thief, or as an evildoer, or interfering in the affairs of other men. But if you suffer as a Christian, then do not be ashamed – but glorify God on that behalf' (*The Making*, p. 45). Scene 22 in the typewritten version of the screenplay repeats this verbatim (see Typescript, p. 15). However, the wording in the same scene in the printed version (and in the film) is different, replacing, among other things, the 'evildoer' and 'interfering in the affairs of other men' with 'a criminal, or an informer' (*The Making*, p. 190).
249 This has been made but not elaborated upon in a student feedback after the viewing of *One Day* at the Department of Slavonic and Baltic Languages and Literatures, University of Helsinki, on 15 November 2007, see Appendix II, Student 5.

home.²⁵⁰ There is even a zooming in shot of all this food made from Ivan Denisovich's point of view when he is looking down on Tsesar's treasured earthly possessions from the top bunk (Typescript 209; Print 203). Thus, the film positions Ivan Denisovich somewhere in between Alyoshka's spirituality and Tsesar's materialism²⁵¹ (it is symptomatic in this respect that Tsesar shares his delicious food with Ivan Denisovich in return for his services, while Ivan Denisovich passes some of that food on to Alyoshka solely for altruistic reasons).²⁵² Therefore, although it is hard to dispute the remark that the 'entire camp is a diabolically-designed unit',²⁵³ it is not the devil but God that discerning members of the public are likely to find in the film's minute details. This message does not appear to clash with Solzhenitsyn's own intentions, which could not be expressed openly in the censored version of *One Day*, published in the Soviet Union. However, when the YMCA Press brought out the revised, uncensored 'canonical' version of *One Day* in Paris in 1973 (i.e. three years after the film had been completed), it was found to be 'more religiously coloured'.²⁵⁴ A fairly recent study of the story re-examines it in the light of the tradition of Eastern Orthodox Christian asceticism, demonstrates convincingly how its 'discursive narrative layers serve subtly to introduce a number of religious notions which are central to the story as a whole'²⁵⁵ and ar-

---

250 Cf. 'Tsezar's thoughts center on his material possessions, which are the source of his well-being, he is not free from the material world' (Svitlana Kobets, 'The Subtext of Christian Asceticism in Aleksandr Solzhenitsyn's *One Day in the Life of Ivan Denisovich*', *The Slavic and East European Journal*, vol. 42, No. 4 (1998), p. 668).
251 As an American critic puts it, Ivan Denisovich 'survives on an untutored existential faith' (S<tefan> K<anfer>, op. cit.).
252 To be fare, Tsesar is not entirely alien to things spiritual, as he discusses cinema and theatrical art with prisoners X-123, Pyotr Mikhailich and the Captain, and shares his tobacco and the content of his food parcel with the Captain out of pure kindness (all these scenes have been kept in the script and the film, see *The Making*, pp. 91-92, 118-19, 120, 136, 155, 220-21, 238-39, 251, 260).
253 Weisman, op. cit., p. 66.
254 Kern, 'Solženicyn's Self-Censorship', p. 430; cf. also: 'from other works of Solzhenitsyn <...> we can understand that Alyoshka's message is very close to the heart of the author' (Kern, 'Ivan the Worker', p. 27). Religious overtones can also be felt in the film's visual images. Thus, the guards are mostly dressed in white sheepskin and look like angels, while the prisoners wear the grey and black attire, as appropriate for the sinners.
255 Kobets, op. cit., p. 662.

gues that *One Day* is an 'essentially religiously-oriented narrative'[256] which has the ideals of Christian asceticism at its very core:

> Ascetic ideals, being inescapably ethical and religious, not only inform the spiritual stance of the story's protagonist <...> but furthermore are identified in the text as an indispensable condition for survival in the Gulag. <...> Shukhov's fortitude in the face of active and rampant evil is truly ascetic. Just like a medieval holy man he resists and overcomes the terrors and blandishments of evil and attains a higher level of spirituality.[257]

Wrede seems to have been trying to get a similar message across almost twenty years before the appearance of this article (which does not mention the film at all). An observant film critic stated upon *One Day*'s release in the US that the film possessed 'an almost religious, mystical simplicity, and the lives of both guards and prisoners <are> <...> almost monastic. <...> Like some monks, <prisoners> undergo changes in the spirit because of systematic deprivation of the body and mind'.[258] Another critic noted: 'Wrede is alert to the little touches of kindness between prisoners that inform Solzhenitsyn's work with its Christian humanism'.[259]

To deliver this covert message successfully, Wrede needed the assistance of an experienced film editor, who could help him to tell the story at a slow but engaging pace, focusing on the small details without letting the overarching idea out of sight. To achieve this, Wrede enlisted the services of Thelma Connell (1912-76), whom he had already collaborated with on *The Barber of Stamford Hill* in 1962. One of the most respected editors in the UK, Connell had been doing editorial work for various film and television companies since the early 1940s. Her credits included Sidney Lumet's *The Hill* (1965), about

---

256 Ibid.
257 Ibid.
258 Ted Mahar, '*One Day* Reflects Attitude of Novel', *The Oregonian*, 13 October 1971.
259 Zimmerman, 'Prisoner's Base'. In an interview, Wrede pointed out that Solzhenitsyn had struck him by his particular combination of 'the man of science and reason and the religious humanist' (Kevin Thomas, 'Director Behind *One Day*', *The Los Angeles Times*, 16 October 1971).

prisoners' survival in the British World War II disciplinary camp in North Africa (starring Sean Connery); Lewis Gilbert's *Alfie* (1966), about the swinging Sixties in Britain (starring Michael Caine); and Anthony Mann's Cold War espionage thriller *Dandy in Aspic* (1968), with Courtenay in a prominent role. Characterising her editing style, Ronald Harwood recalls that Connell's 'only interest was in telling the story as clearly as possible. This would now be regarded as somewhat old-fashioned. She was very good at pacing the story and therefore accurate about how long or short a scene should be'.[260] In 1969, Connell was editing a couple of films for Columbia Pictures, such as the comedy *The Virgin Soldiers* (John Dexter, 1969) and the drama *The Buttercup Chain* (Robert Ellis Miller, 1970), but, according to Peter S. Katz's letter to Wrede of 22 August 1969, was delighted to hear that Wrede had been thinking of working with her again and said she would be available in January 1970. When in Røros, she was 'beside the camera, watching every setup, every shot, <...> muffled up to her eyebrows, conferring, advising, absorbing'.[261] Her presence throughout the filming proved to be highly effective in the editing suite, when, in April 1970, 'in a very short space of time, she assembled a cut version of the film in which Wrede did not interfere'.[262] It was some time at this stage that Wrede sent a thank-you letter to Demin, via Bureau Littéraire D. Clairouin, presumably informing him that the project had entered the post-production stage. Unfortunately, the letter itself could not be located, but we know of it from Marie Schébéko's response of 23 April 1970, sent to Wrede at the Norsk Film address in Oslo (59, Kirkeveien). In her letter, Schébéko communicated the gist of Demin's reaction to Wrede's earlier missive. According to Schébéko, Demin had asked her to tell Wrede 'that the film director who is as much of a poet as you are cannot have betrayed the original author and that he is confident that the "grand child" will be up to the highest expectations'.

---

260 Harwood's email to Andrei Rogachevskii of 12 July 2007.
261 *The Making*, p. 22.
262 *The Making*, p. 24. Connell's editing of *One Day* was later found to be 'as spare and taut as a tourniquet; the hour and three quarters running time, despite the grimness of the subject, doesn't seem a second too long' (Eric Braun, 'One Day in the Life of Ivan Denisovich', *Films and Filming*, April 1972, p. 50).

Wrede's Finnair and SAS ticket stubs show that he was in Oslo from 31 March to 13 April 1970, then went to London where he stayed for a while, then returned to Oslo and stayed there until 13 May, when he went to Helsinki via Copenhagen, to return to Oslo again on 19 May. On 19 May 1970, Wrede's son David, then a pupil at primary school, wrote to him:

> Dear Daddy,
>
> I hope everything is going well in Norway. Here I have just finished doing an assembly for college. I am also doing a Stuart pageant with the rest of my form.
>
> Much love,
> David

Wrede remained in Oslo until 31 May, when he left for London. On 7 June, however, he had to come back to Norway again. Wrede spent so much time in Oslo that he even applied for a permanent work ID at Norsk Film. However, the application was turned down on the grounds that he was a foreign film director, engaged by the company only on a temporary basis (see Arnljot Engh's letter to Wrede of 20 May 1970). Over a long period, Wrede and Connell

> worked together, refining, experimenting, deciding <...> the final cut of the film. Their deliberations were conducted in private; they refused to allow the film to be seen by any of the interested parties until they themselves were satisfied. Only Arne Nordheim, the brilliant young Norwegian composer, was exempted from this rule by virtue of his professional involvement.[263]

Nordheim (b. 1931), paid NOK25,000 (USD3,500) for his musical score for *One Day*, was not the only possible candidate for the job. On 14 July 1969, the Norwegian composer Sven Libaek (b. 1938), a graduate of the Juilliard School of Music in New York and an Australian resident, approached Wrede

---

263 *The Making*, p. 24.

at the suggestion of the Bergen-born film producer George W. Willoughby (1913-97) who worked for Group W on several projects, such as the already mentioned *A Taste of Excitement* (1969) and *Squeeze a Flower* (1970), as well as *Wake in Fright* (directed by Ted Kotcheff, 1971). Libaek volunteered to compose the soundtrack for *One Day*, suggesting that Wrede could listen to some of his LPs featuring the music he had already written for films and television in Australia. The composing job, however, went to Nordheim. Presumably, Libaek's music, which included pop songs and jazz, as well as some more serious orchestral works, seemed somewhat lightweight to Wrede in comparison with Nordheim's atmospheric avant-garde electronic compositions, whose main themes had been 'solitude, death, love and landscape'.[264] It is also possible that Nordheim was partly chosen because of his direct experience with Eastern Europe (since 1967 he had been paying regular professional visits to Polish Radio's Studio Eksperymentalne in Warsaw to record his music).[265]

In June 1970, Richard M. Pack came to Oslo to exercise his *droit de seigneur* with the film. The first screening of the final cut was also watched by a number of other Group W and Cinerama executives. Wrede and Courtenay were present too. After the screening, 'Courtenay – wrung out and weeping from what he had just seen – surveyed the men who had backed the film and found them emotionally wanting. "Do you <...> know what you have just seen?"',[266] the actor asked. Richard M. Pack may have looked indifferent, but, judging by Harwood's letter to him of 17 June 1970, he enjoyed the experience. Harwood wrote: 'I cannot thank you enough for your cable from Oslo after you had seen *Ivan Denisovich*; it gave me a great deal of pleasure, although I have to say that I think all the credit is due to Casper, Tom and Sven'. In August 1970 *One Day* was officially delivered to Group W and Norsk Film. Soon everyone involved was to find out what the critics and audiences thought of it.

---

264 Hallgjerd Aksnes, 'Nordheim, Arne', *The New Grove Dictionary of Music and Musicians*, ed. by Stanley Sadie, vol. 18, London: Macmillan, 2001, p. 34.
265 In her statement of 27 January 2009, obtained by Ben Hellman via Nordheim's agent, Hilde Holbaek-Hanssen, Nordheim's wife Rannveig Getz testifies that the soundtrack to *One Day* was 'much performed' in its own right after the film's release.
266 Bell, op. cit.

6 RECEPTION

On 8 October 1970, it was announced that Solzhenitsyn had become a Nobel Laureate 'for the ethical force with which he had pursued the indispensable traditions of Russian literature'.[267] The news arrived in the middle of preparations for the film's opening.[268] Wrede wanted to organise a simultaneous first night across Scandinavia shortly before Solzhenitsyn's arrival for the official award ceremony in Stockholm on 10 December 1970, but the author could not leave the Soviet Union for fear that he would be stripped of his Soviet citizenship and would not be allowed to return, and the plan was abandoned.[269] The world premiere of One Day in the Life of Ivan Denisovich took place in Oslo (and six other Norwegian cities) on 26 November 1970, accompanied by a short Norwegian documentary about the making of One Day, directed by Carsten E. Munch and photographed by Erik Solbakken. Less than a fortnight later, on 7 December, the film opened in Stockholm.

The reception of the film was very positive, overall. Everyone agreed that the film had been scrupulously faithful to both the letter and the spirit of Solzhenitsyn's book. In the critics' opinion, Wrede had succeeded in creating a film version of an essentially un-dramatic work depicting the monotonous life in a prison camp, while keeping the right atmosphere and using the same low-key tone and the same focus on small, concrete details as Solzhenitsyn

---

267 http://nobelprize.org/nobel_prizes/literature/laureates/1970/index.html. Anticipating Solzhenitsyn's success, the Kremlin attempted to discredit him in Sweden, 'among other things dispatching Mikhail Sholokhov, <a> 1965 Nobel Prize winner, to Stockholm in September. His efforts to block Solzhenitsyn produced the opposite effect, and in fact became instrumental in the Swedish Academy's decision to advance the date of election and thus cut short further interventions' (Marc Slonim, 'European Notebook', The New York Times, 8 November 1970).

268 Following the Nobel awards announcement, the Italian journalist Raffaello Uboldi visited Wrede in his London home and published a gist of their conversation about One Day in Il Giorno of 21 November 1970 ('Ivan accusa Stalin dallo schermo').

269 See Anthony Lewis, 'Solzhenitsyn Hailed Despite Absence at Presentation of 1970 Nobel Awards', The New York Times, 11 December 1970. Solzhenitsyn was finally able to receive his Nobel insignia at the Nobel festivities in Stockholm on 10 December 1974.

did. When Sven Nykvist afterwards summarized the critics' judgement of the film, he did it with one word: 'honest'.[270]

Before the premiere in Oslo, Wrede said in an interview that the strength of his film was in its universality: 'For me, the film is a story of imprisonment – and it can be an imprisoned man anywhere. The film wants to show that man possesses an invincible strength. But he must preserve his integrity. To lose it means to die, in a way'.[271] The Norwegian critics did notice this universal aspect. According to them, the film told the audiences not only about hunger, fear and deprivation of human rights in the Soviet Union under Stalin, but also said something important about the human condition in general.[272] Without 'hatred, bitterness or loud accusations',[273] the film dealt with the will to live, with a powerful sense of individuality and the strength one gets from belonging to a collective. Pride, hope and an inextinguishable spark of life were all to be found in the film, as well as the story.

The actors' performance got praise, especially that of Tom Courtenay in the lead. Discreetly, without any exaggeration, he acted Ivan Denisovich, both when his character was totally engrossed in his highly-skilled bricklaying work and when he was merely one of the prisoners' collective. Courtenay looked completely genuine in the role of the camp's 'little man',[274] acting unsentimentally but with a strong feeling of human dignity.[275] Sven Nykvist's subdued colours were commended for bringing out effectively the coldness and the in-

---

270 Nykvist, op. cit., p. 118.
271 The unsigned article 'Première idag på "En dag i Ivans liv"', *Aftenposten*, 26 November 1970.
272 For one of the story's translators, 'the political setting and implications, as well as the time and place in which the action of <One Day> is set, are incidental to its artistic purpose. It is as symbolic of human existence as is Kafka's *Trial*. The one day in the life of Ivan Denisovich is a day in *anybody*'s life. The majority of the human race are trapped in a monotonous daily routine which differs from that of a concentration camp only in the *degree* of its unpleasantness and hopelessness' (Max Hayward, 'Epilogue', in Max Hayward and Edward L. Crowley (eds), *Soviet Literature in the Sixties*, London: Methuen, 1965, p. 206).
273 Gunvor Gjessing, 'God film om livsvilje', *Aftenposten*, 27 November 1970.
274 Liv Herstad Røed, 'En ypperlig "gjengivelse" av "En dag i Ivan Denisovitsj' liv"', *Morgenbladet*, 27 November 1970.
275 Cf. Wrede's own understanding of the character: 'Ivan makes no pretence of being a hero. He does just enough to last another day. But this requires integrity' (John M. Lee, 'Solzhenitsyn Novel Before Cameras', *The New York Times*, 13 January 1970).

hospitableness of life in the camp. Afterwards you could not even remember, whether it was a colour or a black-and-white film, one critic noted.[276] The music of Arne Nordheim was felt to accentuate the dominant mood of the film, underlining its atmosphere and creating a feeling of 'unreal reality'.[277] Rarely had electronic music been so powerfully used in a motion picture, one critic wrote.[278]

The Norwegian critics paid little attention to the film's minor deviations from the book. The helicopter shots of the camp zooming in and out at the beginning and end of the film were seen to be stressing the desolateness of the prisoners' predicament. The scene with the Captain in an isolation cell, trying to survive the cold Siberian night, was singled out as a rare dramatic addition to the story. Slightly embarrassing to the ears of the Norwegian critics was the Norwegian accent heard in many actors' spoken English.[279] The general

---

276 Herstad Røed, op. cit.
277 Arvid Andersen, 'Overbevisende film-versjon av Ivans hverdag som fange', *Dagbladet*, 27 November 1970, p. 5.
278 Ibid.
279 Oddly enough, upon *One Day*'s release in Britain, a London critic found that 'the voices of the English actors jar more than those of Scandinavian actors in the cast' and that 'visual realism is destroyed by English accents – Mr Maxwell talking a bit posh because he is a naval captain, and Mr Courtenay dropping an occasional "h"' (Felix Barker, 'Ivan the Miserable', *Evening News* of 14 January 1972). A similar opinion was proffered by *The Guardian*: 'It comes as a shock sometimes to hear a bit part played in accents more appropriate to Kensington than, well, Mongolia' (Derek Malcolm, 'Almost Magic Roundabout', *The Guardian*, 13 January 1972). *The Observer*'s George Melly echoed this in the issue of 16 January 1972, characterising some actors' accents as 'the only insurmountable flaw. <...> Courtenay's flat Midland accent works but to hear Russian guards sneering away as if they'd just passed out of Sandhurst is hard to accept'. After the film's release in North America, it has also been noted that 'those variegated British accents of the actors (from cockney to cultivated) make it difficult at first to accept the fact that one is in Siberia rather than in Germany during the war' (*The Motion Picture Herald*, 16 June 1971, p. 568). Arguably the most perceptive judgement on the issue of accents was pronounced by Les Wedman in the Vancouver *Sun* of 5 January 1972: 'a cast of mixed <...> accents, not one of them Russian, <...> matters little because each of them is representative rather than definitive'. Wrede acknowledged that he '"had to think a lot about this aspect, <...> and to use Eastern European accents would really be defeating the purpose and it would be difficult to understand". He also pointed out <...> that the reason for an odd Cockney accent here and there was that there were people of every class and rank in these labour camps' (Dewar, 'Life in a Siberian Labor Camp'). A US critic applauded the fact that no attempt was made in *One Day* to alter the actors' accents 'to correspond to what the American public wants to believe an English-speaking Russian should sound like. Courtenay, as Ivan, has a pronounced Yorkshire accent.

opinion after the world premiere, however, was that the 'intuitive and intelligent film version'[280] of Solzhenitsyn's *One Day in the Life of Ivan Denisovich* was 'powerful, rich and full of atmosphere'.[281] As one journalist put it, 'this is a film that everyone should see. It has something important to tell us, and it has been made with an artistic ambition that has been fulfilled unerringly, absorbingly and movingly'.[282]

The Swedish critics were likewise very complimentary after the opening night in Stockholm. Again, it was the film's closeness to the original that impressed. 'This is probably one of the most exact cinematic interpretations of literary work ever done',[283] a critic wrote. The film was perceived to be true to Solzhenitsyn's plot, form and dialogue, refraining from both over-dramatizing the events and striving to shock the viewers. With 'great humbleness',[284] Wrede 'calmly and resolutely stuck to what had been said on the pages of the book. The film is somewhat angular and un-rhythmic and does not show off with any high points'.[285] The inner substance of Solzhenitsyn's text was recreated through specific details. As a result, the strength of the film manifested itself in its honesty and 'the harsh totality that it makes out of all these details'.[286]

Tom Courtenay received praise, and so did Nykvist's camera work with its soft colours and 'plain closeness to the events'.[287] Nordheim's score was said to reinforce the film's mood 'in a rather suggestive way'.[288] Yet again, special attention was paid to the opening and closing scenes, with the camera either drawing closer and closer, or retreating from the camp's small circle of light, surrounded by dense impenetrable darkness. Some critics felt that the opening scene visualized the complete isolation of the camp perhaps even better

---

This is all very good, because it breaks down a useless stereotype' (Bob Kalfus, '*Ivan Denisovich* Superbly Filmed, Acted', *Phoenix* (Flushing, N.Y.), 19 October 1971).
280 Andersen, 'Overbevisende film-versjon av Ivans hverdag som fange'.
281 Ibid.
282 Torgny Varen, 'Vesentlig og ekte filmverk', *Verdens gang*, 27 November 1970.
283 Ulf von Strauss, 'Krönika över människan', *Svenska dagbladet*, 8 December 1970.
284 Göran Börge, 'En dag i Ivan Denisovitjs liv', *Aftonbladet*, 8 December 1970.
285 Hanserik Hjertén, 'Äkta filmhyllning av Solzjenitsyn', *Dagens nyheter*, 8 December 1970.
286 Ibid.
287 Ibid.
288 Ibid.

than the book. The beginning and the end of the film were interpreted as visual translations of a literary thought, expressing the human universality of the action and, at the same time, the restrictions imposed by the geographical area. It created a symbol of the small individual and his endless Sisyphean task in society.[289]

In the critics' view, Wrede, just like Solzhenitsyn, had managed to talk about terrible conditions without much bitterness but with an unexpected optimism, avoiding both pathos and propaganda. Abstaining from open accusations, the film, just like the book, brought forth a growing feeling of anger in its audiences. The surprising warmth and vital force of Ivan Denisovich and his team mates created an atmosphere of hope and defiance.

On the negative side, what was felt to be lacking in Wrede's film was a treatment of the hierarchy in the hut, involving complicated relationships between prisoners.[290] An opinion was also voiced that Nykvist could have succeeded even better had he chosen to shoot the film strictly in black and white.[291] Courtenay was found to use a too elegant theatrical English on occasion.[292] Still, on the whole, the Swedish reception was highly positive. In the words of one journalist, 'this is a film that I wish a large audience would see. It does not only tell about the Soviets under Stalin but about every country where people are imprisoned and degraded for political reasons'.[293]

On 16 May 1971, *One Day* opened in the 68th Street Playhouse in New York (a film theatre with 360 seats on Manhattan's East Side), with the Cinerama Releasing Corporation acting as distributors. *Life* magazine, with a circulation of seven million copies, greeted its release with the following verdict:

---

[289] Cf. a similar point of reference used in an American response to *One Day*: 'What animates <Ivan Denisovich> is what moved Camus' Sisyphus: the prisoner fails because failure is immanent in man; he endures because he must' (S<tefan> K<anfer>, op. cit.)
[290] Hjertén, op. cit.
[291] Lasse Bergström, 'En positiv överraskning', *Expressen*, 8 December 1970.
[292] Ibid.
[293] Börge, op. cit.

> To say that *One Day in the Life of Ivan Denisovich* is an austere and understated movie is itself an understatement. At a moment when the fashion, especially abroad, is shifting to a plain and unadorned style of film making, director Casper Wrede has outrun everybody. <...> It's an undramatic movie, boring and unpleasant a great deal of the time, as was the novel on which it is faithfully based. It is, however, a singular experience and, I think, a quite daring film. <...> One comes to admire Ronald Harwood's script for its stubborn refusal to moralize, sentimentalize, psychologize or overtly politicize this material.[294]

Variety also found the film 'strangely unmoving, the kind of material to which the viewer wants to respond but doesn't'.[295] Harwood himself admitted, in a letter to the London *Times*, that both Wrede and he, when working on the adaptation of *One Day*, felt 'obliged and determined to duplicate' Solzhenitsyn's 'dispassionate' treatment of 'horrendous events'.[296] However, it is precisely this emotional detachment that some North American critics had a problem with. 'Scenes are shot from a vast emotional distance', one of them reported, 'as if Director Casper Wrede flinched at the pain of showing pain'.[297] Another noted: 'There is little emotional involvement in the plight of the prisoners and nothing in the film that would move one to cheers or to tears'.[298] Roger Greenspun's review in *The New York Times* was even suggestively (and ambiguously) entitled 'Film *Ivan Denisovich*: Best at Long Distance'.[299] Other crit-

---

294 Richard Schickel, 'Boiled Grass and Basic Humanity: *One Day in the Life of Ivan Denisovich*', *Life*, 25 June 1971, p. 12.
295 Verr., 'One Day in the Life of Ivan Denisovich', *Variety*, 19 May 1971.
296 Ronald Harwood, 'Ivan Denisovich', *The Times*, 22 January 1972. Similarly, Courtenay reminisced about the sequence containing the argument over faith between Ivan and Alyoshka the Baptist: 'When I first played that scene, <...> I was really giving him what for, and Casper stopped me and said, no, not that way. You've had a good day, and you've just added it up. You aren't angry. So don't have a go at him. Be gentle. <...> Casper was always having to hold me down when we were making this film' (Bell, op. cit.).
297 S<tefan> K<anfer>, op. cit.
298 Les Wedman in *The Sun* (Vancouver) of 5 January 1972.
299 Greenspun believed that the detachment occurred because, where the book 'sees through the eyes of its Ivan Denisovich <...> the movie chooses mostly to look at him. <...> The result is that what had been "point of view" in the book becomes in the movie something less meaningful and more grand – something like "image of man"' (Roger Greenspun, 'Film *Ivan Denisovich* Best at Long Distance', *The New York Times*, 17 May 1971).

ics – and ordinary members of the public – did feel moved, although not always in a similar way. Frances Herridge of *The New York Post* remarked: 'Tom Courtenay plays the part with such conviction that you soon empathize', and promised to the prospective viewers that the film would 'leave you feeling happier – happier, that is, about your own life'.[300] A *New Yorker* journalist, however, thus expressed the feelings that were likely to be experienced during a viewing of *One Day*: 'grief floods you, and anger', and described how 'a pretty girl built like a koala bounded out of a screening room at the end of the film <...> and shivered, and held her stomach, and said, "It made me feel hungry. I'm on a diet"'.[301]

Also, there was disagreement concerning the actors' performances. According to one opinion,

> Tom Courtenay in the title role[302] and a large cast of supporting players have been extraordinarily successful in submerging themselves in their roles, in making themselves anonymous – surely the most difficult discipline that can be required of actors.[303]

Time magazine, however, insisted that 'the very facelessness of the Scandinavian and English cast lessens the film's power to shock'.[304] Either way, the adaptation was defined as 'a horror film'[305] and 'a slice of death',[306] and no one rushed forward to dispute *Life*'s prediction that 'there is no way to sell a

---

300 Frances Herridge, 'Solzhenitsyn's *Day* on Screen', *The New York Post*, 17 May 1971.
301 Gilliatt, op. cit.
302 Extolled as 'hauntingly effective' (William Wolf, 'One Day in the Life of Ivan Denisovich', *Cue* (New York), 22 May 1971, p. 64).
303 Schickel, op. cit. Cf. 'Courtenay's performance is magnificent but other members of the cast come close to his achievement in spite of the fact that their roles are limited, compared with that of Ivan. Alfred Burke, James Maxwell and Eric Thompson are outstanding' (Frances Taylor, '*One Day* is Grim Tribute', *The Long Island Press*, 17 May 1971).
304 S<tefan> K<anfer>, op. cit. This effect could be put down to the fact that *One Day* tends to treat its characters more 'as exemplars of the human condition and less as individuals' (Greenspun, op. cit.).
305 Joseph Gelmis, 'Superb Survival', *Newsday*, 17 May 1971.
306 Zimmerman, 'Prisoner's Base'.

movie like this one',[307] except for the Philadelphia *Film Bulletin*, which pronounced that the film's success 'probably will be limited to specialised, highly sophisticated art and campus markets. Sensitive, intellectual audiences in such situations will respond and *One Day* should enjoy steady (if not outstanding) grosses – being the sort of film to which admirers will be returning again and again'.[308]

However, in the *New York Magazine* of 24 May, Judith Crist expressed her belief in *One Day*'s wider appeal: 'This is a beautifully made film that anyone interested in humanity should see'. The ever pragmatic *Variety* seems to have anticipated this kind of reaction to the film when it declared: 'critics who value theme over treatment will wax poetic, and that could give this stark Cinerama release some urban legs'.[309] *Variety*'s own verdict was rather dismissive. Wrede's direction was deemed 'lackluster'; Harwood's script, 'so sparse it almost seems non-existent'; and the acting, 'often sounding like a British schoolboy version of *Crime and Punishment*'.[310]

Still, the anchor man and film and theatre critic John Schubeck of WABC-TV announced in a broadcast on 18 May 1971 that *One Day* was 'simply the best film I've seen this year. <…> It has more in any five minutes from beginning to end than most pictures I've seen lately could muster in their entirety'. The film was not doing too badly at the box office, grossing USD19,636 in its opening week[311] and 'averaging more than seven thousand pounds a week'[312] after its first month at the 68th Street Playhouse. It was decided that the film should go on release in key American cities beyond New York. Wrede took an active part in the promotional campaign. According to his Cinerama

---

307 Schickel, op. cit. Cf.: 'Commercially speaking, the picture will have to surmount the disadvantage of its grim subject matter' (*The Motion Picture Herald* of 16 June 1971).
308 <S. n.>, 'One Day in the Life of Ivan Denisovich', *The Film Bulletin* (Philadelphia, PA), June 1971, p. 38.
309 Verr., op. cit.
310 Ibid. According to *Variety*, the only standout elements in *One Day* were 'Nykvist's photography, Per Schwab's grimly accurate art direction and Ada Skolmen's ragtag wardrobe design'.
311 See the chart of fifty top-grossing films in *Variety* of 2 June 1971 (p. 11; *One Day* is in the 49th place).
312 <S. n.>, 'Courtenay's "Ivan" is a Hit in New York', *Kinematograph Weekly*, 26 June 1971. In 1971, one US dollar roughly equalled 0.41 British pound sterling.

Releasing schedule, on 20 September – 1 October 1971 he went to New York (several times), Washington D.C., Philadelphia, Boston, San Francisco and Los Angeles. The New York campaign involved, *inter alia*, Wrede giving interviews, sometimes by telephone, to the NYU, YMCA and WHBI/FM radio stations, the Associated Press agency, the Rocky Mountain News (Denver) and the Buffalo Courier-Express newspapers, as well as a live appearance on the Today show (the NBC network), accompanied by a *One Day* clip. In Washington, Wrede talked to News Radio, National Public Radio and the Voice of America, gave a live TV interview on the Panorama programme and had lunch with the critics from the *Washington Post* (Kenneth Turan), the *Washington Star* (John Segraves) and the *Washington Daily News* (Milton Berliner). In Boston, Wrede was interviewed by the WRKO, WHDH, WILD, WBZ, WCOP, WEZE, WCRB and WMEX radio stations, attended a special screening and seminar for students and educators at the Cheri Theatre complex, and a press luncheon with George McKinnon of the *Boston Globe*, Cameron Dewar of the *Boston Herald-Traveler*, Ann Beierfield of the *Record-American*, Janet Maslin of *Boston After Dark*, Connie Gorfinkle of the *Quincy Patriot Ledger*, Kay Bourne of the *Bay State Banner* and Nora Taylor of the *Christian Science Monitor*.[313] In San Francisco, Wrede responded to questions from the KKHI, KSAN – AM and FM, KSAY, KFRC, KDIA, KUSF, KCSF, KCBS, KSFX-FM and some half-a-dozen other radio stations, and either dined or lunched with journalists from the *San Francisco Chronicle*, the *San Francisco Examiner*, the *Daily Californian*, the *Sun-Reporter*, the *Contra Costa Times*, the *Hollywood Reporter*, the *Sacramento Observer* and a number of other local periodicals. Tom Courtenay was also flown to the US for a four-day promotional visit, filled with interviews to the media (including appearances on Group W's David Frost Show and ABC's Dick Cavett Show).[314]

---

313 One of those present at the luncheon at the Sheraton Plaza recalled that 'Wrede was half an hour late and a disgruntled press had begun to eat when <he> arrived <...>. But the tall, elegant, bearded cosmopolitan soon changed irritation to pleasure, at least for the distaff writers, and we were soon basking in his charm' (Dewar, 'Life in a Siberian Labor Camp'). Another witness reported that Wrede even 'let his food go cold and uneaten while politely answering questions' (McKinnon, op. cit.).

314 Ibid. Regardless of Courtenay's 'almost evangelistic fervour about *Ivan Denisovich*', publicity trips was not something he particularly liked and excelled at, hence engaging 'in a series of pregnant silences with Dick Cavett on television <...> he remembers as a minor disaster' (Bell, op. cit.).

The Cinerama campaign aimed at a wide cross-section of American society, encompassing, among others, liberals and conservatives (because of the film's controversial subject matter), college students (as a frequent cinema-going social group), film industry employees (as a matter of course, for professional reasons), housewives (apparently for their enhanced ability to be compassionate) and the black minority (who were presumably expected to feel solidarity with the oppressed).[315]

All this 'whirlwind of activity' (to use an expression from a letter to Wrede, written on 16 November 1971 by Carol Schmidt, a Cinerama employee) seems to have paid off. On 6 October, *Variety* reported that *One Day*'s gross box office takings after the first week of its release in thirty-five cinemas in and near New York were heading for USD125,000, while in Boston the film made USD15,000; in Chicago, USD11,500; in Denver, USD11,000; and in Washington and St Louis, USD10,500 each.

The critics' response was mostly enthusiastic. *Rolling Stone* magazine praised the 'striking, objective, lean, sardonic craft' of the film, as well as Courtenay's performance: 'pathetic without being maudlin, frighteningly real, he achieves a kind of level in this film he's never managed before'.[316] The *San Francisco Chronicle* called Courtenay's acting 'a moving blend of vigor and sensitivity'.[317] The *Honolulu Star-Bulletin* lauded him as 'one of those rare actors who looks completely commonplace but is able to make a character real through mannerisms and sheer implication'.[318] *The Daily Pennsylvanian* claimed that 'Courtenay's haggard face, pinched lips and half-dazed eyes bring alive visually the politics of hunger and cold of Ivan Denisovich's world in a way that Solzhenitsyn's novel can only hint at'.[319] *The Daily Planet* said:

---

315 According to one critic, 'were it not for the Russian setting, and some sentimentality hung over from the thirties, when liberals deluded themselves over the nobility of the Stalinist experiment, Comrade Ivan would just seem to be another Uncle Tom' (Myron Meisel, 'A Day in the Life', *The Chicago Reader*, 15 October 1971).
316 Weisman, op. cit., pp. 65-66.
317 Paine Knickerbocker, '*Ivan Denisovich*: A Somber Film on Soviet Prison Life', *The San Francisco Chronicle*, 30 September 1971.
318 Pierre Bowman, '*Ivan Denisovich* Rare, Masterly Filmed', *The Honolulu Star-Bulletin*, 27 October 1971.
319 Eglick, op. cit.

'Courtenay shows us the full emotions of a man who refuses to be reduced to an animal. It is a change-of-pace role for Courtenay, but one that he fills to perfection. If there ever was any doubt before, *Ivan Denisovich* establishes Tom Courtenay as one of the finest actors in the world'.[320]

Courtenay's fellow actors received their share of attention too. 'His supporting cast is as good as he', the *Los Angeles Herald-Examiner* wrote. 'Each actor has not simply thrown on his role like a patched mantle or grimy makeup. Each seems to have understood the suffering and deprivation of <the convicts>, and to have let it flourish like a cancer from within'.[321] The 'splendid' Skjønberg was singled out 'as the tough work boss who is expert at padding the work rate',[322] and Eric Thompson was applauded for his 'fine performance as the cynical but very likeable Tsesar'.[323] Maxwell and Burke also got an honourable mention.[324]

One Day's camera work was lavished with praise throughout the country. *The Oregonian* stated: 'Nykvist works in a lean style that emphasises both the barrenness of the life of the prisoners and the almost perverse beauty that comes when both lives and landscape have been stripped to the barest essentials'.[325] *The Chicago Reader* wrote in a similar vein (Nykvist 'has made the wastelands of a Siberian labor camp about as chillingly beautiful as it could be without turning the whole show into a Gasoline Alley Ice Follies'),[326] and so did the Boston-based *Christian Science Monitor* (Nykvist 'makes it a harrowingly beautiful film despite the grimness of his subject. He opens and closes the film, for instance, with shots of the camp looking like some glitter-

---

320 Lewis Beale, 'One Day in the Life of Ivan Denisovich', *The Daily Planet* (Philadelphia, PA), 5-11 October 1971.
321 Bridget Byrne, '*Life of Denisovich*: Absorbing Wrede Fare', *The Los Angeles Herald-Examiner*, 15 October 1971.
322 Cameron Dewar, 'Ivan Denisovich', *The Boston Herald-Traveler*, 4 October 1971.
323 Beierfield, op. cit.
324 See Louise Sweeney, '*Denisovich*: Searing Solzhenitsyn Film Epic', *The Christian Science Monitor*, 2 October 1971. Incidentally, this article had already appeared in the same newspaper, on 2 June 1971, during the film's trial run in New York, under a slightly different title ('Searing Solzhenitsyn film'). The later version of the main text had only several more words added: 'now on screen at Boston's Cheri complex'. Even the misprints were not corrected.
325 Mahar, op. cit.
326 Meisel, op. cit.

ing subzero space station, all navy-blue sky, sparkling geometry of lights and everlasting snow. Even a scene in a dark grey room, where Ivan is scrubbing the floor, has a certain bleak beauty'[327]). *The Detroit Free Press* observed with admiration: 'Sven Nykvist's inspired camera busies itself making analogies between the prisoner's food and the mortar they slap on bricks, between the beige, gray, and white streaks in the weathered wood of their barracks and the beige, gray, and white streaks on their weathered faces'.[328] However, Nykvist was criticised in some quarters for shooting the film in colour. The issue had already been discussed at the time of *One Day*'s release in Scandinavia. In New York, doubts were voiced by the music, film and theatre critic Stewart Klein, who said in his WNEW-TV broadcast: 'As bleak as the surroundings are, the colour film is far too cheery. The movie should have been shot in black and white'. The Philadelphia *Daily Planet* even alleged that *One Day* would have been 'a masterpiece but for one minor error: the decision to shoot the film in color. <...> Its use tends to dissipate the horrors of the film'.[329] *The Miami News* held a similar view: 'The picture may have been better off as a black-and-white venture, which would have enhanced the drab existence of the men, the men's appearances, and the artistic technique'.[330]

Nordheim's music was not to everyone's liking either, at least not all of it. As *The Daily Pennsylvanian* put it, 'the saintly chorus of high-pitched voices that occasionally cuts into the screen's otherwise straightforward soundtrack seems out of place, representing a minor concession to martyr-conscious

---

327 Sweeney, op. cit.
328 Susan Stark, 'Man Survives – in Noble *One Day*', *The Detroit Free Press*, 8 October 1971.
329 Beale, op. cit.
330 Hubert Norton, 'Courtenay is Ideal Ivan', *The Miami News*, 16 October 1971. It is possible, however, that the decision to film *One Day* in colour was made simply in order to remain faithful to the book. Cf.: 'Nine colours are referred to in the text: black, yellow, white, blue, green, red, brown, pink, and grey. The camp's basic colour scheme is composed of the blackness of the night, the whiteness of the snow and the brightness of the numerous yellow lights dotting the compound. Few of the other colours are vivid. The hues of dawn are "blurry"; the gruel Shukhov eats at breakfast is "yellowish"; the glass on the desk in the sick bay is "greenish"; the Tartar's blue shoulder tabs are "grubby"; the power station is a "grey skeleton"; the sun is "dim"' (Richard Tempest, 'The Geometry of Hell: The Poetics of Space and Time in *One Day in the Life of Ivan Denisovich*', in Klimoff (ed.), op. cit., p. 65).

schmaltz'.³³¹ Even if this interpretation is the only possible one (which it does not appear to be), it has to be stressed that, on principle, Wrede did not manipulate his audiences. Student newspapers were particularly appreciative of this aspect of his directing, for some reason. *The Chronicle*, published by Hofstra University (New York), wrote: 'Much of the movie is shown with no dialogue, just letting the audience see what is going on. The silence is louder than any din could be. The audience is allowed to form its own opinions'.³³² *The Campus Slate*, published by the New York Institute of Technology, described *One Day* as 'a form of the audience participation theatre through the media of film', because 'it gives the audience insight and it makes them contemplate'.³³³ Needless to say, this corresponded significantly with Hønningstad's ideas about theatre competing with places of worship as an alternative location for a communal spiritual experience. In Wrede's own words, 'What I want the audience to come away with is a sense of community'.³³⁴

Such an effect was not easy to achieve, partly because the experience depicted in *One Day* was, by and large, very remote from what the film's viewers could readily relate to. This point had been raised by Solzhenitsyn himself, in Ivan Denisovich's comment made when the medical assistant Vdovushkin denies him sick leave: 'There is no point in expecting someone who's warm to understand someone who's cold'.³³⁵ A *Detroit Free Press* film critic explained:

> The <phrase>, of course, uses the word 'understand' to mean fully realize, to realize beyond sympathy, certainly, and even beyond empathy. On those terms, <...> you and I could never fully understand the coldness, not to mention the total experience, of Alexander Solzhenitsyn in a Siberian labor camp of the Stalin era. <...> In great part, however, the failure or success of a work of art depends upon its power to pull us into

---

331 Eglick, op. cit.
332 Susan Giniger, 'Prison Story Premieres Locally', *The Chronicle* (Hempstead, N. Y.), 30 September 1971.
333 James Bachteler, '*Life of Denisovich*: Movie of Rare Quality', *The Campus Slate* (Westbury, N. Y), 19 October 1971.
334 Thomas, op. cit.
335 *The Making*, p. 43.

vicarious experience, to activate our intelligence and emotions, to place us on the brink of understanding. This, Wrede's film does.[336]

Yet the mere brink of understanding would every so often result in a lack of understanding, which in turn would lead to a lack of compassion. It seems that if there was anything unifying about *One Day*'s audiences it might well have been the sensation that the film was either largely lost on many filmgoers, or (mis)interpreted and reacted to in a number of different ways. A *Chicago Sun-Times* contributor summed up his (and presumably some other people's) impressions thus: 'Visually we are involved <...> but emotionally we are distanced and even, perhaps, indifferent'.[337] A *Miami Herald* journalist recorded the opposite: 'We don't view the film, we feel it'.[338] *The Oregonian* occupied a middle ground: 'Just because emotion must be suppressed does not mean it can be eradicated. <...> Unstated, but unmistakeably, a silent, almost telepathic passion seethes through the film'.[339] A reviewer from *The Los Angeles Herald-Examiner* expressed her hope that everyone would 'find one particular moment in this film <...> at which point the objective appreciation of the brilliant craftsmanship will melt into emotional reaction, comprehension of the mind will tumble down, and understanding will be reborn in the heart'.[340] However, very few critics felt sufficiently moved by *One Day* to admit, at least publicly, that 'the personal involvement is so great that one is astonished on leaving the bitter dreariness of the Siberian winter in the theatre that the sun is shining in 70 degree temperatures'.[341]

Yet the universality of the film's message was frequently recognized.[342] Wrede's intention was to show that 'we're all them – the prisoners. Take away the trappings – motor cars, going to the moon, Marxism and Leninism – and there we are. We are all there. I want the audience to experience the meta-

---

336 Stark, op. cit.
337 Gary Houston, 'One Day in the Life...', *The Chicago Sun-Times*, 13 October 1971.
338 John Huddy, *'Ivan Denisovich* Is Sobering Tale of Prison Life', *The Miami Herald*, 19 October 1971.
339 Mahar, op. cit.
340 Byrne, op. cit.
341 Dewar, 'Ivan Denisovich'.
342 Cf.: 'as a film of universality, *One Day in the Life of Ivan Denisovich* occasionally succeeds' (Houston, op. cit.).

phor of the prison as a reality'.³⁴³ *The Miami Herald* came close to appreciating this, when its reviewer stated: *One Day* 'is not about one prison but all prisons, not about one victim but many victims';³⁴⁴ and so did Louise Sweeney of *The Christian Science Monitor*, who said that the film 'leaves you wondering over the unconquerable spirit of all the Ivans in all the prison camps'.³⁴⁵

In fact, the words about prisoners'/human beings' ultimate irrepressibility in *One Day* were repeated so often that it prompted an interesting polemic against the cliché (which the film had been closely identified with). In the opinion of Myron Meisel (*Chicago Reader*),

> there is a little too much of 'the indomitable spirit of Man' and 'Man's will to survive' and other such pseudo-liberal clichés lurking around the edges of this film. This isn't a new message, God knows, and I'm not at all sure that such sentiments are all that true, either. But more importantly, this message has been haunting far too much of the world's art in the last twenty-five years, and further demonstration strikes me as not only unnecessary and repetitive, but dangerously self-indulgent. We all need to be told that our spirit is indestructible just so many times – before we know it, we'll begin to believe it. And in the confidence of our eventual triumph over the forces of repression and oppression, we may well find ourselves with a lot more repression and oppression to have to triumph over. Or triumph in spite of. Being told that Man will always survive, whatever torture and evil he may endure, does hell for the initiative.³⁴⁶

---

343 Thomas, op. cit. Cf. a remark of a *One Day*'s translator, made soon after the book's publication: 'the concentration camp <in Solzhenitsyn's story> is to be seen not just as a microcosm of life in the Soviet Union but of life everywhere. The majority of the human race are condemned to a daily grind, a rat-race, of which the concentration camp is the ultimate and most intense expression' (Max Hayward, 'Solzhenitsyn's Place in Contemporary Soviet Literature', *Slavic Review*, vol. 23, no. 3 (1964), p. 436).
344 Huddy, op. cit.
345 Sweeney, op. cit.
346 Meisel, op. cit.

Independently of Meisel, Paine Knickerbocker arrived at a similar conclusion, the only difference being that, according to the latter critic, the film does not advocate a mixture of humility and perseverance as a desirable answer to the duress but instead 'suggests that rebellion may be the ultimate dignity: that Attica[347] perhaps reveals far more courage and accomplishment than do the acquiescent political prisoners in this frightful Siberian establishment during the Stalin regime'.[348]

Needless to say, these mutually exclusive interpretations of the film's meaning can easily be traced back to the ambiguity of the message of the book itself, so perceptively characterised by Dariusz Tolczyk:

> Is this perpetual understatement and focus on the mundane practicalities of day-to-day existence in the camp, this systematic exclusion of the element of moral outrage, a reflection of an atrophied ethical sense in the protagonist? Could it be an indirect indication of Ivan's inner submission to slavery to the point of accepting his own victimization without a thought of protest? Is it an indication of Shukhov's confusion about what is wrong and what is normal? In other words, does *One Day* stand as a testament to the victory of human dignity over totalitarian dehumanisation or to its ultimate defeat?[349]

The jury, as it were, is still out on this one.

Meanwhile, in early 1972, it was announced that the US National Board of Review of Motion Pictures, *Newsweek* magazine and the influential film critic Judith Crist of the *New York Magazine* had included *One Day* in their lists of the best films of 1971.[350] This was a formidable achievement, considering that Wrede's film was released in the same year as Sam Peckinpah's *Straw*

---

[347] That is, the Attica prison riot at the Attica Correctional Facility in Attica, N. Y., in September 1971.
[348] Knickerbocker, 'A Somber Film on Soviet Prison Life'.
[349] Dariusz Tolczyk, 'Who Is Ivan Denisovich? Ethical Challenge and Narrative Ambiguity in Solzhenitsyn's Text', in Klimoff (ed.), op. cit., p. 78.
[350] See the unsigned notes 'National Board's Bests; Russell for *Devils*, *Boy Friend*' and 'Year-End Ratings by Various Papers' in *Variety* of 12 January 1972.

Dogs, Woody Allen's *Bananas*, William Friedkin's *The French Connection*, Roman Polanski's *Macbeth*, Federico Fellini's *The Clowns*, Bernardo Bertolucci's *The Conformist*, Luchino Visconti's *Death in Venice*, Peter Bogdanovich's *The Last Picture Show*, Miloš Forman's *Taking Off* – and Stanley Kubrick's *Clockwork Orange*, which, in Ronald Harwood's opinion, 'got all the attention'.[351]

In the UK, the film opened at midnight on 12 January 1972, at the Curzon cinema in the Mayfair area of London. The premiere was attended, among others, by 'members of Parliament and top names in the film industry'.[352] A reviewer for the industry's periodical *Cinema TV Today* greeted *One Day* rather warmly:

> It is a measure of the director's skill, the tautness of the script and the sensitivity of the actors' performances that, at the end of a long day, I soon became interested in the minutia of Ivan's life and the widely differing characters of his fellow prisoners. Although the situation is tragic, the film is too stalwartly courageous in tone, too resolutely matter-of-fact about the sufferings endured to provide the audience with the easy comfort of tears. Indeed, if we wept, the film would have failed in at least part of its purpose. Knowing that the story is based on the author's own experiences, we may be permitted to feel anger; but overriding anger there must be pride and joy in man's ability to survive as a thinking creature. *One Day in the Life of Ivan Denisovich* has this inspirational quality, and I welcome it as an antidote against the multitude of films that may be more overtly entertaining but leave me without much hope for any of us.[353]

As for the box office ratings, the same critic stated that *One Day* 'cannot be judged by any ordinary standard but should arouse a great deal of interest

---

351 Harwood's email to Andrei Rogachevskii of 12 July 2007. Curiously, the *Films and Filming* magazine called *Clockwork Orange* the 'most over-rated film of the year' (see the anonymous report 'Films and Filming Honours for 1972', *Films and Filming*, January 1973, p. 42).
352 See the anonymous report 'Prisoner C 854 Goes to a West End Premiere', *Cinema TV Today*, 15 January 1972, p. 12.
353 Marjorie Bilbow, 'The New Films', *Cinema TV Today*, 22 January 1972, p. 28.

amongst the discriminating and all who admire fine acting',[354] expecting the film to do well in 'carefully selected intimate cinemas and art houses'.[355] Judging by a letter to Wrede of 24 February 1972 from Robert Scott, the administrator of Wrede's Manchester-based 69 Theatre Company, this prediction came true, at least as far as Manchester was concerned: '*One Day* has had its run extended in Manchester and was full to bursting last night (Wednesday and in the middle of damned power cuts – pretty good, eh?)'. Scott and his family went to see the film, and here is a summary of their impressions, given in the same letter:

> At the risk of understatement we just want to say that we were thrilled. It was a marvellous film, and if you don't mind me saying so, it shows the strength of Solzhenitsyn's narrative in that the film seemed exactly as we imagined it in the book. The last image of Max <the actor James Maxwell as the Captain in the punishment cell. – BH, AR> is very upsetting and lingers on. We all thought it was simply a great movie.

Professional film critics were, on the whole, somewhat less enthusiastic. Writing to Wrede from his Antibes residence on 6 October 1972, Graham Greene (whose play *The Potting Shed* Wrede had directed and produced at the Olympia Theatre in Dublin in June 1958) even felt compelled to say: 'I can't imagine why the reviews <of *One Day*> in England were so tepid. I think it was one of the most memorable films I've seen in years'. While recognising the adaptation's 'fidelity'[356] to Solzhenitsyn's book, some reviewers commended Harwood's script for its 'economical efficiency',[357] but others noted that it 'broaden<ed> and simplif<ied> some of the details'[358] and called it 'literate and sensible rather than imaginative',[359] believing that it did not 'wholly catch the spare eloquence of the original'.[360] While applauding the fact that the adaptation consciously avoided the clichés normally associated with

---

354 Ibid.
355 Ibid.
356 John Coleman, 'Kubrick's Ninth', *New Statesman*, 14 January 1972, p. 56.
357 See Alexander Walker, 'Bleak Day', *Evening Standard*, 13 January 1972.
358 John Russell Taylor, 'A Death in the Family', *The Times*, 14 January 1972.
359 Malcolm, 'Almost Magic Roundabout'.
360 Ibid.

prison camp films ('this one has no escapes, no great clashes of will among the prisoners, no mutinies. And, of course, no women'[361]), some critics also complained about what they saw as the screen version's 'over-faithfulness'[362] to the original. Taking the line that less does not always mean more, David Robinson of *The Financial Times* explained what, in his view, hampered Wrede's adaptation:

> Perhaps Solzhenitsyn himself has misled the film-makers, with his method (effective enough in the novel) of understatement, of eschewing drama, of describing the camp not at its sensational worst, but at its destroying ordinary best. To attempt the same kind of understatement in the film proves a trap, forfeiting the audience's interest and concern and belief. The result is one of those heart-breaking films that are so honourable, so exceptionally decent in their intentions, so painstaking in execu-

---

361 Barker, op. cit. Cf. also: 'this is a film which could legitimately have wallowed in the discomfort and viciousness of the guards etc; Wrede deserves a medal for not having done so' (Braun, op. cit, p. 50). Billy Wilder's *Stalag 17* (1953), John Sturges's *The Great Escape* (1963) and Bryan Forbes's *King Rat* (1965; also starring Tom Courtenay) were named among the commercial blockbusters in the prison film genre, regarded by some to be inferior to *One Day* (see Les Wedman, op. cit.). It is curious that in 1959 Solzhenitsyn wrote a screenplay called *The Tanks Know the Truth* (Znaiut istinu tanki), which can be considered an action-driven companion piece to *One Day* as it merges a description of the real-life 1954 uprising in the Kengir labour camp with several scenes that in fact took place in 1951-52 in Ivan Denisovich's Ekibastuz camp (for a comparison between Solzhenitsyn's *One Day* and *The Tanks*, see Curtis, op. cit., p. 144). *The Tanks Know the Truth* employs with abandon all the above-mentioned prison film clichés and more, including escape attempts, a revolt crushed by the tanks of the title, heroic deaths, cowardly betrayals, prisoners being tortured, informers being killed and even (heterosexual) love episodes (a wall separating the male and female sections of the camp gets destroyed during the rebellion). First published in 1981, in the eighth volume of Solzhenitsyn's collected works edited in Cavendish, VT, *The Tanks Know the Truth* has not been turned into a film to this day.
362 George Melly in *The Observer* of 16 January 1972. Cf. the opinion of Dimitrii Panin, who served time in the same Ekibastuz camp as Solzhenitsyn and was used as a prototype for the character of Sologdin in Solzhenitsyn's novel *First Circle*. After his release from prison Panin moved to the West, where in 1972 he saw *One Day* in Geneva: 'The actors are good, the director is conscientious, <but> the scriptwriter is too diligent. His diligence has let the film down: it's a timid illustration of the book' (Dimitrii Panin, *Zapiski Sologdina*, Frankfurt am Main: Possev-Verlag, 1973, vol. 1, p. 492; this passage has been omitted from the English translation of the book by John Moore, *The Notebooks of Sologdin*, published in 1976 in London by Hutchinson & Co).

tion that the spectator feels miserably guilty to feel so little involved with them.[363]

Very few critics found the fact that the film was 'cold and sombre <...> superb'.[364] *The Sunday Telegraph* called it 'desperately moving'.[365] The majority opinion, however, begged to differ. *The Times* stated unequivocally: 'Somehow the vital spark is lacking. <...> The film never manages to achieve the intensity necessary to hold our interest, let alone move us, in default of external happening'.[366] *The Evening Standard*'s verdict was no more complimentary: 'It is a quiet film offering no serious experience – more to be measured by an egg-timer than an earthquake scale'.[367] If the film raised any singular, overwhelming emotion among professional reviewers, it seems to have been depression. An *Evening News* critic admitted, referring to the camp's inmates, that for the first half-hour he 'felt as bowed down as these wretched victims of pointless cruelty'.[368] Still, the scenes at the worksite made him understand why the prisoners 'had the impetus to go on living'.[369] Arthur Thirkell of *The Daily Mirror* confessed that he 'did not feel uplifted' and at the film's end felt as if he too 'had served a couple of years in Siberia'.[370] He concluded: 'I was glad to escape from the Curzon cinema'.[371] Writing for *The Daily Express*, Ian Christie remarked that the film should put things into perspective for the filmgoer who perhaps 'shouted at <his> wife because the toast was burnt' or

---

363 See David Robinson, 'The Clockwork before Us', *The Financial Times*, 14 January 1972. Cf. a similar judgement pronounced almost two decades later and reprinted in the subsequent editions of the authoritative *Time Out Film Guide* ever since: 'in his efforts to be accurate and restrained, Wrede forsakes passion and creates a film as cold and clinical as the environment it observes' (G<eoff> A<ndrew>, 'One Day in the Life of Ivan Denisovich', in Tom Milne (ed.), *The Time Out Film Guide*, London: Penguin, 1989, p. 432).
364 Celia Roberts, 'Cinema', *What's on in London*, 14 January 1972, p. 24.
365 Margaret Hinxman, 'Grim and Glorious', *The Sunday Telegraph*, 16 January 1972.
366 John Russell Taylor, op. cit.
367 Walker, op. cit.
368 Barker, op. cit.
369 Ibid.
370 Arthur Thirkell, 'To Siberia with No Love!', *The Daily Mirror*, 13 January 1972.
371 Ibid.

'groaned over an electricity bill <he> can't pay'.[372] At the same time, the film critic conceded that One Day was hardly suitable 'for a jolly night out'.[373]

Appreciation of the actors' performance varied, ranging from The Tablet's summary pronouncement that 'the acting <...> is beyond praise'[374] to The Daily Telegraph's grumpy (but not unreasonable) opinion that the actors do not 'manage to convey – have they ever seen it, I wonder – a continual state of near-starvation'.[375] Apart from brief remarks about James Maxwell ('a somewhat introvert actor who is not always suited to some of the actionful parts that fall his way on television,[376] he is perfectly suited to the well educated and slightly reserved but disastrously outspoken Captain'[377]) and the auxiliary cast ('the only weakness in this harrowing account of men hanging on in hell is in the strangely stagey playing of several of the minor roles, particularly in a feeble guard-room scene'[378]), it was Tom Courtenay, the film's star, whose achievement was singled out, for obvious reasons.

Courtenay as Ivan Denisovich was almost unanimously admired for, in the words of The Sunday Times, 'resolutely denying himself any vestige of heroic individuality'.[379] Yet, owing to his 'flinty'[380] performance, his character, 'with his shaven head and unshaven face, his dehydrated voice and his babyish way of cramming great spoonfuls of revolting fish stew and boiled grass into his mouth, <stood> out firmly but unostentatiously from the rest of the crowd

---

372 Ian Christie, 'If You Had a Tough Time Yesterday, Read on...', The Daily Express, 12 January 1972.
373 Ibid. Cf. also: 'it is not a film for those in search of a jolly night out' (Thirkell, op. cit.).
374 Maryvonne Butcher, 'Cinema', The Tablet: The International Catholic Weekly, 15 January 1972, p. 36.
375 Patrick Gibbs, 'In the Ice', The Daily Telegraph, 14 January 1972. On the contrary, a Newsweek reviewer thought that 'unlike the prisoners of so many American films who look like rich actors wearing soldier suits, <the labour camp inmates in One Day>, with their shaved heads, carry the scars of severe internment' (Zimmerman, 'Prisoner's Base').
376 In 1964-67, for instance, Maxwell appeared in several episodes in the popular spy show Avengers and a crime series called The Saint.
377 Braun, op. cit, p. 51.
378 Coleman, op. cit.
379 Dilys Powell, 'Roots of Terror, Paths of Survival', The Sunday Times, 16 January 1972.
380 Malcolm, 'Almost Magic Roundabout'.

<of prisoners>'.³⁸¹ *The New Statesman* called Courtenay's Ivan Denisovich 'a revelation because it is so sparely touched in, not just a matter of a cropped head and filthy hands'.³⁸² Eric Braun made a perceptive comment that 'Courtenay's unique facial bone structure – accentuated here by hunger and his shaved head to the point of emaciation – his keenly expressive eyes, and oddly musical voice with its faint echoes of his native Yorkshire, are the ideal instruments <for the role>'.³⁸³ Furthermore, in Braun's view, the part of Ivan Denisovich turned out to be so appropriate for Courtenay because he, 'more than any actor in this country, suggests the extraordinary common man with his own inner vision which is going to carry him through to moral victory, even if material success eludes him'.³⁸⁴

Braun must have known that, by Courtenay's own admission, to adopt Ivan Denisovich's frame of mind, he had to follow Wrede's advice to

> think of my father. I started off as a working-class boy in Hull and I've come a long way from there in every sense. But my father is still a working-class man. He has had a much harder life than I have, so I tried to think myself back into his world. <...> As we went on <filming>, <...> I began to realise that it was going to be all right.³⁸⁵

In another interview, Courtenay admitted to an intense affinity with his character:

---

381 Cecil Wilson, 'No Violence, No Sex, Just Freezing Hell', *The Daily Mail*, 12 January 1972.
382 Coleman, op. cit.
383 Braun, op. cit., p. 51.
384 Ibid., p. 50.
385 Norman, op. cit. In his book *Dear Tom*, Courtenay recalls how he said to his father once: 'You're not the average working man, you're below average' (Courtenay, op. cit, p. 20). In the chapter 'Dad', Courtenay describes his father, who spent much of his life painting trawlers, as a 'man who scarcely knew what a theatre was' (ibid., p. 373). This characterisation is reminiscent of Ivan Denisovich's perception of the discussion between Tsesar and prisoner X-123 about cinema (see *The Making*, pp. 91-92). Also, Courtenay's father apparently had 'that northern thing of keeping thoughts close to your chest' (Bell, op. cit.) Curiously, Wrede had not even met Thomas Courtenay Sr. (Tallmer, op. cit.).

> Ivan Denisovich and me are very much alike, I believe. He has little to say – instead he acts. I am just like that, with difficulties to talk about things and formulate my thoughts and feelings in words. I like Ivan's strong backbone, his instinctive capability to survive. But he does not only just manage to do that; at the same time, he demonstrates, perhaps without his own knowledge, the existence of <…> a deep brotherly feeling for all men (*medmänsklighet*).[386]

In yet another interview, Courtenay elucidated his perception of Ivan as a human type by drawing a comparison from nature:

> I'd like to think of it in term of three trees. The first is very strong, stiff and erect against the wind; it has no give in it at all, and when the wind blows hard enough, the tree will snap and break – as did the captain in *Ivan Denisovich*. The second bends totally under the wind, from whatever direction it comes, until finally it blows over. And the third tree is strong enough to stand but pliant enough to give so it can be neither broken nor blown over. This is Ivan.[387]

Sure enough, those who were discerning and well disposed rightly observed that Courtenay's 'understanding of the nature of Solzhenitsyn's incurable optimism warms <the film's> properly bleak exterior like some supernatural central heating'.[388] There was only one dissenting voice, that of *The Daily Telegraph*, arguing that Courtenay gave Ivan 'Denisovich too much of a hang-dog expression, rather at odds with the spry spirit suggested by <Solzhenitsyn's book>'.[389] Otherwise, the tenor of the general approval of Courtenay's contribution can be summed up by quoting *The Sun* newspaper, aimed primarily at a working class readership: the actor 'turns in the best performance of his career. If he does not get an award for this, then there ain't no justice in filmland'.[390]

---

386 Ekstrand, op. cit.
387 Bell, op. cit.
388 Malcolm, 'Almost Magic Roundabout'.
389 Gibbs, op. cit.
390 Fergus Cashin, 'It's a Triumph for Bald Tom', *The Sun*, 13 January 1972.

This judgement was broadly in agreement with what Courtenay too must have felt when he saw the finished picture for the first time. Courtenay recalls: 'I woke up the next morning and I thought, "All right. That's it. Now I don't care. That will do me. If I never do anything better, it won't matter."'[391] Alas, the 'no justice in filmland' caveat proved to be insurmountable, and Courtenay did not receive any awards for his role. Although deemed 'worthy of many prizes',[392] the film itself fared only marginally better, in no small measure due to a political intervention on the part of the Soviet Union. By his own admission, Wrede felt – not unjustifiably, we hasten to add – that he had done 'Russia a great service culturally' because *One Day* 'shows more about Russians that we generally get to find out. It depicts them as human beings, not merely political beings of another order'.[393] It could be assumed with some confidence, though, that Soviet officials did not feel particularly grateful. In his review of the film, televised on 17 May 1971 on the Today show (NBC-TV), the film and book critic Gene Shalit pointed out that the 68th Street Playhouse, where *One Day* had opened, was located just around the corner from No. 136 East 67th Street, home to the Soviet mission to the UN, and urged every member of the mission to attend the screenings. It is not clear how many mission employees heeded this advice, although it is known that at least one reporter from the Soviet news agency TASS was persuaded to watch *One Day*. Richard Pack recalled that 'afterwards, the man would not offer comment on the film's content. The truth hurts'.[394] The reaction of the Soviet authorities was already known by then, and it was not a warm welcome. The film was scheduled to open at the Cannes Festival, held on 12-27 May 1971,

> but the Russians, to whom Solzhenitsyn's name was <...> anathema, made it clear that if it was shown they and all the other Eastern bloc

---

[391] Norman, op. cit. By early June 1971, Courtenay watched the film four times, admitting: 'If I'm too harassed <...> I'd rather see the film than take a pill. It sustains me' (Tallmer, op. cit.).
[392] Bachteler, op. cit.
[393] Jeanne Miller, 'A Film He Had to Make', *The San Francisco Examiner*, 29 September 1971.
[394] Kalfus, op. cit. Wrede's film remains virtually unknown in Russia to this day.

countries would withdraw their entries. So, sadly, Wrede's film never appeared at the venue where it might easily have carried off some award.[395]

However, *One Day* was awarded a 1971 prize by the Office <now Organisation> Catholique Internationale du Cinéma (OCIC, a Roman Catholic Church film reviewing body, established in the Hague in 1928[396]). Its past recipients included Pier Paolo Pasolini's *Teorema* (1968) and John Schlesinger's *Midnight Cowboy* (1969). The artists Edmond Becker (France) and Jean Grégoire (Canada), the journalist Sergio Trasatti (Italy), the priests Anton Kochs (West Germany), Léo Lunders (Belgium) and Joseph Mazloum (Egypt) were among the members of the 1971 jury, which had to choose a winner from all the contenders nominated by the national Catholic Film Offices in many parts of the world. In the jury's opinion, *One Day* emerged victorious not only because of its 'sober and objective manner in communicating to audiences the utter cruelty of prisoners in a concentration camp', but also thanks to achieving a 'universal impact in helping the attentive spectator recall numerous analogous situations under diverse political regimes in all parts of the world where many suffer the abuses of power to express their convictions'.[397] This was evidence that both the specific and the universal aspects of *One Day*'s message had been understood, at least by some viewers, very much the way the film director intended. Wrede must have been particularly pleased with this award because, coming from a religious organisation, it meant that *One Day*'s discreet religious overtones in its exploration of the theme of achieving grace through suffering had been identified and recognised.

---

395 Ronald Harwood, 'Northern Light for the Theatre', *The Guardian*, 30 September 1998. Among the Soviet bloc's films competing at Cannes in 1971 were *Beg* by Alov and Naumov, *Szerelem* by Karoly Makk and *Zycie rodzinne* by Krzysztof Zanussi. Wrede mistakenly believed that the Cannes management had been persuaded by the Soviet offer to bring the hitherto suppressed Andrei Tarkovsky's film *Andrei Rublev* (1965) to the festival 'if the Solzhenitsyn film was quietly dropped' (Appendix I, 'Russia on My Mind', section '1971'). In fact, *Andrei Rublev* was presented at Cannes in 1969.

396 For more on this organisation, see Gaye Ortiz, 'The Catholic Church and Its Attitude to Film as an Arbiter of Cultural Meaning', in Jolyon P. Mitchell and Sophia Marriage (eds), *Mediating Religion: Conversations in Media, Religion and Culture* (2003), pp. 179-88. In 2002, OCIC merged with UNDA (International Catholic Organisation for Film and Television) to become SIGNIS.

397 See the unsigned report 'Int'l Catholic Film Office Awards Group W's *Ivan* Its Annual Grand Prize' in *Variety* of 24 November 1971.

One Day also received the highest prize of the Prix Fémina Belge du Cinéma, L'Olivier d'or – Grand Prix of the city of Brussels (see the letter from René Silvera of Cinerama Releasing Distributors to Wrede, dated 31 January 1973). In addition, *One Day* was nominated for a 1972 award by the Society of Film and Television Arts (SFTA, now known as BAFTA) in the category 'United Nations Award for the best film illustrating one or more of the principles of the United Nations Charter' (previous recipients included Robert Altman's *MASH* in 1970 and Gillo Pontecorvo's *La Battaglia di Algeri* in 1971). In 1972, the United Nations Award was won by Vittorio de Sica's *Il Giardino dei Finzi-Contini* on the life of Jews in pre-World War II Italy.

Meanwhile, political considerations continued to put serious obstacles in the way of Wrede's film, demonstrating, among other things, that censorship can also serve as a form of reception. In Wrede's native country, wary of upsetting its irritable neighbours east of the border, the Finnish Board of Film Classification banned *One Day* from release by a unanimous vote (four to nil) in February 1972. The decision was taken not so much because of the film's (deeply hidden if at all present) potential to incite anti-Soviet activity but more because Solzhenitsyn was considered an enemy by the Soviet Union. In such a context, showing a film based upon one of his works, could be seen as a political provocation. According to the acting director of the Board Paavo Tuomari, there were allegedly hints in the film that the reality depicted in it was not only of historical significance but also reflected part of modern Soviet life.[398]

The importer of the film, Jörn Donner of the Filmkino company – a writer, film director and a co-founder of the Finnish Film Archive – appealed against the decision, pointing out that the film's release in other Northern Countries had done their relations with the Soviet Union no harm, that the book on which the film was based had originally been published in the Soviet Union and that it was still being freely sold in Finland. Nevertheless, the Appeal Board of Film Classification, which included representatives of the Finnish Foreign Ministry,

---

[398] See Peter Kankkonen, *Finlandiseringen – "frivillig" underkastelse*, Uppsala: Pro Veritate, 1979, s. 266-67.

reconfirmed the ban with five votes in favour and four against. Although Donner was offered FIM5,000 in compensation, he made an appeal to the Supreme Court, but the case was dismissed the same year. The whole issue was seen as a question of national survival and it was believed that the film's release could damage Finland's relationship with the Soviet Union.[399] With few exceptions,[400] the film's ban was not publicly discussed, the newspapers only neutrally reporting the decision.[401] When the film was broadcast on Swedish television in 1972, the signal on the Åland islands (the monolingual Swedish-speaking province in Finland on the border with Sweden and within the range of Swedish television transmitters) was deliberately jammed, so that the islands' inhabitants could not watch the film.[402]

Wrede was evidently mystified by the ban. Not knowing much about the film certification procedures in Finland, he was not sure how to react. He was informed, however, that the film was banned for its alleged tendentiousness and partisanship. To this Wrede replied that the Finnish Film Classification Board must have found something in the film that had not been there in Solzhenitsyn's book. Reportedly, this took Wrede by surprise, because neither the book nor the film (in the countries where it had already been shown) had apparently been blamed for being political and taking sides.[403]

---

399 Andres Küng, *Mitä Suomessa tapahtuu*, Helsinki: Kirjayhtymä, 1976, s. 147.
400 In his article 'Filmcensur och neutralitet', published in Finland's largest (and rather liberal) Swedish-language newspaper *Hufvudstadsbladet* on 27 February 1972, Stig G. Carlson pointed out that Finland could not pretend to be neutral when criticism of racial inequality in the USA and of the war in Vietnam was readily available in the Finnish media, while information programmes about the Eastern bloc remained superficial and glossed over sensitive issues. Carlson suggested that censoring films, such as *One Day* (although he did not specifically name it), demonstrate Finland's dependence on the Soviet Union.
401 See, for example, the unsigned reports 'Ivan Denisovitsh poliittisesti arka esitettäväksi' and 'Donner valittaa elokuvakiellosta heti KHO:hon' in *Helsingin Sanomat* of 17 February and 1 March 1972 respectively, and Heikki Eteläpää's 'Elokuvan esityskielto hyvin hämmästyttävä' in *Uusi Suomi* of 20 February 1972 (s. 1, 19).
402 See the unsigned note 'TV-stopp för film på Åland', *Hufvudstadsbladet*, 24 September 1972.
403 See the unsigned note 'Denisovitj är inte en tendentiös film' in *Hufvudstadsbladet* of 22 February 1972. It is not clear how serious Wrede was when denying a political affiliation to Solzhenitsyn, who can arguably be said to have never published anything apolitical in his life. Perhaps this was merely the tactics that the director chose to defend his film under the circumstances. On the other hand, there is no reason to doubt Wrede's words that his picture 'has nothing to do <with> the Stalinist camps. <...> It's about the way we tend to divide humanity. Like the apartheid in South Africa. The

One Day eventually received a public screening at the Film Archive in Helsinki in December 1993 and was broadcast on Finnish television on 27 October 1996. The reception was fairly restrained. In *Helsingin Sanomat* the film was perceived as outdated and incapable of captivating the audience with its 'lengthy gloominess'.[404] The setting did not seem Siberian enough and Courtenay looked too well fed for a Russian prisoner. It was pointed out that Wrede had turned Solzhenitsyn's story into a universal tale of woe, leaving out its political associations.[405] The Communist newspaper *Kansan Uutiset* expressed remorse that the film had not been shown in the 1970s: 'From today's point of view, the decision <to ban the film> can be seen as an excessive measure and an example of unnecessary cringing'.[406] Although not a masterpiece, Wrede's film let a strong and important theme speak for itself, concluded *Kansan Uutiset*.[407]

Whatever journalists and members of the public anywhere in the world may have thought of the film, its most discerning and implacable judge was, of course, Solzhenitsyn himself. He saw the film for the first time in a cinema in Oslo, on 25 February 1974, shortly after his expulsion from the Soviet Union.[408] At the time, Wrede was in Oslo too, working on his film *Ransom* (a.k.a.

---

point is that we have this capacity to relate to human beings as if they were not' (Thomas, op. cit.). It is hard to disagree with Joy Gould Boyum's opinion that the film 'has little concern with ideology' (Joy Gould Boyum, 'On Film', *The Wall Street Journal*, 18 June 1971).
404 Mikael Fräntti, 'Ivan Denisovitsh vihdoin ensi-iltaan', *Helsingin Sanomat* of 27 October 1996.
405 Ibid.
406 Harri-Ilmari Moilanen, 'Päivä Ivan Denisovitshin elämässä', *Kansan Uutiset: Viikkolehti*, 25 October 1996.
407 Ibid. Strangely enough, Wrede seems to have been beyond caring in 1996. His widow Karin thinks the TV premiere just passed by without them noticing anything!
408 Solzhenitsyn's expulsion generated a new wave of world-wide interest in him, and on the crest of this wave *One Day* was re-released in Norway, as well as premiered in West Germany in May, in Denmark in July, and in Italy in September 1974. Before that the film's progress across and beyond Europe had been slow (it had opened in France in September 1972 and in Turkey in March 1973), which suggests that its box office figures were not spectacular but the producers and distributors would not give up on it. For French reviews, see, for example, Patrick Loriot, 'Sisyphe en Sibérie', *Le Nouvel Observateur*, 4-10 September 1972, pp. 50-51; Gilles Jacob, 'Un jour dans la vie d'Ivan Denissovitch', *L'Express*, 4-10 September 1972, p. 11; M. E., 'Ivan Denissovitch au cinéma: Tom Courtenay, celui qui ne dit pas "oui"', *Le Monde*, 7 September 1972; Robert Chazal, 'L'étape d'un esclave', *France-Soir*, 18 September 1972; and the unsigned note in *Paris Match* of 9 September 1972 (p. 64). For German re-

The Terrorists, 1975). Per Egil Hegge, a Russian-speaking *Aftenposten* reporter who met Solzhenitsyn when working in Moscow in the late 1960s – early 1970s, accompanied Solzhenitsyn on his visit to Norway. Hegge's letter to Wrede of 26 February 1974 makes it clear that there was an attempt to arrange a meeting between Solzhenitsyn and Wrede after Solzhenitsyn had seen the film. Wrede was staying at Oslo's Continental Hotel. Hegge and Solzhenitsyn tried to telephone him but he was not in his room. Then Solzhenitsyn left a hand-written note for Wrede, summing up the former's first impressions of the adaptation:

> Dear Wrede,
> It's a great pity we could not meet. Naturally, it is impossible to please the author. He imagines his characters differently, and some of them do not look right (Alyoshka, for example, should be younger). However, you've made a *good* film, faithful to the truth, to the mood, to the feeling. Thank you and congratulations on your success! They say the film did not have a long-lasting success in many countries, but this *is not* your fault, it's simply because care-free Europe is not yet capable of empathising with a great tragedy.
> I shake your hand and embrace you.
> Tom Courtenay is rather good, but Russian humour ('for us, troubles are like water to the goose'[409]) is missing.

The note was written in Russian. Hegge provided its typewritten translation into English (not the one we have used above). In his above-mentioned letter to Wrede, Hegge also added some of the things Solzhenitsyn had said immediately after the viewing:

> The necessary abbreviations had been done very well, the milieu was true, the types were slightly different in his imagination (he did praise

---

views, see Friedrich A. Wagner, 'Wredes Spielfilm: Solschenizyn matt verfilmt', *Frankfurter Allgemeine Zeitung*, 20 May 1974; -ft, 'Die Hölle läßt sich nicht abfilmen', *Die Welt*, 21 May 1974; and H. G. Pflaum, 'Zwei Stunden im Leben des Iwan Denissowitsch: Caspar Wredes Solschenizyn-Verfilmung', *Süddeutsche Zeitung*, 21 May 1974; etc.

409 A Russian proverb (*s nas beda kak s gusia voda*).

Tsesar Markovich), he was very content with the music and asked you to transmit that to Arne Nordheim, both the musical *genre* and the fact that there was music only when there should be. And perhaps the greatest compliment of them all: 'The film gives the spectator just that very feeling (*imenno to chuvstvo*), it was almost painful to experience it again'.[410]

The second time Solzhenitsyn watched the film was in Paris on 9 March 1976, when it was broadcast on French television and he took part in a question and answer session afterwards, on the Les dossiers de l'écran programme. Responding to a request to assess the adaptation, Solzhenitsyn praised the director and the actors for approaching their task

> with honesty and great insight, given that they themselves did not experience <life in a labour camp under Stalin>, did not live through it. Still, <they> were able to guess that melancholy mood and convey the slow rhythm of life of a convict with a ten- or a twenty-five-year sentence.[411]

He added, however, that Westerners could not successfully imagine such a life in every detail. Thus, to him

> quilted jackets looked too clean and had no holes in them; also, almost all the actors were, as a rule, thick-set men, whereas in the camp people are on the verge of death, with sunken cheeks and no strength left. In the film, it is so warm in the hut that the Latvian sits there with his bare arms and legs. This is impossible, you'd freeze.[412]

---

410 In his email to Ben Hellman of 25 January 2009, Hegge says that Sean Connery, who acted in *Ransom*, was in the Oslo cinema at the same screening of *One Day* as Solzhenitsyn, and when he came up to Solzhenitsyn to shake his hand, the Russian author only shook his head, making it clear that this was not the right occasion. In his book, Nykvist recalls that when Solzhenitsyn and Connery eventually shook hands, Connery noticed that his name did not mean anything to Solzhenitsyn, and added: 'My name is Bond, James Bond'. As no James Bond film had been on show in the Soviet Union at the time, Solzhenitsyn remained none the wiser (see Nykvist, op. cit., p. 123).
411 A. I. Solzhenitsyn, *Publitsistika v trekh tomakh*, Iaroslavl': Verkhne-Volzhskoe knizhnoe izdatel'stvo, 1996, vol. 2, p. 383.
412 Ibid., p. 384.

Solzhenitsyn also declared that 'the film, unfortunately, was not only about the past, but also about the present',[413] referring to the Soviet penitentiary system after Stalin – and inadvertently confirming that the 1972 decision of the Finnish Film Classification Board to ban *One Day*'s release was based on more than just a misguided hunch. Nevertheless, in an interview to *France Soir*, given the next day, Solzhenitsyn stressed that for him the film had a personal dimension, as it made him think about his own past, revisit the camp in his thoughts, reminisce about his fellow prisoners and feel emotional.[414]

He reserved his most critical judgement of the film for the first part of his private memoirs *Between the Rock and the Hard Place* (Ugodilo zernyshko promezh dvukh zhernovov), written in 1978 but published only in September 1998 in *Novyi mir*. There he described what he really felt when he saw *One Day* in Oslo for the first time:

> Courtenay and the rest of the film crew have tried honestly and very hard to keep the film as faithful to the original as possible. But what they manage to convey is only cold, cold and a conventional sense of doom.[415] As for the rest (including the everyday details and the atmosphere of life in prison), they just could not grasp it, struggling to bridge the <cultural> gap, and have made it look false (*takaia neskhvachennost', takaia neoborimaia otdalennost', podmennost'*)![416]

Explaining why he had not expressed his disappointment there and then, Solzhenitsyn said: 'Well, I praised <the work, because> the film participants had not done a hack job, they had put their hearts and souls into it (*ne khalturili, staralis' ot serdtsa*)'.[417] Incidentally, his reaction does not seem to have been affected by financial considerations. By the time he saw the film for the first time, he had not received any royalties for the film adaptation of *One*

---

413 Ibid.
414 See ibid., p. 408.
415 Cf. the claim of a *Daily Telegraph* reviewer that the film did not 'quite succeed in suggesting the extreme cold' (Gibbs, op. cit.), which must have caused a veritable stir among the *One Day* crew members.
416 Solzhenitsyn, 'Ugodilo zernyshko promezh dvukh zhernovov', *Novyi mir*, no. 9 (1998), p. 56.
417 Ibid.

Day, of which he had known from BBC Russian Service and Voice of America radio broadcasts.[418] As early as January 1970, a *New York Times* journalist openly stated:

> The novel is regarded as in the public domain, since the Soviet Union refuses to adhere to international copyright conventions. Mr Wrede said there was no question of trying to pay Mr Solzhenitsyn, lest the author's position <with regard to the Soviet authorities> be further compromised.[419]

However, on 22 February 1974 – almost as soon as Solzhenitsyn was expelled from the Soviet Union (he had been arrested on 12 February and flown to West Germany the next day) – Wrede sent a telegram to Solzhenitsyn's legal representative, Dr Fritz Heeb, at 48 Todistrasse in Zürich, Switzerland, stating:

> In 1970 I produced and directed a motion picture based on Alexander Solzhenitsyn's *One Day in the Life of Ivan Denisovich*. The film was financed seventy five percent by the Westinghouse Corporation of America and twenty five percent by Norsk Film of Norway. The total cost of the film was dollars 500,000. The film has been successfully released in a number of countries including the United States and the United Kingdom, Norway and Sweden. At this time picture has not made a profit on its investment though we are hopeful that over its long theatrical and television life it will eventually show substantial profit. I am sending this telegram to inform you that I as the producer director, Tom Courtenay the star of the film and Norsk Film of Norway the co-producer have today agreed to donate one third of any profits that might arise from our participation in this film to Mr Solzhenitsyn. If Mr Solzhenitsyn will accept this offer I would be happy to arrange for copies of distribution statements and statements of accounts to date to be sent to him. I am inviting the Westinghouse Corporation of America to make a similar gesture and I

---

418 See Reshetovskaia, op. cit., p. 390-91.
419 Lee, op. cit. Wrede went on record as saying that at the start of the *One Day* project he had 'conferred with at least 50 lawyers from various countries, <...> and I believe what I've done is legal' (P<aine> K<nickerbocker>, op. cit.).

would be happy to arrange for a colour print to be given to Mr Solzhenitsyn should he wish to see it. I am currently at the Continental Hotel, Oslo, Norway, where I would appreciate hearing from you. Meanwhile I would be happy to give you any further information you may require.

Solzhenitsyn's uneasiness about certain aspects of Wrede's adaptation must have been dictated by reasons other than pecuniary. Among them, the unavoidable lack of authenticity should be mentioned. In Solzhenitsyn's own words, 'it became crystal clear to me that this could only be filmed with our actors, that is, those with a Soviet background. I saw a yawning gap in outlook and experience, unbridgeable after Soviet decades. <…> Will I ever see a genuinely accurate (*istinnaia*) film version in my lifetime?'[420]

It is true that for a long time no Solzhenitsyn-related film project could either come to fruition or please Solzhenitsyn sufficiently. His own 1968 screenplay *The Parasite* (Tuneiadets), commissioned by the Mosfilm studios – a satirical comedy about a car accident and the car owner's subsequent attempts to repair the damaged vehicle – could not be filmed because Solzhenitsyn had fallen out with the Soviet authorities by the time he had finished it.[421] His 1959 film script *The Tanks Know the Truth* could not be filmed or even published in the Soviet Union because of its topic (the 1954 rebellion in the Kengir labour camp). After Solzhenitsyn's expulsion, the Czech director Vojtěch Jasný and the Polish director Andrzej Wajda (both working abroad at the time) considered shooting it in 1974 and 1980-81 respectively. According to Solzhenitsyn, Jasný could not quite cope with the task, while Wajda eventually gave up the idea, fearing that otherwise he would not be allowed back into Socialist Po-

---

420 Solzhenitsyn, 'Ugodilo zernyshko promezh dvukh zhernovov', *Novyi mir*, no. 9 (1998), p. 56. Unsurprisingly, on his visit to Taiwan in October 1982, Solzhenitsyn praised the 1982 Taiwanese film *Portrait of a Fanatic* (directed by Wong Tung), based on a book called *Unrequited Love*, by Bai Hua, banned in Communist China for political reasons: 'Such films can only be made by people who have suffered a great deal. This film could not have possibly been made in America or anywhere else. China's essence can only be revealed from a free Chinese territory. I envy you: we Russians do not have such a territory and cannot do anything like that' (Solzhenitsyn, 'Ugodilo zernyshko promezh dvukh zhernovov', *Novyi mir*, no. 12 (2000), p. 121).
421 See Reshetovskaia, op. cit., pp. 311, 330, 365-66. For a published version of *The Parasite*, see A. I. Solzhenitsyn, *Sobranie sochinenii v deviati tomakh*, Moscow: Terra – Knizhnyi klub, 2005, vol. 9, p. 474-554.

land.[422] In late 1983 – early 1984, a television company in West Germany planned to adapt the Lenin chapters from *The Red Wheel* and the Stalin chapters from *The First Circle* for the small screen, but it did not happen. In March 1989, the Lenfilm studios asked for Solzhenitsyn's permission to film *The Cancer Ward*, but he refused, insisting that this should be preceded by a Soviet publication of *The Gulag Archipelago*.[423] As for the 1973 Danish-Swedish film adaptation of *The First Circle* (*Den Foerste kreds*, directed by Aleksander Ford), Solzhenitsyn described it as 'hurled into the world by callous mercenaries', and branded it 'shameful'.[424]

With time, Solzhenitsyn became more and more sceptical about anyone's chances, outside Russia, of producing a film adaptation of his works that he would be completely satisfied with.[425] He was partly concerned about the Western tendency to alter the original to achieve a more dramatic effect, partly about the risk of over-politicising the film, but most of all, about the danger of making the film appear anti-Russian, rather than anti-Communist.[426] Numerous proposals to turn *The Gulag Archipelago* into a film (including the idea – suggested by Herbert Brodkin, the executive producer of the 1978 award-winning American TV series *Holocaust* – to focus only on Georgii Tenno and Nikolai Zhdanok's escape from the Ekibastuz camp in October 1950, described in chapter 7 of Part V of the book) were repeatedly

---

422 See Solzhenitsyn, 'Ugodilo zernyshko promezh dvukh zhernovov', *Novyi mir*, no. 9 (1998), p. 61; and no. 9 (2000), p. 118; as well as his *Sobranie sochinenii v deviati tomakh*, Moscow: Terra – Knizhnyi klub, 2005, vol. 9, p. 558. In 1988-89, Wajda returned to the idea of filming *The Tanks* – and then abandoned it again, for unknown reasons (see Solzhenitsyn, 'Ugodilo zernyshko promezh dvukh zhernovov', *Novyi mir*, no. 11 (2003), pp. 56-57).
423 See Solzhenitsyn, 'Ugodilo zernyshko promezh dvukh zhernovov', *Novyi mir*, no. 12 (2000), p. 151; and no. 11 (2003), p. 51.
424 Solzhenitsyn, 'Ugodilo zernyshko promezh dvukh zhernovov', *Novyi mir*, no. 9 (1998), p. 56; see also ibid., no. 11 (1998), p. 110.
425 As early as 1971, Wrede had predicted the main thrust of, and the reasons behind, Solzhenitsyn's reaction to Western film adaptations of his labour camp books: the 'author is so close to his work that he might be a bit dubious about anyone making a film of it and <...> he might depress the situation by expressing a feeling that only the worst could be expected. Besides, <...> the author had never been out of his own country in his life and how then could he evaluate <such a film>? Solzhenitsyn had been in one of these camps himself <...> and his emotions could be a bit mixed on the subject' (Dewar, 'Life in a Siberian Labor Camp').
426 See Solzhenitsyn, 'Ugodilo zernyshko promezh dvukh zhernovov', *Novyi mir*, no. 9 (2000), pp. 118-19.

turned down by Solzhenitsyn because he felt that the difficult task of keeping the right balance between the adaptation's documentary and feature components, as well as selecting episodes, arranging them in a proper order and making sure that the 'general purifying cathartic spirit'[427] of the book remained intact, required his own input and control at every stage in the process. And Solzhenitsyn had no time for this, because he wanted to give priority to his work on the multi-volume epic *The Red Wheel* about World War One and the Russian revolution.

It is possible that Solzhenitsyn's highly sensitive attitude to film adaptations of his works derives not only from a special significance he attached to his own words and ideas, whose integrity could, he felt, be easily compromised by an outside interference, but also, to a certain degree, from what appears to be his unfulfilled ambition to act as a film director himself. In autumn 1959, when working on the screenplay *The Tanks Know the Truth*, Solzhenitsyn carefully and deliberately detailed the key aspects of technical direction in it, because he doubted if it would ever be made into a film in his life time, and wanted to help the reader imagine what it would look like on the screen. The nature of many shots (such as their length, angles and the manner in which they were linked to each other) was meticulously characterised throughout the script, with instances of musical accompaniment and other sound effects also indicated.[428] Although Solzhenitsyn attached to the script a note stating that any future director, cameraman, composer and actors should feel free to ignore his directions, he applied the same technique ten years later in his *Parasite* script, which was expressly commissioned for filming by a professional studio and therefore did not require the same level of technical specification. The

---

427 Solzhenitsyn, 'Ugodilo zernyshko promezh dvukh zhernovov', *Novyi mir*, no. 9 (2000), p. 119.

428 'To make the reader see and hear, I've introduced a system of margins, or indents. The lines that contain references to music and sound effects, except for the speech, would begin on the left side of the page, without an indent. The first indent to the right, in bold script, would indicate the camera's angle and movement, the frame's scope and any change in the screen size. The next indent, further to the right, would describe what can be seen on the screen. The "=" sign would mark a cut, i.e. an abrupt transition from one shot to another. The absence of such a sign would mean a gradual transition from one shot to another. The last indent, even more to the right, would indicate a dialogue, which is all italicised' (A. Solzhenitsyn, *Sobranie sochinenii v 9 tomakh*, Moscow: Terra-Knizhnyi klub, 2005, vol. 9, p. 357).

film director Aleksandr Alov, co-head of an Artistic Association at the Mosfilm studios, reportedly claimed that, in his experience, only two or three scripts were as ready for immediate production as *The Parasite*.[429]

Partly inspired by Dos Passos's Camera Eye 'stream of consciousness' sections from his *USA Trilogy* (1930-36),[430] Solzhenitsyn employed the skills honed on *The Tanks* and *The Parasite* in his *Red Wheel* epic (whose title, incidentally, might well have been inspired by Abel Gance's 1923 four-and-a-half-hour-long feature film *La Roue*). Conscious of the fact that it was impossible to retain the reader's attention across the ten-volume expanse of *The Red Wheel* by using 'only the traditional third-person narration',[431] Solzhenitsyn introduced, among other things, chapters that looked like film sequences, which essentially transformed the reader into an eyewitness. Among the events chosen for cinematographic treatment were battle scenes from *August 1914* and scenes of revolt from *October 1916* and *March 1917*.[432]

Solzhenitsyn's cinematographic vision is evident even in some sections of *The Red Wheel* that do not overtly use the screenplay format. According to John Kohan,

> In attempting to make a distant and unfamiliar era more accessible <...>, Solzhenitsyn experiments with modes of narrative that seem more derivative of photography and cinema than traditional historical fiction. Rather than constructing the novel in a linear pattern with successive events joined together in chronological order, Solzhenitsyn creates an impression of the age by providing heaps of detail that coalesce into 'literary photographs' in the mind's eye. When the depiction of war demands movement and action, events cluster together in associational

---

429 See Reshetovskaia, op. cit., p. 366.
430 For more on the influence, see Curtis, op. cit., p. 150.
431 Solzhenitsyn, 'Ugodilo zernyshko promezh dvukh zhernovov', *Novyi mir*, no. 2 (1999), p. 89.
432 See, for example, A. Solzhenitsyn, *Sobranie sochinenii v 30 tomakh*, Moscow: Vremia, 2007-2008, vol. 7, pp. 290-95; vol. 8, pp. 30-33, 55-59; vol. 9, pp. 354-61; vol. 11, pp. 17-24, 87-90, 719-22; and vol. 13, pp. 135-38, 253-56.

units independent of their place in the overall time schema — a style resembling the cinematic montage.[433]

The cinematographic dimension of some of Solzhenitsyn's other works, including *One Day*, has also been noted. Professor Curtis says of *The First Circle* that 'the extent to which film suffuses the narration as well as the consciousness of the characters' is greater 'than in any other novel ever written in the Soviet Union'[434]; and of *One Day*, that its entire text can be read as 'Ivan Denisovich's movie, for he perceives most of the action'.[435]

This is not an isolated opinion. A critic has observed that *One Day* 'is short, simply written, and yet so detailed that it is almost a screenplay in itself'.[436] A scholar has asserted that *One Day*'s 'use of interjections like *da* and *zhe* together with the elliptical grammar generally make for a cinematographic <...> quality'.[437] Another scholar believes that the shifting point of view in *One Day*'s narrative (mentioned in Section 5 of our work) warrants a comparison with standard types of shots employed by cinematographers:

> When the narration is moved towards the protagonist's subjective sphere, the epic distance is dramatically reduced and close-ups are used. Conversely, when Solzhenitsyn switches over to the point of view of the narrator who epitomizes the prisoners' milieu, the representation resorts to medium or long shots.[438]

The same scholar observes that, in the scene depicting the altercation with Der, 'a distinctive cinematographic manner of rendering the event is used. The general picture consists of several frames — "silent episodes" unfolding

---

433 John Kohan, 'The Writer as Cameraman: Pictorial Narrative in *August 1914*', *Modern Fiction Studies*, vol. 23, no. 1 (1977), p. 74.
434 Curtis, op. cit., p. 166.
435 Ibid., p. 165.
436 Eglick, op. cit.
437 Porter, op. cit., p. 28.
438 Viktor Iurovskii, 'Stilistika rasskaza A. I. Solzhenitsyna „Odin den' Ivana Denisovicha"', in Patrick Sériot (ed.), *Contributions suisses au XIV congrès mondial des slavistes à Ohrid, septembre 2008 / Schweizerische Beiträge zum XIV. Internationalen Slavistenkongress in Ohrid, September 2008*, Bern: Peter Lang, 2008, p. 348.

before Ivan Denisovich's eyes, as well as expressively intense dramatic acts'.[439]

In 1992-94, the film director Evgenii Tsymbal and the independent filmmaking company Kontakt (formed by Vladimir Grammatikov and Mikhail Zil'berman) intended to adapt Solzhenitsyn's story 'An Incident at Kochetovka Station' for the big screen, using the facilities of the Gorky film studios in Moscow and starring Aleksandr Filippenko in the role of Tveritinov. To arrange this, Tsymbal and his colleagues conducted lengthy negotiations with Solzhenitsyn and his literary agent. It transpired that the sale of the film rights to Kontakt at a preferential rate would depend on the film director agreeing to follow Solzhenitsyn's instructions on what exactly the screen version should look like. This amounted to little else but directing the film by proxy, using professional film-makers as technical executors of Solzhenitsyn's will. In addition, Solzhenitsyn wished to reserve the right to veto the film's release if he did not like it. When Solzhenitsyn was told that no financier would underwrite the project on these conditions, he suggested that he could stay away from it altogether (except for expressing publicly his opinion about the film version when it comes out) – but the Kochetovka film rights would be offered to Kontakt at the standard rate. Tsymbal and Kontakt agreed to the second option but failed to raise the amount requested.[440]

Curtis ascribes the persistence of Solzhenitsyn's cinematographic vision (and ambitions, we hasten to add) to his passionate desire to counterbalance the lack of pictorial evidence serving to expose Communist crimes in a sufficiently memorable way:

---

439 Ibid., p. 350.
440 Evgenii Tsymbal's email messages to Andrei Rogachevskii of 17 and 18 January 2009. Solzhenitsyn liked to be in control even in the areas where many others, inhibited by a lack of qualifications, would not dare to interfere. Thus, he wrote to his friends the Zubovs about undergoing chemotherapy in a cancer hospital in Ryazan in April 1958: 'I took the treatment into my own hands, prescribed myself everything that was necessary and arranged that via either my doctor or the head nurse. Taking notice of my doggedness (*v"edlivost'*), the head of unit gave in and let the nature take its course. After administering myself <the medicine> three times and withstanding it well, I have discharged myself from the hospital for the remaining four intakes and continue the treatment as an out-patient' (L. Saraskina, *Aleksandr Solzhenitsyn*, Moscow: Molodaia gvardiia, 2008, p. 442).

> The verbal equivalents of visual images in Solzhenitsyn give his work an immediacy that has been absent from our sense of twentieth-century Russian history. Whereas we have films of the opening of Hitler's concentration camps, and even Nazi-made films of the destruction of the Warsaw ghetto, we have no films of Stalin's concentration camps.[441] Instead, we have <Eisenstein's> *October*, whose power in this age of visual images convinced people that it was documentary history, not art. It is as though <Leni Riefenstahl's> *The Triumph of the Will* were our only source of visual information about the Third Reich. Solzhenitsyn's use of film technique attempts to overcome this disparity.[442]

It is therefore hardly surprising that Eisenstein serves as a negative inspiration for Solzhenitsyn on a number of occasions, both providing an (often inconspicuous) point of departure for Solzhenitsyn's imagery and coming under Solzhenitsyn's open attack because of the political and aesthetic divide between them. For example, Curtis argues convincingly that *The Tanks Know the Truth* has consistent parallels with Eisenstein's most famous film, *The Battleship Potemkin*:

> The zeks in *The Tanks Know the Truth* rise up in righteous protest against the food and working conditions, just as the sailors do in *Potemkin*; both groups enjoy a heady, but temporary, success, and then are defeated by overwhelming force. The famous Odessa steps sequence in *Potemkin*, in its sustained tension and unflinching portrayal of the authorities' disregard for human life, closely resembles the tank attack in *The Tanks Know the Truth*. But *The Tanks Know the Truth* does not, of course, have the optimistic finale of *Potemkin*.[443]

Potemkin is also discussed in *One Day*, by Tsesar and the Captain. Tsesar praises Eisenstein's visually striking frames and sequences, such as the

---

441 Those did exist but had been concealed from a wider public until shortly before the collapse of the Soviet Union; see, for example, the documentary film *Solovki Power* (Vlast' solovetskaia, 1988) by Marina Goldovskaia, partly based on the genuine OGPU (state security) footage.
442 Ibid., p. 166.
443 Curtis, op. cit., pp. 144-45.

pince-nez hanging from the ship's rigging and the pram going down the Odessa steps, while the Captain maintains that some scenes on the ship look contrived (e.g. the maggots on the rotten meat are too large to be real).[444] In addition, Solzhenitsyn's polemics with Eisenstein manifests itself in Tsesar's conversation with prisoner X-123, this time about the second part of Eisenstein's *Ivan the Terrible* (1946). Once again, Tsesar admires the beauty of Eisenstein's images, such as the *oprichniks*' dances and the cathedral scene, while X-123 criticises both the film's message (justifying tyranny in an attempt to please Stalin) and the film's creator for sycophancy. When Tsesar remarks that 'art isn't a question of *what*, but of *how*', X-123 retorts: 'To hell with your 'how' if it doesn't arouse any decent feelings in me'.[445]

The appearance of not one but two conversations about Eisenstein in a compact book with very little room for superfluous detail might seem an unaffordable luxury. Moreover, the discussion of the second part of *Ivan the Terrible* in a distant labour camp in 1951 appeared improbable to a discerning eye, because that very second part had been banned by Stalin and could be screened publicly for the first time only in 1958. Forgetting that Tsesar was a film director who might have seen the film through purely professional channels, and that the only information given by Solzhenitsyn about X-123 is the length of his term (twenty years of hard labour), which does not automatically mean that he had been imprisoned since 1931,[446] David Robinson of *The Financial Times* picked up on what he thought of as a glaring anachronism making those in the know feel 'irritated by such improbabilities as that intellectuals in a Stalinist camp should be self-consciously discussing Part II of *Ivan the Terrible*, which was still suppressed many years after Stalin's death'.[447] *The Times*' John Russell Taylor, considering the same episode, wisely made the reservation that 'engaging in a detailed discussion, or any discussion at all, of the then unseen second part of Eisenstein's *Ivan the Terrible*' would be

---

444 See *The Making*, p. 120.
445 Ibid., p. 92.
446 Leona Toker makes such an assumption, claiming that X-123's 'intellect, ascetic idealism, uncompromising position, and twenty years in the camp' probably make him 'a member of the Socialist Revolutionary party' (Toker, op. cit., p. 278).
447 Robinson, op. cit.

too early 'for anyone in Russia except a few privileged specialists'.[448] This, however, did not save Russell Taylor from the wrath of Ronald Harwood, who submitted a letter to the editor of *The Times* to defend Solzhenitsyn, 'too meticulous a writer to be as careless as your critic suggests'.[449] In Harwood's view, Solzhenitsyn made a deliberate anachronism 'in order to state unequivocally a theme that is central to all his work',[450] namely that the artist has a moral responsibility to the society he or she lives in to reflect reality as it is, objectively, without embellishing or blackening it on demand.

While agreeing with Harwood in everything but the anachronistic nature of the discussion of the second part of *Ivan the Terrible* (for the reasons outlined above), it is possible to go a little further and suggest that Eisenstein held what might appear a somewhat disproportionate significance for Solzhenitsyn because the former exemplified for the latter the Socialist Realist style, dominant in the Soviet Union and its satellite countries in the early 1930s – late 1980s.[451] Solzhenitsyn had a difficult relationship with this style, marked by preferences for certain topics (such as propaganda of the Marxist-Leninist philosophy of history) and genres (e.g. production novel[452]), as well as requirements for easier accessibility by the widest possible audience. On the one hand, Solzhenitsyn loathed what Socialist Realism had come to represent, in particular its constant endeavour to instil in the public a sense of the inevitability of the radiant Communist future. On the other, he was obliged to conform to Socialist Realist formal constraints, to get at least some of his work past the censors. It also has to be added that Socialist Realism's tendency to define unambiguously what is good and what is evil, and its overreliance on the traditions of classical nineteenth-century Russian literature,

---

448 John Russell Taylor, op. cit.
449 Harwood, 'Ivan Denisovich'.
450 Ibid.
451 On Socialist Realism, see, for example, Régine Robin, *Socialist Realism: An Impossible Aesthetic*, transl. by Catherine Porter, Stanford, CA: Stanford University Press, 1992; and E. Dobrenko and H. Günther, *Sotsrealisticheskii kanon*, St Petersburg: Gumanitarnoe agentstvo "Akademicheskii proekt", 2000. According to Robert Porter, 'Socialist Realism is achieved when the "message" (socialist, capitalist, liberal, religious or whatever) in a given work outweighs its artistry, when it tries to direct the reader's imagination instead of stimulating it' (Porter, op. cit., p. 44).
452 For more on this genre, see Katerina Clark, *The Soviet Novel: History as Ritual*, Bloomington: Indiana University Press, 2000.

fitted in rather well with Solzhenitsyn's conservative literary taste and moralistic inclinations. When Solzhenitsyn's friend Lev Kopelev said of an early version of *One Day* that it reminded him of a 'typical Socialist Realist <...> production novel',[453] he had a point.

The allegations that Solzhenitsyn's otherwise impeccably anti-Communist art was tainted with Socialist Realism largely hinge on the episode when Ivan Denisovich and his teammates work on the construction of a brick wall. The episode does indeed look as if it belongs to the Socialist Realist canon, which habitually eulogizes collective manual labour braving the elements. It is true that this scene particularly impressed Khrushchev, who thought that it glorified Socialist construction, and might well have helped the typescript of *One Day* to be approved for publication.[454] The scene, however, is autobiographical. Solzhenitsyn worked as a mason in a labour camp, and, to his own astonishment, was himself carried away in the process of forced labour,

> ensuring that the wall was flat enough and doing more work <than was asked of me>. As for Ivan Denisovich, who does not have any other interests apart from work, he'll die spiritually if he does not get carried away. For him this enthusiasm for slave labour is a way of saving himself.[455]

In the words of a shrewd Solzhenitsyn scholar, 'the satisfaction with which <Ivan Denisovich> lines up the breeze blocks and judges the exact amount of mortar has nothing to do with the construction of the future: it is simply pride at doing a job properly'.[456]

---

453 Saraskina, op. cit., p. 465. For a comprehensive analysis of Solzhenitsyn's involvement with Socialist Realism, see Michael Nicholson, 'Solzhenitsyn as "Socialist Realist"', in Hilary Chung (ed.), *In the Party Spirit: Socialist Realism and Literary Practice in the Soviet Union, East Germany and China*, Amsterdam: Rodopi, 1996, pp. 55-68.
454 Solzhenitsyn, 'Vystuplenie po frantsuzskomu televideniiu (Parizh, 9 marta 1976)', in his *Publitsistika v trekh tomakh*, vol. 2, p. 391.
455 Ibid.
456 Geoffrey Hosking, *Beyond Socialist Realism: Soviet Fiction since Ivan Denisovich*, London-Toronto-Sydney-New York: Paul Elek / Granada Publishing, 1980, p. 47. Gary Kern explains why the wall construction should not be seen in a Marxian light: in the scene, 'Ivan confirms himself as a good worker and derives dignity and spiritual strength therefrom. This aspect of his work can only be called spiritual in that it is

This is exactly the way the episode is presented in Wrede's film.[457] The observant Paul D. Zimmerman of *Newsweek* magazine noted correctly that the film director 'shares the author's fascination with the process of prison work. His footage on the building of the wall takes on the clarity and purpose of a ritual dance, damaged only by the inclusion of cacophonous neo-Carl Orff lamentations'.[458] Myron Meisel of *The Chicago Reader* defined the wall sequence as 'almost hypnotic' and 'exhilarating'.[459] Joy Gould Boyum of *The Wall Street Journal* called the wall construction 'the film's most memorable scene' and interpreted its message as follows: 'While suggesting through its narrative that the development of collective interests through the team idea <...> is simply a device of the authorities, the film nevertheless makes the joint effort a glorious expression of both man's joy in his work and his responsibility to his fellow human being'.[460] Charles Champlin of *The Los Angeles Times* said that the sequence was 'in fact at the heart of the film' and declared it 'thrilling, as the completion of the Kwai bridge is, <...> despite the same kind of ironic awareness that their defiant good work is also a compliance with the overseers they presumably hate'.[461] Not everybody was so perceptive. *The New Yorker* called Ivan Denisovich's wall 'useless',[462] Queens College's (CUNY) newspaper *Phoenix* stated that the scene did 'not quite

---

quality freely given, without calculation or coercion <...>. Obviously this contradicts the theory of Marx, which assumes that one can realise himself in his labor <...> only when he can use his product or exchange it at a fair rate – in other words, when the worker himself has control over his product of labor' (Kern, 'Ivan the Worker', p. 24), which of course does not apply to Ivan Denisovich.

457 In Wrede's own words, *One Day*, to an extent, 'is a practical guide to life. If you want to retain yourself as an individual, no matter how modestly, when you have to do a job, take an interest in it. You need something to be proud of. It can be said you're doing it for Joseph Stalin, for the country, but you're doing it for yourself' (Thomas, op. cit.).

458 Zimmerman, 'Prisoner's Base'. We disagree with Zimmerman's critical remark about Nordheim's soundtrack, though.

459 Meisel, op. cit.

460 Gould Boyum, op. cit.

461 Charles Champlin, '*One Day* a Tribute to Spirit of Survival', *The Los Angeles Times*, 13 October 1971. The reviewer refers to David Lean's 1957 film *The Bridge on the River Kwai* about the construction of a railway bridge by the British inmates in a Japanese World War II prison camp in Burma.

462 Gilliatt, op. cit.

match in quality the rest of the film',[463] and even Graham Greene in his letter to Wrede of 6 October 1972 said: 'the only longueur I found was exactly the same as I found in the book – the building of the wall for me went on a little too long and in too boy scoutish a spirit, but that's Solzhenitsyn and not you'.[464]

It looks as if Wrede was fully aware of the fact that Solzhenitsyn manipulated Socialist Realist structures to undermine them from within. There are signs that in his version of *One Day*, Wrede also tried to engage with iconic Socialist Realist imagery by the cinematographic means at his disposal.[465] Thus, in the episode depicting the march to the worksite, the contrast between the prisoners' black garb and the guards' white uniforms,[466] underlining their respective roles of 'scum' and 'guardian angels', attributed to them by the Soviet system, can be seen as an ironic reversal of the scene on the quarterdeck in *The Battleship Potemkin*, when the sailor martyrs, about to be fired at, are dressed in angelic white, whereas their tormentors (the officers and the marines) wear devilish black. Similarly, the shot of Alyoshka the Baptist looking at the sun is strongly reminiscent of a scene from *Mother* (1926), a film adaptation of the eponymous classical Socialist Realist novel by Maxim Gorky by yet another world-famous Socialist Realist film director, Vsevolod Pudovkin. In Pudovkin's film, one of the chief protagonists, a factory worker called Pavel, is transported from jail to a provincial court through a snowy landscape to stand trial for revolutionary activity. When he comes out of the carriage, clothed in a prisoner's uniform, he also looks at the shining sun, which he has not seen for a while, and smiles. The analogy invoked by the

---

463 Kalfus, op. cit. ('The quick-moving camera does indeed convey the thrusting, sweating quality of work, but it also disorients the audience visually').
464 A film critic explains, however, that 'if one event like the protracted brick and mortar construction of a structure in the snow and subfreezing temperatures begins to seem nearly intolerable, this is part of Wrede's method. It is designed to subject us to the ordeal that constitutes the bulk of the day's activity, as well as to draw a parallel to the similarly primitive, wasteful, slave labor of constructing the pyramids, as the squad is obliged to haul bricks by hand in lieu of a working hoist' (Kenneth Geist, 'One Day in the Life of Ivan Denisovich', *SHOW* (New York), September 1971, p. 56).
465 An American critic even called Wrede's *One Day* 'an impressive instance of socialist realism, the official Soviet aesthetic that demands actuality and accessibility and above all, the presentation of an inspiring proletarian heroism' (Gould Boyum, op. cit.)
466 Cf. the picture of David Wrede wearing one of the guards' uniforms in Appendix IV.

juxtaposition of the two images is obvious: Stalinism oppresses people, just like tsarism used to do, so has the change of the social order brought any difference? Thus the Socialist Realist formula separating good from evil on the basis of Marxist ideology is turned on its head.

There are reasons to believe that Wrede's *One Day* influenced Andrzej Wajda's award-winning film *Man of Marble* (Człowiek z marmuru, 1976) by its imagery that proved helpful in subverting Socialist Realist demands, which Wajda had to live with unwillingly for quite some time and which *Man of Marble* renounces. *Man of Marble* is about Mateusz Birkut (played by Jerzy Radziwiłowicz), a peasant turned mason who works on a construction site in the Nowa Huta socialist housing development in the late 1940s – early 1950s and is imprisoned on false charges of terrorism. Birkut's bricklaying skills are central to the film, which tells the true story behind the record-breaking achievement that had made him a socialist celebrity (30,509 bricks laid in one shift by a team of five, led by Birkut). The film reveals that special conditions were created for Birkut's team to make their record possible: they were all fed 10,000 calories a day for two weeks, smoked luxury cigarettes and were even shaved and sprayed with perfume, so that they would look their best on camera (which was there to document the record). On the hot summer day the record was achieved (the bricklaying sequence lasts just as long as in *One Day*, if not longer), the team was given mint tea for refreshment, was watched by hundreds of supporters and entertained by a brass orchestra and a folk music band. Nothing could be further from the conditions Ivan Denisovich and Team 104 had to endure when they were forced to build their own wall, and broke their own modest record of sorts, arriving late for the recount before being taken away from the worksite. Yet two documentary films by the fictitious director Jerzy Burski (played by Tadeusz Łomnicki), *A City is Born* and *They Build Our Happiness* – forming part of *Man of Marble* – demonstrate that, as a rule, the Nowa Huta builders lived in cramped conditions in huts filled with bunk beds, and were given only one piece of fish for lunch (not unlike the prisoners' living quarters and diet in *One Day*). A close-up of a tin bowl with some fish in it from *A City is Born* (which, we learn, had remained unfinished, presumably because it had contained more realism than socialism) appears to be a direct visual reference to the corresponding frame in *One Day*, which

Wajda must have had an opportunity to see thanks to his professional connections.

The fact that the *Man of Marble* frame with the fish in the bowl appears in footage stylised as a documentary, brings to mind the dual nature of Wrede's *One Day*, which is a feature film that often looks like a re-enactment of real-life events. This characteristic feature of *One Day* did not go unnoticed. Periodicals as diverse as *The Daily Mirror*, *The Sun*, *Newsday*, *SHOW*, *The Detroit News*, *The Oregonian*, *The Campus Slate* (Old Westbury, N. Y.), *The Wall Street Journal* and *The Financial Times* independently of each other noted the film's 'documentary realism'[467] and called *One Day* 'documentary in style',[468] 'straightforward enough to be almost a documentary',[469] 'a documentary rather than <...> entertainment',[470] a 'dramatised documentary',[471] a 'documentary-style production',[472] 'an impressive and deeply moving document in its own right'[473] and a 'brilliant documentary-style close-up of the struggle to remain an individual'.[474] Wrede had already had some experience as a documentary maker before he commenced work on *One Day*. In 1964, he directed a BBC documentary about the relationship between the sixty-one year old Ibsen (played by Claes Gill) and the eighteen year old Emilie Bardach (played by Camilla Hasse), under the title *The Summer in Gossensass* (aired on 15 September 1964 by BBC1). The programme was based on a text by Michael Meyer, Wrede's regular collaborator. A year later, on the occasion of the centenary of Jean Sibelius's birth, Wrede was asked by the BBC to make a one-hour documentary about his famous fellow countryman. It was broadcast by BBC1 on 5 December 1965. Both films involved actors.[475] This

---

467 Robinson, op. cit.; and Gelmis, op. cit.
468 Ken Barnard, 'A Man Endures in a Siberian Prison', *The Detroit News*, 6 October 1971.
469 Mahar, op. cit.
470 Bachteler, op. cit.
471 Thirkell, op. cit.
472 Geist, op. cit.
473 Gould Boyum, op. cit.
474 Cashin, op. cit.
475 Anthony Burgess, of all people, declared that *The Summer in Gossensass* was 'one of the finest literary documentaries that television has yet given us', and noted that 'contemporary photographs blended beautifully with acted film' (Anthony Burgess, 'The Arts', *The Listener*, 15 October 1964, p. 603; see also Mary Crozier's rave review in

kind of background served Wrede well in successfully adapting Solzhenitsyn's book, which was a piece of fiction but at the same time functioned as 'an anthropologist's guide to an institution'.[476] As one film critic put it, 'anyone wanting to know how to get through a day in a Russian concentration camp with body and soul intact will find <Wrede's> film an enthralling guide'.[477]

There is no doubt that Solzhenitsyn's book presented special difficulties in terms of its screen adaptation precisely because *One Day*'s narrative structure had been shaped to a significant extent by the art of cinema.[478] (As Eisenstein once noted, noone made films of Dos Passos's novels because they were already cinematographic.[479]) That is why, in the words of *The Guardian*, Wrede's adaptation betrayed the strain of 'the effort to reconstruct in visual terms what Solzhenitsyn's words can make the imagination do better'.[480] Nevertheless, Wrede handled the task splendidly. In the opinion of *The*

The Guardian of 16 September 1964). William Trevor, however, took issue with the manner in which the Sibelius documentary engaged actors: 'We saw too much of the young Sibelius playing the violin in woods and by water. It is a fact that he did so, but it does not for a moment follow that the image will bear ruthless repetition' (William Trevor, 'The Arts', *The Listener*, 30 December 1965, p. 1087).

476 Hosking, op. cit., p. 41.

477 Gibbs, op. cit.

478 Other texts by Solzhenitsyn have been affected by the same problem too. When *The Tanks* were published in France, some critics claimed that Solzhenitsyn had succeeded in visualising the action to such a degree that it had virtually rendered the shooting unnecessary (Solzhenitsyn, 'Ugodilo zernyshko promezh dvukh zhernovov', *Novyi mir*, no. 9 (2000), p. 179). A comparison of two television adaptations of *The First Circle*, the 1992 US-French three-hour long one (directed by Larry Sheldon, with F. Murray Abraham as Stalin) and the 2006 Russian seven and a half hour long one (directed by Gleb Panfilov), shows that the US-French version might well be less authentic (although some scenes in it were shot in Moscow) but it is definitely more dynamic of the two, precisely because it was impossible to cram the novel's ninety-six chapters in three hours, and Solzhenitsyn's intrusive cinematographic vision had to be ignored at times. The ten-episode Russian version is extremely close to the original, which does it a considerable disservice, because the lack of action in a confined space (a secret research lab in the GULAG) is compensated by prisoners' (and their gaolers' and relatives') conversations which become progressively longer and harder to follow. Even actors' fine performances (especially Roman Madianov as Abakumov, Vladimir Iakovlev as Khorobrov, Andrei Smirnov as Bobynin, Igor Skliar and Inna Churikova as the Gerasimoviches) cannot rescue the mini-series, although it was apparently approved by Solzhenitsyn, who personally recorded the narrator's voiceover for it.

479 See S. Eizenshtein, 'Kino i literatura: (Ob obraznosti)', *Voprosy literatury*, 1 (1968), p. 93.

480 Malcolm, 'Almost Magic Roundabout'.

New York Times, his film 'is not merely a close adaptation; it has, much of the time, the look and, indeed, the feel of a careful, tasteful, rather sumptuous illustrated edition'.[481] It appears, however, that the film's longevity has been largely secured not so much by its faithfulness to the letter and the spirit of the original, but by Wrede's ability to capture not only the fictional side but also the documentary potential of Solzhenitsyn's book. As time goes on, this documentary aspect of the film seems to become more and more important in preserving the book's visual equivalent for the younger generation, which seems to be reading less and less but increasingly relies on visual aids both for factual information and emotional education. Tom Courtney said of *One Day* once: "That film has got legs. Others will take more money now but they won't have the legs, they won't be around as long as our film will. It's a marvellous film. It makes me weep when I see it'.[482] Although, admittedly, not everyone will be reduced to tears after its screening, the film's lasting relevance is undeniable and can be seen, for example, in the student feedback produced after watching *One Day* as part of the course on Russian fiction (Proosa-analyysi) at the Department of Slavonic and Baltic Languages and Literatures, University of Helsinki, on 15 November 2007 – in Wrede's native country where the film was banned for almost a quarter of the century (see Appendix II).

---

481 Greenspun, op. cit..
482 Norman, op. cit.

EPILOGUE AND CONCLUSIONS

Wrede's immediate post-*One Day* years were marked by the 69 Theatre Company's mutation into the Royal Exchange Theatre (jointly led by Wrede, Elliott, Maxwell and Braham Murray), which opened in Manchester in 1976 in a Victorian building that until 1968 had housed a commodities exchange. The designer Richard Negri turned what is sometimes referred to as the 'largest room in the world'[483] into a new, hyper-modern seven-sided theatre-in-the-round venue. For Wrede and his colleagues this was a dream come true, as their theatre company finally found a permanent home.[484] Wrede's name was closely associated with the Royal Exchange Theatre until his retirement in 1989. Murray recalls that Wrede

> was the link between the architects and the designers. He was the one who led us to the idea of theatre-in-the-round as being the shape for our time. He was the one who had the audacious idea of building our theatre in the Cotton Exchange, thus saving an immense amount of money and creating the tension of old and new that gives the building its unique atmosphere.[485]

Plans for the new theatre were numerous. In Wrede's own words,

> It has taken us more than twenty years to get a theatre of our own. During the next twenty years we hope to be able to stimulate one or two genuine playwrights to give life to the scene that we have created here, playwrights who can talk to our time and express the poetic side of man. I believe that times when a theatre performance could be justified by being social or political are over. I think we are soon going to go beyond that.

---

483 Marie-Louise Fock, 'Casper Wrede på ny teater', *Hufvudstadsbladet*, 17 September 1976. In all likelihood, this is an exaggeration: it probably was the largest trading room in England.
484 Ibid.
485 Murray, 'Wrede Defined', p. 19.

This had its time and its function. Our function here in Manchester is to create a poetic identity of our own.[486]

For the opening of the new theatre building, Wrede chose Heinrich von Kleist's *The Prince of Homburg* with Tom Courtenay in the main role. During the next fifteen years before his retirement, Wrede personally directed nineteen productions in Manchester, including Ronald Harwood's *A Family* (1978), Molière's *The Misanthrope* (1981), Ibsen's *The Wild Duck* (1983) and Sophocles's *Oedipus* (1987). New works by British authors were also included in the repertoire. This was greatly assisted by an international playwriting competition, sponsored by Mobil. The sponsorship links were established by Wrede.

During his years in Manchester Wrede did not have much time left for television productions and film directing. His last film was *Ransom* (1975), also known as *The Terrorists*. In it, one group of terrorists hijacks a British passenger aircraft as it is landing in an unspecified Scandinavian country (the film was shot in Oslo), while another group kidnaps a British Ambassador in that country. A military police chief (Sean Connery) is assigned to solving both problems. Sven Nykvist was responsible for the cinematography again. Of the actors engaged in *One Day*, Maxwell and Cording made an appearance in *Ransom*, and so did Wrede himself, in an uncredited bit part (as one of the terrorists). *Ransom*, an attempt to make a thriller with a difference, was seen as mediocre by the critics[487] and was not successful commercially. In 1980, Wrede wrote an original screenplay for Norsk Film, called *Love Child*, a cross between a sports film and a true romance, about an affair between Robbie Charnock, a middle-aged high-achieving English football manager,

---

486 Ibid.
487 Cf.: 'The more such films try to transcend their own obvious limitations, the less they succeed in satisfying the basic requirements of the genre. Wrede tries hard to examine the morality behind the right-wing approach <of Connery's character> to law and order, and he even tentatively gives the band of kidnappers a vaguely reasoned case. But he only succeeds in substituting one set of compromises for another, so that the film appears weak and flabby on almost every level' (Derek Malcolm, 'Right First Time', *The Guardian*, 27 February 1975); 'even though its last couple of twists are surprising enough, the director <...> throws his advantage away with a confused final shootout' (Russell Davies, 'Fascist Truth', *The Observer*, 2 March 1975).

and Elise Gundersen, a Norwegian teenager. The screenplay has not been filmed.

Russia kept occupying Wrede's mind, too. One of his greatest successes as a theatre director was the 1985 Royal Exchange Theatre production of Chekhov's *Three Sisters*.[488] Wrede worked with a new, specially commissioned translation by Michael Frayn. For *Three Sisters* Wrede chose mainly young actors, such as Niamh Cusack (Irina) and Janet McTeer (Masha), both little known at the time. There also were two Scandinavians in the cast, the Swede Sven-Bertil Taube as Vershinin and the Norwegian Espen Skjønberg – who had acted in *One Day* – as Chebutykin. *Three Sisters* was a critical success.[489] Michael Ratcliffe of *The Observer* called the production 'handsome and lucid', and declared that Skjønberg 'gives one of the best performances I have ever seen by a European actor on the English stage'.[490] *The Sunday Times* asserted that Wrede's direction

> brings out the toughness of Chekhov's imagination, his complete understanding of small people harassed and baffled by massive misfortunes. <...> Wrede has understood that <Chekhov>'s at his most poignant when his people, buffeted by life, cornered, desolate, or simply shy, stumble unconsciously into eloquence. <...> One of the best things about

---

[488] Chekhov was one of Wrede's favourite playwrights. In 1977 Wrede assisted Elliott in the direction of *Uncle Vanya* with Albert Finney as Astrov, and two years later directed *The Cherry Orchard*, with Dilys Hamlett as Ranyevskaya and James Maxwell as Gayev. *The Financial Times* found the latter production 'superficial', and noted, rather unkindly, that Hamlett's 'frenetically Garboesque Ranyevskaya <...> is so insensitive in her treatment of the other characters, it is difficult to understand how she could get so worked up about leaving a lot of fixtures and fittings, let alone her beloved orchard'. Of Maxwell, the critic said that he 'has obviously never been near a billiards table or he would not persist in building those flimsy manual bridges in mid-air' (Michael Coveney, 'The Cherry Orchard', *The Financial Times*, 3 November 1979). *The Guardian* was only partially satisfied: Wrede 'gets the play half right; it is good on social comedy and the Chekhovian appetite for human oddity but curiously lacking in any sense of heartbreak or despair' (Michael Billington, 'The Cherry Orchard', *The Guardian*, 2 November 1979). Curiously, none of the Royal Exchange stage versions has been included in Patrick Miles and Stuart Young's 'Selective Chronology of British Professional Productions of Chekhov's Plays, 1909-1991'; see Patrick Miles (ed.), *Chekhov on the British Stage*, Cambridge: Cambridge University Press, 1993, pp. 237-50.
[489] Marie-Louise Fock, 'Stor regiframgång för Wrede i England', *Hufvudstadsbladet*, 23 May 1985.
[490] Michael Ratcliffe, 'Taking the Pulse', *The Observer*, 14 April 1985.

this production is the actors' way with the silent eloquence of glance and gesture. <...> Such acting is a pleasure to watch <...> because it is so natural and authentic. <...> Such performances as this fully justify the claim of this company that they are the National Theatre of the north.[491]

Of special importance for Wrede was his production of *Hope Against Hope* (1983), about the life and death of the poet Osip Mandelstam (played by David Horovitch), who died in the GULAG.[492] Wrede's stage adaptation was based on the memoirs of Mandelstam's widow Nadezhda (Avril Elgar), works by the Mandelstam scholars Clarence Brown and Jennifer Baines, and a study of Stalin's purges, *The Great Terror*, by Robert Conquest. According to *The Times*, Wrede 'has taken on an extremely difficult task. There is little sustained dialogue in the book<s>; and <...> the detail of the story is signally lacking in dramatic events. In the first half of the production the company have the task of lifting a dead weight'.[493] However, continued the same critic, 'as the production develops and sheds the need to explain basic facts, <...> it takes on some of the qualities of Greek tragedy'.[494] Explanatory remarks on historical events and peripheral characters were given by a chorus dressed in greatcoats and headscarves. The principal characters were introduced by the poet Anna Akhmatova (Dilys Hamlett), who appeared in some scenes as the Mandelstams' devoted friend.

---

491 John Peter, 'Women of Some Importance', *The Sunday Times*, 14 April 1985. The production was not to everyone's taste, though. *The Financial Times* claimed that 'Mr Wrede's direction is of the sheer unpleasantness of the yearning romantic' (Martin Hoyle, 'Three Sisters / Royal Exchange, Manchester', *The Financial Times* of 15 April 1985), while *The Times* stated that 'its separate elements fail to mesh together into a shared dramatic fabric, and not only through the casting of a Norwegian Chebutykin, a Swedish Vershinin, and a Natasha straight out of *Coronation Street*. <...> <The play seems> to be clicking mechanically over pre-arranged points, rather than organically unfolding' (Irving Wardle, 'Frustration for the Sisters', *The Times*, 13 April 1985; Cheryl Prime, engaged in the role of Natasha, did indeed play Kathy Barrett in a 1982 episode of the above-named soap opera).
492 There is an obvious thematic link between this production and Wrede's adaptation of *One Day*, which, to use an American critic's expression, 'has man hoping against hope' (Norton, op. cit.).
493 Irving Wardle, 'Hope Against Hope / Royal Exchange, Manchester', *The Times*, 4 February 1983.
494 Ibid.

FILMING THE UNFILMABLE 139

The lack of dramatic material was compensated by a 'flexible and varied direction and imaginative sound effects'.[495] Wrede managed to create an atmosphere which at times became suffocating. Especially impressive was the deportation scene, in which the prisoners start humming a Russian lament song.[496] The tragic turning point of the play is when Mandelstam sees himself forced, in order to save his own life, to write a eulogy to Stalin – a choice which proves out to be a failure in all respects. Yet, wrote a *Times* journalist, 'we emerge from the theatre not cast down but uplifted, <as> the play also shows that the divine spark in the human spirit can never be extinguished'.[497] Mandelstam's significance for Wrede is evident from the fact that, when Wrede died of pancreatic cancer, for his obituary notice in *Hufvudstadsbladet* of 4 October 1998, a poem by Mandelstam was chosen ("How I wish I could fly...", written in 1937 in exile in Voronezh).

It is curious and at the same time highly intriguing that the above-quoted passage from *The Times* on the indomitability of the human spirit as portrayed in *Hope Against Hope*, as well as the *Sunday Times* observation on the semi-documentary nature of the production ('The result is something short of a play, but far more than a documentary. The inevitable space between what we see on the stage and what we can only try to imagine is always in the director's mind'[498]), are very similar to the gist of the most perceptive pronouncements on Wrede's version of *One Day*, and point at an overarching theme encompassing much of Wrede's creative activity.

Speaking of Wrede's most innovative and lasting contribution to the Royal Exchange Theatre, Murray posits that it probably was the concept of a 'group

---

495 Marie-Louise Fock, 'Casper Wredes giv om Osip M.', *Hufvudstadsbladet*, 23 February 1983. Some critics were left disappointed. *The Financial Times*, for one, was merciless: 'The end result <...> is a gloomy and ponderous saga on a worthy theme. <...> The material proves curiously leaden and intractable for stage purposes' (Michael Coveney, 'Hope Against Hope / Royal Exchange, Manchester', *The Financial Times*, 4 February 1983).
496 Marie-Louise Fock, 'Casper Wredes giv om Osip M.'.
497 Bernard Levin, 'Hope Springs Eternal But Not from This Inky Hand', *The Times*, 25 February 1983. Other critics' reaction ranged from Michael Coveney's statement that it was impossible 'to feel anything resembling involvement in the tragic tale' (Coveney, op. cit.) to Robin Thornber's definition of the production as a 'propagandist sob story' (quoted from Levin, op. cit.).
498 James Fenton, 'Making Art out of Terror', *The Sunday Times*, 6 February 1983.

of individuals pooling their resources to create something better than any of them could achieve. There is no leader except the one who at any moment knows best about the matter in hand'.[499] This may well be true of the Royal Exchange Theatre, but as far as *One Day* was concerned, Courtenay states without hesitation that the film came into being 'mainly thanks to Casper'.[500] Harwood echoes Courtenay's opinion that Wrede's role in making the film adaptation of *One Day* happen was absolutely indispensable:

> On reflection, it was now possible to see why the project had come so far: Wrede possessed all the qualifications for organising and controlling this difficult enterprise. Because of his fluent command of the necessary languages, he would be able to communicate with the English actors in English, the Norwegians in Norwegian, the Swedish cameraman in Swedish. More importantly, being a Finn, the cold, the snow, the freezing conditions were very much part of his inheritance; they held no terror for him; they were elements he understood.[501] This factor alone gave confidence to those who had entrusted him so completely with the making of the film. In a more secret and private sense, his time served as a boy of fourteen in the Finnish army during World War II provided him with insights into a particular kind of harsh experience of communal life under austere conditions.[502]

This appraisal by the people deeply involved in the production of *One Day* is independently confirmed by the judgement of many critics. The film appealed to an astonishingly wide spectrum of periodical publications in many countries, from mainstream, local, religious, student and political parties' newspapers to film industry and women's magazines. Even *Mayfair*, a British adult magazine for men, which had neither a moral stand to uphold, nor a highbrow agenda to pursue, said in its review of the film: 'the director, Casper Wrede,

---

499 Murray, 'Wrede Defined', p. 19.
500 Norman, op. cit.
501 Asked by a journalist, if 'he would have been equally attracted to a similar theme if the setting were in a hot climate, such as Devil's Island, <Wrede> said, "Well, it would not have been so easy. I understand the cold and its effects on people. If it were set in a hot climate I would have had to go there for several months to get the feel of the place, the atmosphere"' (McKinnon, op. cit.)
502 *The Making*, p. 18.

with his control of shape, pace and movement, seems a rare find indeed'.[503] It is a challenge to try and name any other film that would fit the notion of critical acclaim so accurately. In the instances when the film was not liked it often inspired an engaging discussion of the issues that had either been neglected or rarely raised in conjunction with motion pictures. Speaking of Solzhenitsyn's *One Day*, a scholar remarked: 'Perhaps the ultimate test of a work of art's validity is that it <...> is if not "all things to all men", at least "many things to many men"'.[504] This equally applies both to Solzhenitsyn's book and to Wrede's adaptation and their respective receptions.[505]

Owing to Wrede's visionary mind and exceptional commitment, the insurmountable difficulties of Solzhenitsyn's story – which, in the words of Derek Malcolm, is 'not a book I would want to film'[506] – such as its dearth of dramatic and heroic action, the desolate location and bleak weather conditions it describes (compounded by the need to replicate them outside Russia), its heavy demands on authenticity and its apparent unprofitability[507] – were miraculously prevailed over, and what had been assumed to be unfilmable even by the story's author, was filmed. Irrespective of Wrede's major achievements as a theatre director, the ephemeral nature of theatre productions, which appear different every time they are performed and are notoriously resistible to reproduction by other media, means that *One Day* is arguably destined to remain a crucial piece of hard evidence by which his directorial skills – and possibly the durability of Solzhenitsyn's testimonial art (not to speak of the ultimate visual impression of the essence of the entire Stalinist epoch) – will be judged in the future, if there is one.

---

503 David Quinlan, 'Films', *Mayfair*, Vol. 6, No. 10 (1971), p. 15. The American *Playboy* magazine also rated *One Day* highly calling it 'a virtually perfect film' (see the May 1971 issue, p. 42).
504 Porter, op. cit., p. 42.
505 For an overview of critical responses to Solzhenitsyn's story, see ibid., pp. 29-49.
506 Malcolm, 'Almost Magic Roundabout'.
507 To use an American journalist's colourful expression, 'in these days of fluctuating public taste and financial squeeze, no major studio would think of touching such a novel with a ten-foot mike boom' (McKinnon, op. cit.). One could not agree more with *The Sunday Telegraph* about 'the gratitude one feels that the subject, not an easy commercial one, could be financed and produced in the first place' (Hinxman, op. cit.).

ACKNOWLEDGEMENTS

We would like to express our gratitude to Richard D. Davies (for coming to the rescue at short notice); Boris and Ilia Rogatchevski (for their patient and selfless guidance on various linguistic and visual matters); Miranda Collett (for technical assistance); and Ekaterina Rogatchevskaia of the British Library, Gabriel Superfin of the Historisches Archiv at the University of Bremen's Forschungsstelle Osteuropa, Zoran Sinobad at the Library of Congress, Elena Kraineva of the William and Gayle Cook Music Library at the University of Indiana, Colleen W. Seale of the George A. Smathers Libraries at the University of Florida, Tom Whitehead of the Temple University Libraries, Jean Penn of the Pasadena Public Library, as well as members of staff at the Chicago Public Library (for answering many tricky bibliographical queries). Special thanks are due to Dr David Wrede, whose trust, help and encouragement have been absolutely vital for the completion of our work.

In the instances where previously unpublished material has been reproduced, every effort has been made to contact copyright holders to obtain permission. Where this has not been possible, we wish to tender our apologies and thanks.

BH, AR

SELECTED FILMOGRAPHY AND BIBLIOGRAPHY

Primary sources

One Day in the Life of Ivan Denisovich (1970), based on a story by Aleksandr Solzhenitsyn (Group W, Norsk Film A/S, Leontes Productions Ltd; 105 min.)
Crew:
Director and Producer: Casper Wrede
Screenwriter: Ronald Harwood
Photography: Sven Nykvist
Art Director: Per Schwab
Music: Arne Nordheim
Costume Design: Ada Skolmen
Editor: Thelma Connell
Chief Make-up Artist: Nurven Bredangen
Executive Producers: Howard O. Barnes, Erik Borge, Richard M. Pack
Production Executive: Peter S. Katz
Assistant to the Director: Alf Malland
First Assistant Director: Allan Ousby
Continuity: Laila Bull Tuhus
Production Manager: Jac Hald
Production Assistant: Per Gran
Production Secretary: Erik Hurum
Construction Manager: Snorre Skaugen
Props: Jan Mathias
Sound Mixer: Paul LeMare
Boom Operator: Svein Ellefsen
Wardrobe Assistant: Gro Johansen
Make-up Assistant: Kari Hermansen
Camera Operator: Hans Nord
Focus Puller: Karl Christian Qvigstad
Stills Cameraman: Svend Wam
Camera Crane Operator: Jarle Hole
Chief Electrician: Bjarne Kjos

Electricians: Erling Bunes, Arne Olsen
Cast:
Ivan Denisovich – Tom Courtenay
Tyurin – Espen Skjønberg
Fetyukov – Alf Malland
Senka Klevshin – Frimann Falck Clausen
Gopchik – Jo Skønberg
Eino – Odd Jan Sandsdalen
Väino – Torstein Rustdal
Captain – James Maxwell
Alyoshka – Alfred Burke
Tsesar – Eric Thompson
Pavlo – John Cording
Kilgas – Matthew Guinness
Kolya Vdovushkin – Casper Wrede
Actors in bit parts: Roy Bjørnstad, Paul Connell, Sverre Hansen, Ronald Harwood, Wolfe Morris, Kjell Stormoen, etc.

Harwood, Ronald. *One Day in the Life of Ivan Denisovich* <the typescript of a screenplay based on Solzhenitsyn's eponymous book, from the translation by Gillon Aitken>. London: Scripts Ltd, <1969>
Harwood, Ronald. 'Ivan Denisovich', *The Times*, 22 January 1972
The Making of One Day in the Life of Ivan Denisovich <by> Alexander Solzhenitsyn, transl. by Gillon Aitken, Introduction and Screenplay by Ronald Harwood, New York: Ballantine Books, 1971
Solzhenitsyn, A. *Bodalsia telenok s dubom: Ocherki literaturnoi zhizni*, Paris: YMCA-Press, 1975
Solzhenitsyn, A. *Odin den' Ivana Denisovicha*, Paris: YMCA Press, 1987
Solzhenitsyn, A. I. *Publitsistika v trekh tomakh*, Iaroslavl': Verkhne-Volzhskoe knizhnoe izdatel'stvo, 1996, vol. 2; Iaroslavl': Verkhniaia Volga, 1997, vol. 3
Solzhenitsyn, A. I. 'Ugodilo zernyshko promezh dvukh zhernovov', *Novyi mir*, no. 9 (1998), pp. 47-125; no. 11 (1998), pp. 93-153; no. 2 (1999), pp. 67-140; no. 9 (2000), pp. 112-83; no. 12 (2000), pp. 97-156; no. 11 (2003), pp. 31-97

Solzhenitsyn, A. I. *Sobranie sochinenii v deviati tomakh*, Moscow: Terra – Knizhnyi klub, 2005, vol. 9

Solzhenitsyn, A. *Sobranie sochinenii v 30 tomakh*, Moscow: Vremia, 2007-2008, vol. 7, pp. 290-95; vol. 8, pp. 30-33, 55-59; vol. 9, pp. 354-61; vol. 11, pp. 17-24, 87-90, 719-22; and vol. 13, pp. 135-38, 253-56

Wrede, Casper. 'Old Vics Teaterskola', *Handels- och Sjöfarts-Tidning*, 20 August 1951

Wrede, Casper. 'Letter to a Young Actor' (unpublished manuscript, David Wrede's private archive)

Wrede, Casper. 'Russia on My Mind' (unpublished manuscript, David Wrede's private archive)

Secondary Literature on Aleksandr Solzhenitsyn and his One Day in the Life of Ivan Denisovich

Curtis, James M. *Solzhenitsyn's Traditional Imagination*, Athens, Georgia: The University of Georgia Press, 1984

Fiene, Donald M. *Alexander Solzhenitsyn: An International Bibliography of Writings by and about Him*, Ann Arbor: Ardis, 1973

Francis, Damien. 'Solzhenitsyn, Soviet Dissident Writer, Dies at 89', *The Guardian*, 4 August 2008

Hayward, Max. 'Solzhenitsyn's Place in Contemporary Soviet Literature', *Slavic Review*, vol. 23, no. 3 (1964), pp. 432-36

Hayward, Max. 'Epilogue', in Max Hayward and Edward L. Crowley (eds), *Soviet Literature in the Sixties*, London: Methuen, 1965, pp. 203-08

Hosking, Geoffrey. *Beyond Socialist Realism: Soviet Fiction since Ivan Denisovich*, London-Toronto-Sydney-New York: Paul Elek / Granada Publishing, 1980

Iurovskii, Viktor. 'Stilistika rasskaza A. I. Solzhenitsyna „Odin den' Ivana Denisovicha"', in Patrick Sériot (ed.), *Contributions suisses au XIV congrès mondial des slavistes à Ohrid, septempre 2008 / Schweizerische Beiträge zum XIV. Internationalen Slavistenkongress in Ohrid, September 2008*, Bern: Peter Lang, 2008, pp. 345-61

Kaufman, Michael T. 'Solzhenitsyn, Literary Giant Who Defied Soviets, Dies at 89', *The New York Times*, 4 August 2008

Kern, Gary. 'Solženicyn's Self-Censorship: The Canonical Text of *Odin den' Ivana Denisoviča*', *The Slavic and East European Journal*, vol. 20, no. 4 (1976), pp. 421-36

Kern, Gary. 'Ivan the Worker', *Modern Fiction Studies*, vol. 23, no. 1 (1977), pp. 5-30

Klimoff, Alexis. 'The Sober Eye: Ivan Denisovich and the Peasant Perspective', in Alexis Klimoff (ed.), *One Day in the Life of Ivan Denisovich: A Critical Companion*, Evanston, IL: Northwestern University Press, 1997, pp. 3-31

Kobets, Svitlana. 'The Subtext of Christian Asceticism in Aleksandr Solzhenitsyn's *One Day in the Life of Ivan Denisovich*', *The Slavic and East European Journal*, vol. 42, No. 4 (1998), pp. 661-76

Kohan, John. 'The Writer as Cameraman: Pictorial Narrative in *August 1914*', *Modern Fiction Studies*, vol. 23, no. 1 (1977), pp. 73-83

Lakshin, V. 'Ivan Denisovich, ego druz'ia i nedrugi', *Novyi mir*, no. 1 (1964), pp. 223-45

Leighton, Lauren G. 'On Translation: *One Day in the Life of Ivan Denisovič*', *The Russian Language Journal*, vol. 32, no. 111 (1978), pp. 117-30

Lewis, Anthony. 'Solzhenitsyn Hailed Despite Absence at Presentation of 1970 Nobel Awards', *The New York Times*, 11 December 1970

Luplow, Richard. 'Narrative Style and Structure in *One Day in the Life of Ivan Denisovich*', *Russian Literature Triquarterly*, No. 1 (1971), pp. 399-412

May, Rachel. *The Translator in the Text: On Reading Russian Literature in English*, Evanston, IL: Northwestern University Press, 1994

Nicholson, Michael. 'Solzhenitsyn as "Socialist Realist"', in Hilary Chung (ed.), *In the Party Spirit: Socialist Realism and Literary Practice in the Soviet Union, East Germany and China*, Amsterdam: Rodopi, 1996, pp. 55-68

Pike, David. 'A Camp Through the Eyes of a Peasant: Solzhenitsyn's *One Day in the Life of Ivan Denisovich*', *California Slavic Studies*, vol. X (1977), pp. 193-223

Porter, Robert. *Solzhenitsyn's One Day in the Life of Ivan Denisovich*, London: Bristol Classical Press, 1997

Reshetovskaia, N. *Solzhenitsyn i chitaiushchaia Rossiia*, Moscow: Sovetskaia Rossiia, 1990

Rus, Vladimir J. 'One Day in the Life of Ivan Denisovich: A Point of View Analysis', *Canadian Slavonic Papers*, vol. 13 (1973), pp. 165-78

Rzhevskii, L. 'Obraz rasskazchika v povesti Solzhenitsyna "Odin den' Ivana Denisovicha"', in Robert Magidoff, George Y. Shevelov, J. S. G. Simmons and Kiril Taranovski (eds), *Studies in Slavic Linguistics and Poetics in Honor of Boris O. Unbegaun*, New York and London: New York University Press; University of London Press, 1968, pp. 165-78

<S. n.> 'Aleksandr Solzhenitsyn: Indomitable Russian Writer', *The Times*, 5 August 2008

<S. n.> 'Alexander Solzhenitsyn, Voice of the Gulag', *The Daily Telegraph*, 4 August 2008

Saraskina, L. *Aleksandr Solzhenitsyn*, Moscow: Molodaia gvardiia, 2008

Scammell, Michael. *Solzhenitsyn: A Biography*, London: Hutchinson, 1985

Schapiro, Leonard. 'Bent Backs', *New Statesman*, 1 February 1963, pp. 158-59

Scherr, Barry P. 'Aleksandr Solzhenitsyn', *Encyclopedia of Literary Translation into English*, ed. by Olive Classe, London-Chicago: Fitzroy Dearborn, 2000, pp. 1300-02

Shneerson, Mariia. 'Golos Shukhova v proizvedeniiakh Solzhenitsyna', *Grani*, no. 146 (1987), pp. 106-33

Slonim, Marc. 'European Notebook', *The New York Times*, 8 November 1970

Smith, J. Y. 'Nobel Winner Chronicled Tyranny of Soviet Union', *The Washington Post*, 4 August 2008

Tempest, Richard. 'The Geometry of Hell: The Poetics of Space and Time in *One Day in the Life of Ivan Denisovich*', in Alexis Klimoff (ed.), *One Day in the Life of Ivan Denisovich: A Critical Companion*, Evanston, IL: Northwestern University Press, 1997, pp. 54-69

Toker, L. 'On Some Aspects of the Narrative Method in *One Day in the Life of Ivan Denisovich*', in W. Moskovich (ed.), *Russian Philology and History: In Honour of Professor Victor Levin*, Jerusalem: PRAEDICTA, 1992, pp. 270-82

Tolczyk, Dariusz. 'Who Is Ivan Denisovich? Ethical Challenge and Narrative Ambiguity in Solzhenitsyn's Text', in Alexis Klimoff (ed.), *One Day in the*

Life of Ivan Denisovich: A Critical Companion, Evanston, IL: Northwestern University Press, 1997, pp. 70-84.

Werner, Martin (Hrsgb.) *Aleksander Solschenizyn: Eine Bibliographie seiner Werke*, Hildesheim: Olms, 1977

Williams, Carol J. 'Solzhenitsyn, Chronicler of Russia under Communism, Dies at 89', *The Los Angeles Times*, 4 August 2008

Secondary Sources on Casper Wrede and his *One Day in the Life of Ivan Denisovich*

A.O. 'Fremragende Ivan', *Morgenposten*, 27 November 1970

Andersen, Arvid. 'Det fineste og mest profesjonelle film-*miljø* jeg har opplevd! Espen Skjønberg: Solsjenitsyns nøkterne fangehverdag var alltid vår rettesnor', *Dagbladet*, 26 November 1970

Andersen, Arvid. 'Overbevisende film-versjon av Ivans hverdag som fange', *Dagbladet*, 27 November 1970

A<ndrew>, G<eoff>. 'One Day in the Life of Ivan Denisovich', in Tom Milne (ed.), *The Time Out Film Guide*, London: Penguin, 1989, p. 432

Allen, Jack. '*Ivan Denisovich* Film Culmination of Dream', *The Buffalo Courier-Express*, 27 September 1971

Arni, Erkki. 'Nobel-kirjailijan filmaus vaatii näyttelijältä sisua: Suomalainen rakensi Stalinin vankileirin', *Helsingin Sanomat,* 13 December 1970

Bachteler, James. '*Life of Denisovich*: Movie of Rare Quality', *The Campus Slate* (Westbury, N. Y), 19 October 1971

Barker, Felix. 'Ivan the Miserable', *Evening News*, 14 January 1972

Barnard, Ken. 'A Man Endures in a Siberian Prison', *The Detroit News*, 6 October 1971

Beale, Lewis. 'One Day in the Life of Ivan Denisovich', *The Daily Planet* (Philadelphia, PA), 5-11 October 1971

Bell, Joseph N. 'Courtenay's Missionary Zeal for Ivan Denisovich', *Los Angeles Times*, 7 November 1971

Bez. 'En betydelsefull dag i Casper Wredes liv', *Hufvudstadsbladet*, 5 January 1970

Beierfield, Ann M. '*Denisovich* Important Work', *The Record-American*, 2 October 1971

Bergström, Lasse. 'En positiv överraskning', *Expressen*, 8 December 1970

Bilbow, Marjorie. 'The New Films', *Cinema TV Today*, 22 January 1972, p. 28

Billington, Michael. 'The Cherry Orchard', *The Guardian*, 2 November 1979

Bowman, Pierre. '*Ivan Denisovich* Rare, Masterly Filmed', *The Honolulu Star-Bulletin*, 27 October 1971

Börge, Göran. 'En dag i Ivan Denisovitjs liv', *Aftonbladet*, 8 December 1970

Braun, Eric. 'One Day in the Life of Ivan Denisovich', *Films and Filming*, April 1972, pp. 50-51

Burgess, Anthony. 'The Arts', *The Listener*, 15 October 1964, p. 603

Butcher, Maryvonne. 'Cinema', *The Tablet: The International Catholic Weekly*, 15 January 1972, p. 36

Byrne, Bridget. '*Life of Denisovich*: Absorbing Wrede Fare', *The Los Angeles Herald-Examiner*, 15 October 1971

Cashin, Fergus. 'It's a Triumph for Bald Tom', *The Sun*, 13 January 1972

Champlin, Charles. '*One Day* a Tribute to Spirit of Survival', *The Los Angeles Times*, 13 October 1971

Chazal, Robert. 'L'étape d'un esclave', *France-Soir*, 18 September 1972

Christian, George. 'Survival Is Triumph to *Denisovich*', *The Houston Post*, 1 October 1971

Christie, Ian. 'If You Had a Tough Time Yesterday, Read on...', *The Daily Express*, 12 January 1972

Coleman, John. 'Kubrick's Ninth', *New Statesman*, 14 January 1972, p. 56

Courtenay, Tom. *Dear Tom: Letters from Home*, London: Black Swan, 2001

Coveney, Michael. 'The Cherry Orchard', *The Financial Times*, 3 November 1979

Coveney, Michael. 'Hope Against Hope / Royal Exchange, Manchester', *The Financial Times*, 4 February 1983

Crozier, Mary. 'The Summer in Gossensass on BBC-1', *The Guardian*, 16 September 1964

Davies, Russell. 'Fascist Truth', *The Observer*, 2 March 1975

Dewar, Cameron. 'Life in a Siberian Labor Camp', *The Boston Herald-Traveler*, the Show Guide supplement, 3 October 1971

Dewar, Cameron. 'Ivan Denisovich', *The Boston Herald-Traveler*, 4 October 1971

Dickey, Fred. 'Siberian Prison Movie Has Cold Message', *San Jose Mercury-News* of 24 October 1971

Eglick, Peter. 'A Study in "Absolute Insecurity"', *34th Street: The Magazine of The Daily Pennsylvanian*, 30 September 1971

Ekstrand, Nils-Erik. 'Ryskt fångläger filmas i Norge', *Dagens Nyheter*, 13 January 1970

Eteläpää, Heikki. 'Elokuvan esityskielto hyvin hämmästyttävä', *Uusi Suomi*, 20 February 1972

F.S. 'Courtenay: Det kan bli en mektig og gripende film: Norske skuespillere i filmatisering av Solsjenitsyns roman', *Aftenposten*, 29 September 1969

-ft. 'Die Hölle läßt sich nicht abfilmen', *Die Welt*, 21 May 1974

Fenton, James. 'Making Art out of Terror', *The Sunday Times*, 6 February 1983

Film Critic. 'At the Cinema', *The Guardian*, 2 February 1963

Film Critic. 'At the Cinema', *The Guardian*, 9 February 1963

Fock, Marie-Louise. '"Casper" – teater i England', *Astra* (Helsinki), no. 1, 1955, p. 4

Fock, Marie-Louise. 'Casper Wrede retrospektivt', *Hufvudstadsbladet*, 5 April 1957

Fock, Marie-Louise. 'Casper Wrede på ny teater', *Hufvudstadsbladet*, 17 September 1976

Fock, Marie-Louise. 'Casper Wredes giv om Osip M.', *Hufvudstadsbladet*, 23 February 1983

Fock, Marie-Louise. 'Stor regiframgång för Wrede i England', *Hufvudstadsbladet*, 23 May 1985

Fransberg, Klas. *Film på finlandssvenska: Från Stiller till Engström*, Vasa: Scriptum, 1994

Fräntti, Mikael. 'Ivan Denisovitsh vihdoin ensi-iltaan', *Helsingin Sanomat*, 27 October 1996

Geist, Kenneth. 'One Day in the Life of Ivan Denisovich', *SHOW* (New York), September 1971, p. 56

Gelmis, Joseph. 'Superb Survival', *Newsday*, 17 May 1971
Gibbs, Patrick. 'In the Ice', *The Daily Telegraph*, 14 January 1972
Gilliatt, Penelope. 'Worlds Away', *The New Yorker*, 22 May 1971, pp. 71-72
Giniger, Susan. 'Prison Story Premieres Locally', *The Chronicle* (Hempstead, N. Y.), 30 September 1971
Gjessing, Gunvor. 'God film om livsvilje', *Aftenposten*, 27 November 1970
Gould Boyum, Joy. 'On Film', *The Wall Street Journal*, 18 June 1971
Granum, Bjørn. 'Varm film i kuldegrader', *Arbeiderbladet*, 27 November 1970
Greenspun, Roger. 'Film *Ivan Denisovich* Best at Long Distance', *The New York Times*, 17 May 1971
Gripenwaldt, Raoul. 'Soviet Prison Life Subject of Film', *Evening Outlook* (Santa Monica, CA), 11 October 1971
Guarino, Ann. '*One Day in the Life of Ivan Denisovich*: Film Sharply Etches Russian Prison Life', *The New York Daily News*, 17 May 1971
Haddal, Per. 'En god dag i Ivan Denisovitjs liv', *Vårt land*, 27 November 1970
Harwood, Ronald. 'Northern Light for the Theatre', *The Guardian*, 30 September 1998
Hebert, Hugh. 'The Next Media Man', *The Guardian*, 17 April 1970
Herstad Røed, Liv. 'En ypperlig "gjengivelse" av "En dag i Ivan Denisovitsj' liv"', *Morgenbladet*, 27 November 1970
Herridge, Frances. 'Solzhenitsyn's *Day* on Screen', *The New York Post*, 17 May 1971
Hinxman, Margaret. 'Grim and Glorious', *The Sunday Telegraph*, 16 January 1972
Hjertén, Hanserik. 'Äkta filmhyllning av Solzjenitsyn', *Dagens nyheter*, 8 December 1970
Houston, Gary. 'One Day in the Life…', *The Chicago Sun-Times*, 13 October 1971
Hoyle, Martin. 'Three Sisters / Royal Exchange, Manchester', *The Financial Times*, 15 April 1985
Huddy, John. '*Ivan Denisovich* Is Sobering Tale of Prison Life', *The Miami Herald*, 19 October 1971
Norton, Hubert. 'Courtenay is Ideal Ivan', *The Miami News*, 16 October 1971

Jacob, Gilles. 'Un jour dans la vie d'Ivan Denissovitch', *L'Express*, 4-10 September 1972, p. 11

Kalfus, Bob. '*Ivan Denisovich* Superbly Filmed, Acted', *Phoenix* (Flushing, N.Y.), 19 October 1971

K<anfer>, S<tefan>. 'Witness', *Time*, 31 May 1971, p. 41

Kankkonen, Peter. *Finlandiseringen — "frivillig" underkastelse*, Uppsala: Pro Veritate, 1979

Kivinen, Greta. 'Caspar Wreden puheilla: Kalevala on Kalevala englannin kielelläkin', *Kaleva*, 25 September 1970

Knickerbocker, Paine. '*Ivan Denisovich*: A Somber Film on Soviet Prison Life', *The San Francisco Chronicle*, 30 September 1971

K<nickerbocker>, P<aine>. 'A Young Director's Struggle to Make Denisovich', *The San Francisco Chronicle*, 1 October 1971

Küng, Andres. *Mitä Suomessa tapahtuu*, Helsinki: Kirjayhtymä, 1976

Lee, John M. 'Solzhenitsyn Novel Before Cameras', *The New York Times*, 13 January 1970

Levin, Bernard. 'Hope Springs Eternal But Not from This Inky Hand', *The Times*, 25 February 1983

Loriot, Patrick. 'Sisyphe en Sibérie', *Le Nouvel Observateur*, 4-10 September 1972, pp. 50-51

M. E. 'Ivan Denissovitch au cinéma: Tom Courtenay, celui qui ne dit pas "oui"', *Le Monde*, 7 September 1972

Mahar, Ted. '*One Day* Reflects Attitude of Novel', *The Oregonian*, 13 October 1971

Malcolm, Derek. 'Almost Magic Roundabout', *The Guardian*, 13 January 1972

Malcolm, Derek. 'Right First Time', *The Guardian*, 27 February 1975

McKinnon, George. '*Ivan Denisovich* 8 Years in Planning', *The Boston Globe*, 3 October 1971

Meisel, Myron. 'A Day in the Life', *The Chicago Reader*, 15 October 1971

Melly, George. 'Kubrick's Crystal Ball', *The Observer*, 16 January 1972

Meta. 'Åbostoff till story för film om Sibelius', *Åbo Underrättelser* (Turku), 31 October 1964

Meyer, Michael. *Not Prince Hamlet: A Life in Literary and Theatrical London*, Oxford: Oxford University Press, 1990

Miller, Jeanne. 'A Film He Had to Make', *The San Francisco Examiner*, 29 September 1971

Miller, Stephanie. 'One Day in the Life of a Siberian Prisoner', *Seattle Post-Intelligencer*, 8 October 1971

Moilanen, Harri-Ilmari. 'Päivä Ivan Denisovitshin elämässä', *Kansan Uutiset: Viikkolehti*, 25 October 1996

Murray, Braham. 'Wrede Defined', *Plays and Players*, March 1990, pp. 17-19

Murray, Braham. *The Worst It Can Be Is a Disaster: The Life Story of Braham Murray and the Royal Exchange Theatre*, London: Methuen Drama, 2007

Norman, Barry. 'Tom Courtenay in *Ivan Denisovich* – a film with legs', *The Times*, 6 Nov 1971

Nykvist, Sven. *Vördnad för ljuset: Om film och människor i samtal med Bengt Forslund*, Bonnier: Uddevalla, 1997

Pack, Richard. 'Where Is It Colder Than a Sponsor's Heart?: Filmmaking in Røros, Norway', *Variety*, 11 February 1970

Panin, Dimitrii. *Zapiski Sologdina*, Frankfurt am Main: Possev-Verlag, 1973, vol. 1, p. 492

Peacock, Trevor. 'Casper Wrede', *The Independent*, 30 September 1998

Petäjä, Jukka. 'Törmäys Suomen itsesensuuriin', *Helsingin Sanomat*, 4 August 1988

Peter, John. 'Women of Some Importance', *The Sunday Times*, 14 April 1985

Pflaum, H. G. 'Zwei Stunden im Leben des Iwan Denissowitsch: Caspar Wredes Solschenizyn-Verfilmung', *Süddeutsche Zeitung*, 21 May 1974

Powell, Dilys. 'Roots of Terror, Paths of Survival', *The Sunday Times*, 16 January 1972

Quinlan, David. 'Films', *Mayfair*, Vol. 6, No. 10 (1971), p. 15

Ratcliffe, Michael. 'Taking the Pulse', *The Observer*, 14 April 1985

Roberts, Celia. 'Cinema', *What's on in London*, 14 January 1972, p. 24

Robinson, David. 'The Clockwork before Us', *The Financial Times*, 14 January 1972

Rosman, Steve. 'Classic to Low-class', *The Torch* (St John's University, New York), 1 October 1971

Russell Taylor, John. 'A Death in the Family', *The Times*, 14 January 1972

<S. n.> 'A Cry for Help from a Prisoner in the Night', *Today's Cinema*, 25 June 1971, p. 20

<S. n.> 'A Magnificent Performance: Ibsen's *Brand* Seen Clearly', *The Times*, 9 April 1959

<S. n.> 'BBC Television: "Uncle Vanya"' in *The Times*, 21 January 1957

<S. n.> 'Courtenay's "Ivan" is a Hit in New York', *Kinematograph Weekly*, 26 June 1971

<S. n.> 'Denisovitj är inte en tendentiös film', *Hufvudstadsbladet*, 22 February 1972

<S. n.> 'Donner valittaa elokuvakiellosta heti KHO:hon', *Helsingin Sanomat*, 1 March 1972

<S. n.> 'Group W Films to Make "Denisovitch" with Tom Courtenay, Norsk Films', *Variety*, 1 October 1969

<S. n.> 'Hollywood North', *Scandinavian Times*, no. 2, May 1970, pp. 42-43

<S. n.> 'Int'l Catholic Film Office Awards Group W's *Ivan* Its Annual Grand Prize', *Variety*, 24 November 1971

<S. n.> 'Ivan Denisovitsh poliittisesti arka esitettäväksi', *Helsingin Sanomat*, 17 February 1972

<S. n.> 'One Day in the Life of Ivan Denisovich', *The Film Bulletin* (Philadelphia, PA), June 1971, p. 38

<S. n.> 'Playboy After Hours', *Playboy*, May 1971, p. 42

<S. n.> 'Première idag på "En dag i Ivans liv"', *Aftenposten*, 26 November 1970

<S. n.> 'Prisoner C 854 Goes to a West End Premiere', *Cinema TV Today*, 15 January 1972, p. 12

<S. n.> 'Simulating Siberia', *Time*, 2 March 1970, p. 55

<S. n.> 'TV-stopp för film på Åland', *Hufvudstadsbladet*, 24 September 1972

<S. n.> 'What Are the Prospects for Theatrical Adventure?', *The Times*, 3 April 1959

<S. n.> 'Where to Go to Film Cold *Ivan*? Pick the Far Arctic', *The Pasadena Star-News*, 26 September 1971

Sellæg, Arne. 'En film i Solsjenitsyns ånd', *Nationen*, 27 November 1970

Schickel, Richard. 'Boiled Grass and Basic Humanity: *One Day in the Life of Ivan Denisovich*', *Life*, 25 June 1971, p. 12

Shalit, Gene. 'What's Happening: Movies', *Ladies' Home Journal*, no. 8, 1971, p. 18

Smith, Liz. 'Ivan Survives', *Cosmopolitan*, no. 8, 1971, p. 16

Stark, Susan. 'Man Survives – in Noble *One Day*', *The Detroit Free Press*, 8 October 1971

Stognar, Gerd. 'Historien om mennesket Ivan – fange C854', *Kvinner og klær*. 8 December 1970, pp. 17-19

Strauss, Ulf von. 'Krönika över människan', *Svenska dagbladet*, 8 December 1970

Sweeney, Louise. 'Searing Solzhenitsyn Film', *The Christian Science Monitor*, 2 June 1971

Sweeney, Louise. '*Denisovich*: Searing Solzhenitsyn Film Epic', *The Christian Science Monitor*, 2 October 1971

Tallmer, Jerry. 'Tom Courtenay: No More Anti-Heroes, Please', *The New York Post*, 5 June 1971

Taylor, Frances. '*One Day* is Grim Tribute', *The Long Island Press*, 17 May 1971

Taylor, Nora E. 'Denisovich: Wrede's Eight-year Saga', *The Christian Science Monitor*, 29 September 1971

Thirkell, Arthur. 'To Siberia with No Love!', *The Daily Mirror*, 13 January 1972

Thomas, Kevin. 'Director Behind *One Day*', *The Los Angeles Times*, 16 October 1971

Thompson, Eric. 'Frostproof Edition', *The Times*, 15 January 1970

Trevor, William. 'The Arts', *The Listener*, 30 December 1965, p. 1087

Trilling, Ossian. 'Trettondagsafton i BBC i regi av Casper Wrede', *Nya Pressen* (Helsinki), 27 March 1957

Uboldi, Raffaello. 'Ivan accusa Stalin dallo schermo', *Il Giorno*, 21 November 1970

Varen, Torgny. 'Vesentlig og ekte filmverk', *Verdens gang*, 27 November 1970

Verr. 'One Day in the Life of Ivan Denisovich', *Variety*, 19 May 1971

Wagner, Friedrich A. 'Wredes Spielfilm: Solschenizyn matt verfilmt', *Frankfurter Allgemeine Zeitung*, 20 May 1974

Walker, Alexander. 'Bleak Day', *Evening Standard*, 13 January 1972

Wall, Michael. 'Directing for the Actor', *The Manchester Guardian*, 7 May 1959

Wardle, Irving. 'Hope Against Hope / Royal Exchange, Manchester', *The Times*, 4 February 1983

Wardle, Irving. 'Frustration for the Sisters', *The Times*, 13 April 1985

Wedman, Les. <An Untitled Column>, *The Sun* (Vancouver), 5 January 1972

Weisman, John. 'Jail in Siberia: A Smoothly Running, Never Ending Example of Man's Inhumanity to Man', *Rolling Stone*, 11 November 1971, pp. 65-66

Wilson, Cecil. 'No Violence, No Sex, Just Freezing Hell', *The Daily Mail*, 12 January 1972

Wolf, William. 'One Day in the Life of Ivan Denisovich', *Cue* (New York), 22 May 1971, p. 64

Zimmerman, Paul D. 'Prisoner's Base', *Newsweek*, 24 May 1971, p. 46

Z<immerman>, P<aul> D. 'A Last Look at 1971's Movies', *Newsweek*, 3 January 1972, p. 33

Casper och den förbjudna filmen (Casper and the Forbidden Film, 2009), dir. Klas Fransberg, Långfilm Productions, Finland Ab, 55 min.

APPENDICES

I   RUSSIA ON MY MIND

AN AUTOBIOGRAPHICAL ESSAY
BY C<asper> W<rede>[508]

1938

My earliest memory of our neighbour, Russia, begins with waking up to yet another of those hot midsummer days which that year hung suspended from May to September like white linen blowing on a line so long that there seemed to be no end to it. I ran out to play. The great apple orchard, planted by St Petersburg gentry and wiped out to the last tree by the historic frosts of 1940, stood in full bloom. My brother and I had measured an – in Finland – unheard of 40 degrees of heat on Midsummer Eve. Everywhere was dry as tinder and the river, too dangerous to bathe in, flowed much diminished, deep down in its furrow. That morning I felt an acrid taste in my mouth and my eyes began to water. When I looked up I saw the sun burning scarlet in a charcoal sky. A terrible fear that this was the end of the world crawled out from my heart and all over my body. I could not move. Then: I ran. "The forests of Russia are on fire," my mother said. Since that day, until not very long ago Russia was the dark centre of my imagination. The smoke rolled over us for days, weeks perhaps, and soon there were new flames to add to the fire. These flames leapt from Russian bombs that fell on us unannounced one morning, broke up my biology lesson – for which I was grateful as it was my first with a new teacher and I had not prepared myself very well – and ended my childhood. The war took from me my home and my roots. To add to my

---

[508] In preparation of this and the next manuscript ('Letter to a Young Actor') for publication, every attempt has been made to preserve, where possible, the wording and punctuation of the originals.

grief, the enemy occupied and later burnt down our tiny rented holiday cottage by the sand and sea... I lived as a child in peace and plenty next door to a terror and suffering of which I had no knowledge. Yet it cast a shadow of anguish over my soul, just as sensible to me as the forest fires which had darkened the sky and made my eyes water. Only this shadow took a lot longer to dispel.

1940

I remember nine silver planes marked with red stars, marching slowly in formation high across the sky, lit by the February sun which barely managed to get up over the tops of the grandfather Christmas trees on the horizon before it sank back again dismayed at not being able to raise the temperature above the forty below the zero mark. Myriads of barely visible snow crystals tumbled out of the blue, turning each hair of our eyelashes and eyebrows into tiny icicles. The unearthly stillness created in nature by the frost brought the rhythmic drone of the aircraft engines close to us. The planes were returning to base, having set fire to one of our old timber–built towns on the west coast. They must be able to see us standing here in the snow just as clearly as we can see them, I thought. "Look", I said, "they will come down and kill us". The older children laughed and the younger ones, braver than I, kept quiet. "Listen", my brother said, "one of them is sick". Right enough, a plane was sagging behind the others, one of its engines coughing badly. We could hear that ominous sound long after we had lost sight of the planes. That night my father told us on the phone that he had seen the aircraft come down.

1919–1939

There had of course been the emigrants, the leftovers from the table of the revolution, swept across the border and scattered all over my childhood landscape. Homemade Russian ice cream was sold to me in the summer by an aristocrat with a delicate pointed beard. There was a very old man, said to have been one of the richest in the world, living in a poorhouse overlooking the greatest lake in Europe with the domes of an ancient island monastery floating on the horizon and his measureless homeland announcing its presence beyond by a towering row of clouds.[509] I have this picture of him: sitting on a bench, both hands on his stick, gazing out over the water; but I now believe it is in fact an image I carry of myself – with a lifetime of Russia on my mind. I also vividly remember my mother putting on a comic Russian accent when telling her favourite anecdotes of a dotty émigré, <a> Petersburg lady, very deficient in her new language, who married a junior cavalry officer. When her husband asked for someone to take responsibility for some task, she asked: "Responsibility, responsibility, what the hell do you mean, responsibility?" Having listened to her husband's explanation of the concept of responsibility in terms of the planning and execution of a railway journey she said: "Me! I'd much rather carry responsibility than suitcases! Dammit!" She it was who, growing impatient with the ladies' after dinner conversation about absent friends and servants, threw open the door to the general's library, looked over the astonished brandy sipping, cigar smoking, stuffed shirts inside and exclaimed: "How boring you all are! In Petersburg sexual intercourse was much livelier!" I laughed at these stories long before I knew what they meant, let alone before I realised the significance they held for my passionate but principled mother who had grown up between the parental Scylla and Charybdis of imminent eternal damnation and present alcoholic euphoria. It is only now that it occurs to me what a temptation and what a threat these impulsive, life-loving Russians provided for our high–minded, formal, protestant society.

1944

Again it was February and I was again standing in a field of snow, this time in the dark, surrounded by great guns, their barrels wound down to their casemates for temporary want of ammunition. It had been a lively night. I was draped in my commanding officer's parade greatcoat, having arrived in civvies that afternoon, a frozen schoolboy, to make up for the lack of men. I was watching the searchlight next to me catch in its beam a large, angular four–engine bomber. To find the safety of the vast darkness surrounding it, the pilot tried desperate manoeuvres – but too late. Three other beams had joined in and kept the lumbering aircraft captive.

---

509 Wrede is describing Lake Ladoga and the Valaam Monastery, part of the Finnish territory at the time.

Again I could clearly see the red stars on its wings. There was an uncanny pause. No whistling bombs now, no explosions, no gunfire, no heavy breathing of shells travelling far into the night. I was too deafened by the battle even to hear the sound of the fleet of invisible planes, fleeing our shores, light of their load. It was the silence of expectation soon fulfilled: magically, a bright row of pearls appeared in the sky. They ran gaily toward their illuminated target which, receiving them, obligingly burst into flames, outshining all our previous fireworks. It began its spiralling descent, breaking into pieces as it fell. Like a soccer crowd on a Saturday afternoon we cheered and clapped our numb hands. Our night–fighter plane showed up for a moment, crossing a beam of light, on its way back to circling, high and unseen, like a buzzard, waiting for its prey to reveal itself. We hailed it with hoarse shouts of triumph; but it was a feeling of shame that heated my body through and through when it dawned on me that there were people trapped in that ball of light about to hit the ground.

1944–1945

I am running, very light and fast, over the uneven ground. A wonderful feeling to know that my feet will find their way safely even now when the autumn twilight is losing out to the night. It has taken all the years of my life for my feet to soak up the nature of the forest floor so well as to give me complete confidence in their mastery of it. Now I can travel at speed over rock and root looking ahead, letting my feet do their own thinking. I am only halfway there but the path gleams like a black snake in front of me and I have conquered my fear of being alone in the dark. Or, rather, my fear has been replaced by a strange feeling about the great importance of the sealed message I am carrying. This feeling streams to me from the enclosing night, from the whole being of the embracing forest: a feeling of great events in the making, a sense of destiny. Not my destiny alone. No, it is an all-embracing feeling, like the one music gives when it sets one free from thoughts and pictures and floods one with awe. I cannot remember any longer exactly where this journey in the dark takes place or to whom I bring the fateful message: some officer, I believe, at an isolated command post by the sea. All I know is that when I return exhausted and fall asleep that night we are still fighting Stalin with Hitler and when I wake up next morning we are fighting Hitler with Stalin. This desperate last move, in a drawn out game, entails the sacrifice, so to speak, of the castles and the horses, but secures a draw preserving the king, the bishops and what is left of the pawns. It does, of course, leave us in possession of rather less than half of the board. This is the unlikely dawn of a new life for those of us who survived to see the day break. But that is not how I feel when I return to the city and see the Soviet soldiers with their machine guns encamped on the doorstep of the hotel my darling uncle has run throughout the war.[510] The soldiers are guarding Zhdanov, "the butcher of the Baltic".

He is now our creditor and bailiff and when his name is mentioned my mother's face takes on that set expression which in the war years is intended to conceal her knowledge of the nature of the fate that, most probably, lies in store for us. It is Zhdanov, however, who does not survive his Master's persecution mania and we who learn to live with it. Within limits, we are still free.

1946

The city had not yet begun to throw off its post-war want and gloom. The trams entering and crossing the station square rattled and screeched behind me as, one wet and windy evening before Christmas, I pushed open the door to the lobby of a rundown hotel and joined a modest gathering of middle-aged women and men who did not look at home in these surroundings – two world wars ago the fashionable haunt of artists and their rich patrons.[511] I was profoundly uneasy: these were my first secret steps on the road to self-assertion and independence. (Looking now, down the wrong end of the telescope of time, I see that I must have felt very small and needed the most potent ally there was in order to back up and prop up my imminent rebellion. I was indecently young and criminally green in judgement: so naive, according to a friend, my own age, that he feared for me; and I knew of course that I was doing wrong. Asserting my own will against fearful and well-meaning parents was a business fraught with much shame and disingenuity). I thought I had come in order to meet the leading personalities of the circle to which I had re-

---

510 The fourteen-storey Torni Hotel in the Helsinki City Centre (opened in 1931).
511 The Kämp Hotel in the Helsinki City Centre (opened in 1887).

cently been introduced. In fact, I was there to be looked over, and by one person in particular. When I first saw her, the crowd parting before here like the Red Sea in front of Moses, it struck me, like lightning, that I had come in the presence of death. What I actually saw was a straight-backed, strongly built woman in a simple black dress. Her face was large and pale. That was all. She was, however, the red queen of the communist party, daughter of an old associate of Stalin's: member of the original Soviet Central Committee and chief bogey man of my childhood.[512] Today, I am told that she was a warm-hearted woman, a good sort, who devoted her life to the cause of the poor and the disadvantaged, and who suffered grievously in her private life. But then: then she had about her an air of implacable purpose, of impersonal will against which there was no appeal, qualities that are required from an executioner. I fancied there hung a scent of violent death, both past and still to come, around that fine head crowned with dark plaits. The dread I experienced at that moment is not to be compared with the fear that used to squeeze my heart during the war. That fear was cousin to the common fear of the dark. This was for me a virgin meeting with death, my own, which of course had no date stamped on it as yet.

But I had already sat in enough dingy rooms, breathing nicotine and brandy fumes until the early hours listening to the arguments between the fiery party activists and the ominously cool party intellects, to know that "Our Comrades" having taken power from "Them" all over Eastern Europe, "We" now were confident that "We" could do the same here at home. There had even been some talk about what would happen to "Them" afterwards, but it was not encouraged – perhaps for my sake. It was a happy time for "Us", full of hopes and plans and excitement. "They", meanwhile, were lying low. As for "Me", I had to find another way.[513]

---

512 The Finnish Communist politicians Hertta Kuusinen (1904–74) and her father Otto Wille Kuusinen (1881–1964).
513 Representative of the left-wing political leanings of the young Wrede is his article 'Möte med min röst' (Finding My Voice), published on 16 August 1947 in *Folktidningen*, a newspaper of the Demokratiska förbundet för Finlands folk, a socialist alliance that included the Communists. In this article, Wrede wrote that he would like to go inwards and try to find his own voice, but also outwards and work for the establishment of socialism.

1948

In this communist circle I met a lion–hearted poet with a deeply etched face, noble profile, child's eyes and large capable hands. He had spent years in prison for his faith in the Moscow road for Humanity to Justice and he was quietly determined to see it through.[514] This poet was in many ways in character very like that giant of African-Americans[515] whose hand firmly grasped my wrist as mine wrung his fingers when we first met in a hotel, but now, in another country. He was on a cultural tour sponsored by Washington for purposes of its own. I watched at close quarters as he fought, with the eyes of the world on him, a great battle of conscience. He had been ruthlessly manipulated by the communist press on the continent into the position of having to declare where his loyalties lay: in Washington? or, in Moscow? For the public this was – by the propaganda of both sides – made out to be an inescapable choice between patriotism and ideology. For him it was a question of what the cause of the people of his own colour demanded of him. The United States was racist: he knew that from experience. The Soviet Union on the other hand had long ago taken him to its heart as a man and as an artist and had used him to advertise to the world its supposed freedom from racial prejudice. Both sides had made him a symbol of the brotherhood of man. And both had threatened, privately, to disown him as a traitor if he did not come out on their side. He prevaricated, and became the first person in my experience on whom all the media of the world focused their attention on day after day. They hounded him. When at last it became clear that he had to choose, the heart of this Old Lion overruled his head. I sat in on a press conference with some thirty international journalists: there was hardly a word of truth in what I read the next day. His fellow white Americans never forgave him. He at once became useless to Moscow's propaganda machine and he was soon forgotten. These were the early days of the painful time of "Them" and "Us", "Us" and "Them". The war had not ended. It had merely gone cold on us.

1968

---

514 Either Armas Äikiä (1904–65) or Arvo Turtiainen (1904–80).
515 The actor and singer Paul Robeson (1898–1976).

Sunday afternoon in Hyde Park. I am lounging in the grass with a successful Russian writer and former Gulag inmate who had defected from Moscow only a couple of weeks earlier.[516] He is taking great delight in trying to identify the ethnic origins of all the people picnicking and strolling by. His years as an orphan in Soviet institutions and later in the Gulag archipelago have given him a vast knowledge of types and he is very observant. He gets tired of this game and becomes thoughtful. "It is a good thing that the people of the Soviet Union do not know about this place," he says, "and that having been told about it they would not believe it exists." Why is it a good thing? "Because if they would believe it, you would have 200,000,000 people in Hyde Park."

The main reason why we in the West, all of us, were taken by surprise when the great changes behind the Iron Curtain took place so rapidly and almost without resistance is that we had not penetrated behind the stony mask presented to us. We believed in the indefinite will of the people in power there to use force in order to maintain their positions. My first insight into the personal ambivalence that lived under the surface of Stalin's heirs and former servants had come from my father, at whose table the most civilized and subtle of Soviet deputy premiers[517] – on behalf of his bosses – had made the speech of thanks to the host. In it, as it were to praise to the hilt the ample and generous hospitality he and his peers had received, he suggested as a closing pleasantry that he and my father swap jobs. It is difficult now to convey how perfectly everyone at that table understood all that was being said and all that remained unspoken. My father had been forced to learn Russian at school; he had all but lost the use of one leg fighting the revolution of 1917; he had heard his name read out over the radio as one of many on a Moscow death list in 1940; in the same year he had been required by his government to go to Soviet occupied territory, sleep in what had been his own house and assist the Russians to put into production an industrial plant he had supervised the

---

516 The author and artist Mikhail Demin (1926–84; real name Georgii Evgen'evich Trifonov), who made drawings of the labour camp for Wrede's *Ivan Denisovich* (see Appendix III). In fact, having asked for asylum in France in the summer of 1968 (see the unsigned note 'Asylum Sought by Russian Poet' in *The Times* of 15 August 1968), he came to see Wrede in London in mid-June 1969.
517 Probably Anastas Mikoyan (1895–1978).

building of;[518] now he had been required to invite into his home the most powerful people in the post–Stalin Soviet Union and here they were, conceding that theirs was the less enviable lot in life. And so it was. And still is. Everyone laughed heartily and raised their glasses to peaceful co–existence. The time for blood–letting was over.

1961–1970

Nothing remains in my memory of the time when I first read Solzhenitsyn but the experience is with me still. It was a kind of homecoming: "A work of art is its own verification," he says in his Nobel lecture, "works which draw on truth and present it to us... compellingly involve us, and no-one ever, not even ages hence, will come forth to refute it." But it was not only myself I met in meeting Ivan Denisovich. For the first time I met ordinary Russians of my own generation. For the first time I was shown – without bitterness or recrimination – life backstage at the great Soviet show. And I knew with the whole of my being that what I was shown was the truth. My guide did not only possess the necessary experience; he had the genius to convey it in the simplest and most accessible form. I only regret that the political implications of the story had obscured its universal lesson: that we are what we do; that is not what we do but how we do it that makes us what we are. This little book created the first living bond between the Russia of the future and the people in the world outside who chose to believe in forces stronger than violence and murder. I never knew when it was that it chose me to put it into pictures. The process was remarkable: before I knew it I had been joined by all those who were needed to realise the project and the assured impossibility of the task dissolved before us and was overcome at every stage. But it was only later that I began to feel the presence and the power of the host of those who had died in the camps working with us in the dark and the snow: for the first shot on the first day of filming the thermometer nailed to the wooden post in front of the guard's hut showed precisely 27 degrees centigrade below zero as prescribed by Alexander Solzhenitsyn; when our cameraman, after hours of

---

518 Wrede's father, Kenneth Alexander Wrede (1898–1983), supervised the construction, and was the chief executive, of a rayon–manufacturing plant KUITU OY in Jääski (now Lesogorsky, Russia). It became operational in 1937.

preparation in the pitch dark, shouted "the moon, we've forgotten the moon," I could raise my hand and point to the full moon rising from the hills at exactly the required spot; after weeks of work in the open air one of the actors was asked by a newcomer what the weather would be like the next day, the actor turned to me and asked in turn, "what weather do you want tomorrow?" I told him. He turned back to the newcomer and said, "There you are, that is tomorrow's weather." And so it was – night and day for twelve weeks. The locals and the mountain farmers, who were helping, threatened us day after day with the inevitable week–long mid-winter snowstorms – and they were snowed in right enough by terrible blizzards and cut off for a week as soon as we had gone. These were the most spectacular instances of a sequence of most unlikely events that only come once in a lifetime and it is good to remember them.

I specially treasure the memory of one day early on in the filming when, having kept everyone for hours out on the wind-driven icy wastes at an intolerable nearly 40 degrees of frost and finally having achieved what we set out to do, I heard one of the actors say, "Let's go home." It was the barbed wire ringed camp, on a snow–covered mountain plain in the middle of nowhere, which standing high on the platform of a camera crane I could see in the distance, that to this Englishman so soon had become "home." I had to swallow hard as, leaving the camp for the last time, I saw the glorious sun setting on one horizon and a ghostly full moon rising on the other. I took it to be a confirmation.

1971

The film I had made of Alexander Solzhenitsyn's book, One Day in the Life of Ivan Denisovich, had been entered for the Cannes film festival. As the time drew near I was told that it was not going to be shown. The Soviet authorities had not only threatened to pull out of the festival themselves, but they said they would pull out all the Iron Curtain countries as well, if Ivan Denisovich was shown at Cannes. Earlier they had without success tried to persuade my Norwegian partners not to let the film be made in their country. This time they fared better. They made the Cannes festival director an offer he could not refuse: If the Solzhenitsyn film was quietly dropped, then that great, masterly film about the medieval icon painter Andrey Rublev – until then seen only by a very privileged few – would receive its first ever public showing at Cannes.[519] My American partners happily accepted the invitation to show two other films instead.

1972–1983

If it was the war that equipped me for making the film about life in a Soviet labour camp, then it was my years of wandering and searching which followed the war which opened my mind and made me fit to embrace the experiences of Nadezhda Mandelstam and her husband Osip in the Soviet twenties, thirties and forties as she describes them in her memoirs. I even extracted a kind of theatrical event entirely drawn from the prose of Nadezhda and the far less accessible poetry of Osip Mandelstam and their friend Anna Akhmatova. I lived with these books for years, immersed myself in them and extended my reading in order to understand how Russia had arrived at its present state and what had happened there to people like myself.

These two voices, Nadezhda's and Osip's, have spoken to me more directly and clearly about the fundamental experiences of our times than any living person I have met. I think this is because in education and in vocation and in their personalities they were already intimately familiar to me – not that their characters are easy to penetrate; and because, highly sophisticated and intelligent people that they were, they lived – in fear – the lives of the poor and the persecuted, treasuring every moment, suffering every human want and weakness; and above all because – refusing to flee the land – they stubbornly maintained their integrity in the face of events which swept away even the idea of the right of an individual to have his own thoughts and feelings – let alone express them. Osip Mandelstam died for his right to be a poet. Nadezhda said she lived on in order to hide and save her husband's illegal poetry, but that is only the half of it: her own writing makes up the other half. Here is

---

519 In fact, *Andrei Rublev* (1965) by Andrei Tarkovsky was screened at Cannes in 1969.

true agreement between life and work. Two lives: one in poetry, the other in prose; naked witnesses to the times they lived through and died in.

Theirs was the last generation of people in Russia who knew themselves as part of our European civilization. The people who come after them are strangers to us and we to them. Refusing to surrender to terror they and their peers are like pawns buried in the Russian soil, crying to be redeemed. It will take a long, long time. (Just a few years ago I mentioned Osip's name in Moscow only for his memory to be mocked by some grinning anti-Semitic cultural pundit). But the evidence is there. And, "no-one has come forth to refute it". Over this evidence we are all invited to sit in judgement: to condemn, to dismiss, to deny, to argue, to reason and to modify. They are not a few, the doubters and the opponents I have seen wriggle on the barb of this sharp hook, which will not let one go without a blessing.

Two simple stories remain with me for life from all the reading I did during these years. To me they are signposts of what is being done to people now – the whole world over. I re-tell them here in my own words. The first comes from a countryman of mine who on being thrown into the blackness of a cell in the fortress of St Peter and St Paul after a while sensed that he was not alone.[520] A military man, new to this existence, he introduced himself formally to the invisible presence close to him. After a little a voice answered him, saying, "I was a professor of Theology, I know, but you must forgive me, I cannot recall my name".

The other story is much better told in context, by Nadezhda Mandelstam. It takes place in freezing winter in a city in Mongolia at a time before Stalin's death. A good and well qualified teacher, a decent family man, is thrown out of work, with immediate effect, from an institute of higher education. This is done out of prejudice and spite by the head and unanimously approved out of fear by a committee of colleagues. At the moment the teacher knows that noone will employ him again; no-one will speak to him or his family again, except at great and unpredictable risk to themselves and their own. That evening, in the snow outside the buildings of his former place of work, this man,

---

520 Unidentified person.

his wife and little children joined hands and danced and sang children's rhymes, the whole night through.[521]

1972–1974

In the early seventies I met a writer friend who had recently returned from some years in the United States. We brought each other up to date. In the middle of my story he cut me off with some venom, "I don't care if they are ALL killed!", he shouted. I had been talking about suffering Russia as usual. This, from a man who knew a good deal about suffering humanity? I was rather shocked. "How come?" "Racialists, the lot of them. Ask any Arab, African or Chinese, they know". It took me some time to digest this. But not long afterwards I found myself at dinner with, among others, a very distinguished paediatrician, head of a children's hospital in Moscow; a passionate, dedicated man who had given up everything in life for the health and welfare of children:[522] "That's where it begins!" Well, by the time whisky was on the table he was away, holding forth about population problems in the Soviet Union. To illustrate a point he put his forefingers to his temples and pushed up the corners of his eyes: "Breeding so much faster than Russians, you know. You have the same problem in America – and here too." He smiled conspiratorially, expecting sympathy and agreement. But he had fallen among Norwegians: a principled lot. They looked him steadily in the eye, shook their heads and said, "No, we don't know; tell us." Silence. The spectacle was pitiful. Here

---

521 The episode took place in 1953 (shortly after the death of Stalin), not in Mongolia but in the city of Ulyanovsk on the Volga river, where Nadezhda Mandelstam taught at the local Teachers' Training College (*pedagogicheskii institut*). She recalled: 'I noticed a little group of people standing in the courtyard. It turned out to be a short-legged Jewish couple, who worked in the mathematics department, and their numerous children. Only recently they had wept bitterly at the news of the Leader's death, and now, the previous night, they had been dismissed from their posts at a special faculty meeting <in the course of the anti-Semitic campaign of 1949-53. – BH, AR>. Both of them, taking on trust everything they had always been taught, had decided to have a large family in the confident expectation of a happy future. Unable to stand the blow that had now fallen, they had gone off their heads and were dancing hand in hand around the courtyard, yelling at the top of their voices – to the genuine amusement of their student onlookers' (Nadezhda Mandelstam, *Hope Abandoned: A Memoir*, translated from the Russian by Max Hayward, London: Collins and Harvill Press, 1974, p. 385).
522 Unidentified person.

was this man – who in the actions of his life without the slightest doubt was morally superior to all the rest of us put together – drowning in silent disapproval. And the poor man in his confusion did not even know why. I felt for him, coming as I do from a country where the arrival of two foreigners is a cause for celebration, but the appearance of five a sinister harbinger of invasion. The revolution of 1917 left many things in Russian society basically unchanged and the ensuing isolation has if anything re-enforced anti-Semitism and racial prejudice. The really alarming thing to me, though, is that the disease which had its seat in the heart of Russia, "the Kremlin", has infected every part of the former empire and every individual within it. This is what makes them strangers to us, to each other and to themselves. Take the paediatrician: as I drove him back to his lodgings he was silent at first, tired obviously and invaded by black thoughts and feelings. We arrived. He did not get out of the car. We sat there in the dark. "They do not understand", he said. (Now I had become an emigrant member of the family whom one could talk to because one would never see him again). "You see, at home we have to be able to speak three languages fluently and to be able to distinguish between them very exactly. They are all in Russian, of course. The first we speak at work and in the street for anyone to hear. The second we speak to our family and friends. The third we speak only to ourselves. This is our life, and what does it make of us? Terrible. Terrible". We embraced and parted, but the question remained with me: what has it made of them?

Russia had produced the few great personalities of my day. They were forged in the hottest of furnaces, the coldest of deep freezes, never able to count on support from anyone, always exposed to the severest physical and moral danger and yet finding ways to speak out for the sake of the fearful, ignorant and passive multitude which was and is as ambivalent to them as it was and is to its masters. But the price of this strength and integrity lies in the isolation in which it has been achieved. Never to be forgotten is the boredom and the contempt, uninhibitedly displayed on the podium by the feted, prize-winning expatriate Russian poet,[523] for his academic peers – British, American, Conti-

---

[523] Possibly Joseph Brodsky (1940–96).

nental – over matters he knew more about. They, it was clear, had not graduated from his university. In fact, they had never even applied.

When confronted with or about each other these great men and women always express both a kind or solidarity and rigidly irreconcilable views. And when speaking to any of these luminaries and expressing admiration for another – a friend of theirs – I have never failed to provoke this response, "Yes, but..." followed by an – often endless – exposition of their own unique and highly entertaining point of view on any subject under the sun. Such people provide inspiration, but they are incapable of joining together. And they cannot lead. For in our day people will only be lead from below and within the ranks. And they will not stoop to command.

1989

What about the ranks? What have the Soviet years made of them? One twilight evening as we were driving through the outskirts of Moscow, I saw a big complex of rather superior low level buildings. "What is that?" I asked. "I don't know", said my guide, gazing vaguely in the right direction, "but I have been told that <this> is where the secret services train their recruits". Told? Oh, yes? This, from the man who knew everything. To reveal other people's secrets always was easier than confessing one's own. I had another guide, female and admirable also, but in a different way. She was assigned to me, I think, because the great film star from the West did not like her and had been told she was a notorious informant to the powers residing around Dzerzhinski's statue (as if the next one wouldn't be). She was small, dark, lively and dominant, hard as if she had been dipped in stainless steel. A miracle worker, able to fulfil one's every wish and to add some of her own on top. But she was never frank – except once. I had been speaking at some length about things one did not talk very much about in Moscow at the time. She interrupted me and said, with some pride: "My father was one of Bukharin's aides". On this remark novels might be written. What happened to the children of fathers who had received their ration of lead in the back of the neck and whose names had been cast into the outer darkness? All I will say is, it does not make for frankness, but it heightens – in some – the flame of the will to live to an almost unbearable brightness.

Sitting in an old Lada, next to the interpreter, parked beneath the statue of Dzerzhinski – now removed – with the new headquarters of the secret services behind me on the left, the great emporium of children's toys in front of me, and on the right, the immaculately restored facade of the prison in the cellars of which so many people have been shot in the back of the neck (Nadezhda Mandelstam often thought of this moment for "the noble head of Isaac Babel"); or they departed in a vehicle – disguised as a butcher's van in order not to upset people – for a life behind the wire; some of course left by the front door, but most of them had signed lists of names, of family, friends, acquaintances or persons not know to them, in order that the quota of names be fulfilled and there be addresses enough to drive to for the nightly arrests... Who can blame them who never saw the inside of that building in the hour of its darkness?

Watching the yellow leaves glued to the tarmac, I listen and descend in my mind through the floors of the vast repository beneath me which, I was being told, houses all the files of every last person who has ever attracted the attention of the organs of safety of the power whose guest I now am: my own name is here in some footnote; the manuscript of Alexander Solzhenitsyn's novel, The First Circle, is here; here is the slip of paper on which someone scribbled down a mangled version of Osip Mandelstam's poem in which he calls Stalin a murderer and which he never wrote down, only recited once among friends. It earned him his first arrest and exile and made a certainty of his early death to be accomplished at a later and more convenient moment. Osip was last seen, unhinged mentally, scavenging for scraps at the staging post, on the sea of Okhotsk, for the ultimate destiny of Kolyma in the Arctic, where much gold was found, and a pile of worn-out Gulag boots at a burial site to this day bear witness to the fate intended for the poet Mandelstam – had he lived so long. If there were a Dante alive today, this is where he would descend. But this is hell with a difference: it is the hell of the victims. The perpetrators are not here. They are respected citizens of all classes and many nationalities, ceremoniously buried or living on state pensions, their chests covered with medals. There are no files on them. My guide was an agricultural engineer with Bulgaria as his speciality. He was a knowledgeable man: he showed me the building in which the secret work took place that inspired The First Circle; he had a friend who sold me a padded jacket, a model originally supplied to Gulag prisoners but now the height of fashion – and great against the winter frost; I brought it back as a keepsake for my old friend who was Ivan Denisovich in the film; most valuable of all, he presented me with a concrete example of what had happened to the Russians under Stalin. At the end of our tour he stops the car in a large open space near the Kremlin walls.

Pokerfaced he asks me to get out and thoroughly scrutinise the facade facing me of one of those tall, heavy buildings, characteristic of Soviet architecture and to tell him what I see. I look, but not knowing what I am looking for, I see only this huge uniform facade, here and there tarted up with some detailing which is too minute too provide any relief from the pervading dreariness. My guide is disappointed with me and asks me to look again. I can tell from his face that there is some great and pleasurable satisfaction to be had from this mystery so I look very hard, cursing myself, for I know I am no good at this game. I never know what clothes people wear, or what colour their eyes are, or their hair. In the end he draws my attention to a certain detail high on the left of the building and then to its symmetrical counterpart on the right. Hallelujah! The veil falls from my eyes: they are not the same. Although the volume of the building is symmetrical, the detailing is different one side from the other. Why? My guide has the answer, of course: the building was commissioned by order of the Boss himself and when the final plans were presented to him by the architects, to flatter the All-seeing Little Father, they had given him the choice of two alternatives: on the right, alternative A; a line down the middle; on the left, alternative B. The great man studied the drawing, took up his pen and signed it: "Joseph Stalin". No more was said. And that is how it was built – asymmetrical.[524] There is no disease without symptoms. Who has not seen examples of socialist art? Posters or statues of men and women, marching forward, heads erect, strong, harmonious faces and bodies, decently covered, well differentiated male and female, perfectly symmetrical fea-

---

[524] Wrede is referring to the hotel 'Moscow', designed by A. V. Shchusev, L. I. Savel'ev and O. A. Stapran, built in 1932–38 and demolished in 2003–04.

tures expressing nothing – except an absolute faith. In what? An idea? A science? A leader, perhaps?

1992

Sitting comfortably in a sofa and turning on the local television station I happened on a little documentary interview. Two young people in a comfortless room, St. Petersburg, I think it was. There was a girl, not at all twenty yet and a young man, not yet thirty. She was a whore and he was a pimp. That was made clear. She was also a nice family girl and he a fully qualified microbiologist. That one could see. Both of them were, in the conventional sense, unemployed. He had been very fortunate, he said, someone in the organisation he now worked for had "dropped out" and he had been invited to step into the empty shoes. "Yes, this was a great piece of luck". He was a tall, lean young man and looked like the friend of the anti–hero in a modern French film. He was of course, among other things, intellectually superior to the interviewer, and both he and the girl had clearly had been chosen for their looks and told to do the interview as an advertisement for the services of their organisation.
"What was his job?" He was a salesman. He found the client, he made the deal and delivered the goods. "Was it not true that he was pimping for this girl?" "You do not understand. I am a businessman. There is nothing personal in what I do. I find a buyer and I deliver the goods, that is all". Implacable, even–tempered, polite even. The interviewer tried to rile him. Nothing doing. She insulted him. He chose to overlook it. "Would he get married?" "No, in this life, no. In theory, sometime, perhaps, yes, but, now, no". What about her? She sat still and expressionless, looking straight in front of her as paralysed as the rabbit in my garden, being stalked by the neighbour's cat. "Was she not frightened doing this?" Little nod. "Yes". "Very frightened?" Quickly, "Yes". "Then why did she do it?" Silence. Very long silence. "Did she then like what she did?" Stare. "Like it?" Silence. "Well, if she was frightened and did not like it, why did she do it?" She wetted the lipstick on her lips. At length: "Was she forced to do it?" Credible shake of the head. "Well, then?" This torture went on for quite a while. Then the resentment – not visible – became vocal: "What do you <think> I should do? No work. No money. Walk <the>

streets? Eat from bins? No life. No clothes. No fun. Nothing for life. Nothing. Nothing!" "Did she not know how dangerous it was to do what she did?" She knew. "Did she not know how often doing what she was doing ended, used up and discarded?" She knew. "Or worse?" She knew. "Well then?" She was saving. She had plans. She was doing it for a few years only. "Did she go with Russians also?" Outraged, vigorous shaking of the head. "Foreigners?" Nod. "Only foreigners?" Double nod. Silence. Pretty girl, so young, the skin of her face white, already deadened a little. "So she had not given up hope?" Stare. "She had hope?" Nod. "Hope, yes". "For the future?" "For the future, yes". Nod. Little smile. Young man sitting on <the> bed, knees drawn up to his chin, smoking. There was more, but the question I ask myself is this: How will these four people – my guides and the youngsters on TV – learn to speak to each other frankly in all their three languages, given their situation and their personal histories? And what about those other 199,999,996 who would have come to Hyde Park that day in June and whom I have not met and know nothing about?

1993

Russia has become a stranger to me. All my life she has provided for me: a theatre, for laughter and suffering; work, which has given me satisfaction and money; an education, in ways of life I would not have had the strength to sustain; a place, safely to house my imagination and my inner conflicts. And now she has left me to go on with her journey for which I have nothing to offer her, except my gratitude.

November 1993

LETTER TO A YOUNG ACTOR

For some time now I have had it in my mind to write you a letter and, in as few sentences as I am able, try to convey to you my experience of what makes an actor in the theatre.

I am not concerned with the training of actors or the continuing exercises of body and voice, which only become unnecessary when an actor has the opportunity to work on the stage most nights of the year. Then, his breathing moves deeply and his body responds freely to the demands made on it. When he is out of practice, acting on the stage becomes difficult and irksome and he is tempted to restrict himself to working in the media, which require less of him physically than mentally. In addition, not only does he earn more money but the severity of criticism that is meted out to the actor on the stage seldom or never touches him in films or television. There it is usual to single out the program or the movie for blame or praise and it is more often the actor's personality rather than his talent or skill which marks him out for success or the lack of it. For the actor who wishes to master the art of working on the stage, the first hurdle consists of maintaining a voice and a body equal to the challenges of the classical repertoire and a large audience. Once he possesses these tools – which are as necessary for the small part as for the great – he is also equipped for any other task his profession may throw his way.

The stage actor's body and soul are his medium; there is no screen, canvas, brush, chisel, musical instrument or pen and paper between him and his work. Like all other artists, to begin with, he learns to practice a craft. For the actor, however, the end result of his apprenticeship lies in overcoming his self. For acting becomes an art only the moment the actor is able to forget and abandon his own conscious being, in order to put himself totally and completely at the disposal of the character he is playing. With the proviso, of course, that his intelligence remains his own sovereign tool with which he oversees the planning of his performance and with which he – in the event – imperceptibly guides the execution of it: never interrupting, interfering with or dictating to the character, but remaining wide awake, still and watchful at the centre of his being, fully in control. Without developing this faculty, which has the treble function of stage manager, creative critic and imaginative spectator, the actor is at the mercy of the whims of the moment: his own state of mind, his digestion and any passing distraction. – And the way the performance of a play, however well rehearsed, can drift off course after a very few performances is well know to all who work in the theatre. It is remarkable how difficult

– and therefore rare – it is for actors themselves to notice such changes and to correct them before the balance and, sometimes, the whole purpose of the work is lost. In fact these changes mostly occur through something happening spontaneously on the stage, something which may be felt to be "good" at that moment. Few actors, however, have developed the capacity afterwards to reflect coolly on whether such a moment of satisfaction is right for their character, good for the play, the other performers or the audience and therefore worth persisting with. For instance, to make the public laugh – at what, it matters not – is, in itself, considered by many to be an achievement. And contrary to the, by critics, often expressed conviction that after the first night things will soon be well, in fact, they seldom do improve much without determined work on the part of everyone involved. Against this I must put the fact that I have never seen a performance that could not be improved upon. Rehearsal time is usually inadequate to the requirements of the play; it is often in the very moment of action that an actor is informed, by the character he is playing, about the true nature of that moment (spontaneous enlightenment about the deep layers of life is provoked in acting them out rather than thinking them out); the potential of a comedy cannot be realised without an audience, and so on and so on... What is more, actors are notoriously in a difficult position, exposed as they are face to face with an audience, night after night, whatever the quality of the play or the state of the production: they naturally cover up cracks; they have to convey sense where the material they work with only provides nonsense; they have to generate energy in situations where none is to be found, and, having to earn a living, they can hardly be blamed for the present confusion and the lack of standards in a world which offers them the highest financial reward for the most contemptible product. But, in the end, it is the actor himself who is the pair of scales on which the balance has to be struck between the disciplined form necessary to sustain a sequence of performances and the appearance of spontaneous life, which cannot be achieved without creative freedom. These paradoxes are of course inherent in all art. The more self-contradictions an actor can sustain between what he is saying, doing, thinking and feeling, the more interesting the character he is playing becomes. Indeed there have been actors whose whole career and success have been based on the enigma presented by their personality.

It is a feature of our time to value thinking and abstract intellectual activity above all the other capacities we possess. The attention and importance that the intellect has been awarded has had a not inconsiderable effect on the acting profession and the theatre as a whole – not forgetting the theatre schools. The trouble is that it has seldom been made clear enough to the student that human thought in itself has no life. There <sic! – BH, AR> attaches neither vitality nor feeling to it. The point I am making is this: if the actor has approached a play and a character as in an intellectual task, he by definition has cut himself off from the very source of acting in himself, namely, his creative imagination in all its human contradictions, and instead, he has – perhaps without knowing it – committed himself to reproduce on the stage a blueprint, which he has thought out from reading the text. The result can only be a demonstration of a product of his brain, however he dresses it up, not acting. That is why, in acting, pure thinking needs to be forged into <a> separate weapon in the actor's armoury which I have already described. Conveying a thought on the stage is a different proposition. If we study the playwrights who have wrestled with the problem of transmitting purely intellectual conceptions through their plays, writers like Shaw, Brecht or Stoppard, we soon find that wit, humour, farce and bathos have been used as the theatrical leaven in order to make palatable the intellectual bread. Indeed, in requires great displays of talent in quite different fields for us not to reject the "boring bits". The actor therefore is advised to interweave some more personal attitude or feeling with his understanding of what he is saying when he is required to express intellectual conceptions. (The quality of wisdom, being a thing of the spirit, is given <to> only few actors to embody).

Do not misunderstand me: the more an actor uses his perceptiveness and intelligence in life, the broader the material he will have at his disposal will be for his work but the kind of intelligence that an actor needs most in approaching a play and a part is an intelligence of the heart, the widest possible warmhearted understanding of himself and of others of which he is capable. Prejudice and fear of life are the enemies of acting. They make a personality narrow and timid. In order to act a character who is narrow and timid the actor should be able not only to embrace him with sympathy but also to intensify and bring out into the open these qualities of fear and timidity which the fearful and timid as a rule do their utmost to conceal from others. Apart from his own experience of life, by reading the great authors, poets and playwrights, listening to the great composers, soloists and singers and studying the great painters and draughtsmen the actor will learn about and enrich his work. Throughout his life he has these most rewarding and pleasurable occupations to aid him. Reading allows him to share in the experiences of the ages and acquaints him with characters of such potency and fascination that they have a life far longer than any mortal being. Music teaches him about feeling in sound and the – for an actor – vital art of phrasing and variation of tone. Painting and the graphic arts train his eye and his judgement in respect of appearance and the importance of detail for the whole. And, of course, much, much more than this, for it is only through learning to recognise all that which raises us above the ordinary that we ourselves can aspire to rise above the trivial.

When it comes to studying a part the first thing, for me, is losing myself in the words. (For others, pictures, appearances, relationships and whatever may come first). A play, a part comes to life for me through the words. The word – to me, you understand – is a living thing. At each moment, in each mouth, it has a different sound and different meaning. It is only by forgetting oneself and sinking deeply into the lines that the character begins to speak within one. It is now that one needs the ability to concentrate totally on the material one has been given to work on. (Exercises in meditation, that is, acquiring control over one's mind through practicing inner stillness and forgetfulness of oneself and the world outside, are a sure way to increase one's powers of concentration). The aim for the actor in studying his part will be to penetrate so profoundly into the text that the words he is going to speak begin to sing within him with such might that, when he utters them on the stage they will reach right into the heart and mind of the most indifferent member of his audience. Such speaking may be loud but it need not be. Speech can be luminous in any mood or tone of voice as long as it is true to the moment. For myself, I can only proceed to action when I have a sure sense that the life of the play (read: part) has taken root inside me. Then it is exciting to find out the how of the action. (For some actors it may be a hat that reveals the character, and the voice and all the rest comes to him as a consequence of finding the hat. Working like this from the outside in is as good a way as the other – provided it leads the actor into the character in the end).

The role which the actor's own personality plays in his work is becoming an increasingly urgent subject for exploration. The subject might be expressed like this: acting is based on the notion that the actor is able to forget himself and inhabit someone else; performing is based on the ability of the performer to be himself unreservedly and naturally in front of an audience. The actual truth of the matter for everyone lies in somewhere between these two extremes. It is the nature of the time in which we find ourselves that accomplished performers are at a premium. The cinema and television as a rule demand performances indistinguishable from the behaviour of people in daily life. Even the exaggerations of violent or villainous behaviour must be kept within the bounds of the believable, which leads actors capable of it into psychopathic exhibitions. I have heard of an actor, known for her work on the stage, who at an interview for a film job was told by the director – famous for the faithful imitation of life in his films – "I know you are an actor but, never mind, I think you can do it". Now, it is in the nature of a naturalistic performance that the actor to a very high degree has to base it on himself. It need not be his innermost private self that he is exhibiting but, to all intents and purposes, he has to lend his own self as material for the performance.

How is it then that there is a difference between acting and performing? For when we see an actor truly acting a part we know that nevertheless there is a person present at the heart of the character who cannot be anyone else but the being of the actor. After all, he is not a medium who allows himself to be possessed from outside by some other being. What we see on the stage in a genuinely acted character is palpably a living person who cannot in the final analysis be anyone but the actor in the part. And on the other hand, when we see, say, an amateur performance we may be shown a character and at the same time recognise the personality of the actor who is showing us this character. In acting the secret then must lie in the ability of the actor to forget, withhold or conceal his private self and – in creating and making room for the character to use his body and soul – nevertheless enter into his creation with some essence of his own being to give it life, presence and authenticity.

These are processes which escape beyond the limits of our consciousness and are concealed from our view. We cannot will them into being, yet it is possible for us to make them come about, but it takes time, often a very long time, to refine and change one's own self. What is required is that we rid ourselves of our prejudices. Everything we think we know once and for all; the whole range of what and whom we like and whom we dislike; our firm ideas of right and wrong; all this stands in the way of becoming an actor, because we need to be free to imaginatively discover everything about the character we are to play. Now we see what makes a performer: he is tied to his private self in a way which means that he is forced to pass character and situation through his own personality, such as it is. Only in this way can he appear before an audience. The true stage actor, however, who is open to all that is human, finds his way into a character through the study, concentration and practice of self-forgetfulness which takes place as much in private as in rehearsal.

The secret of art is this: that we penetrate deep enough into our own being to reach some stream from the source we share with others and that we find our own individual expression for what we have there experienced.

Here are <the> contradictions we have to understand and come <to> terms with. Anything that is true, real and valid but expressed in general terms is both lifeless and unconvincing, when applied to human beings. On the other hand, the merely personal may amuse, annoy or arouse indifference. Only that which arises from our deepest experiences of the inner and the outer world when they are harmoniously fused together and expressed in a way uniquely individual to ourselves, is endowed with the power to convince and enlighten.

I hope you will forgive that in trying to articulate my thoughts and experiences I have used at times words too uncompromising to reflect the tangled and imperfect realities which apply to myself and you in equal measure.

II STUDENT FEEDBACK

(Produced after watching Wrede's *One Day in the Life of Ivan Denisovich* as part of the course on Russian fiction (Proosa-analyysi) at the Department of Slavonic and Baltic Languages and Literatures, University of Helsinki, on 15 November 2007.)

Student 1:

Like the novel, the film refrains from revelling in the horrors of the camp life and from dramatizing events. It remains true to the plot and the narrative mode, and the result is that it feels as genuine as the book.

Especially moving is the scene when in the Siberian cold the prisoners are walking towards their working place with the guards on all sides and surrounded by white snow. The film dwells upon this scene without trying to explain it; you can only guess what is going on in the minds of the prisoners.

Student 2:

The film is even more impressive than the book. It goes deeper and makes you realize how hard life was in the camp. Hardly anything is added or taken away from the novel. The film does not accentuate any part of the novel, but has the same documentary touch. One of the most moving and beautiful scenes, both in the novel and in the film, is when Shukhov gives the rest of his cigarette to his deaf friend Senka. The Norwegian winter landscape with the light from the lamps of the camp is especially good. The dialogue functions better in the film than in the book. Ivan's thoughts are given through a narrator, a solution which gives the story depth.

Student 3:

The book and the film are fairly different. The atmosphere of the film is very depressing. It focuses on the miserable and cruel side of the Soviet system. This is to be sure also to be found in the book, but there the accent is different. The overall message of the book is more positive and the atmosphere is brighter. In the film the atmosphere is created by long, silent scenes. These scenes give an idea of an endless row of days ahead. The colours are either dark or cold blue. Tom Courtenay is good and credible in the main role. It is the same kind of calm and thoughtful character <as Ivan Denisovich in the book>.

Student 4:

The film is a successful rendering of the novel. It delivers the message in a straightforward way, without any "lakirovka" <varnish>.

Student 5:

The film is true to the events of the book. Still, the narrative solution is different. In the book you have a narrator, who at times comes close to Ivan's point of view. Sometimes the narrator closely relates Ivan's thoughts and feelings in Ivan's own language, sometimes there is a distance between them, as when the narrator talks about Ivan, using his surname. The other characters are presented through the dialogue.

The hierarchy of Alyoshka sleeping above Ivan and Tsesar below him is important. It is symbolic when you think of Solzhenitsyn's later development, but it is also interesting that he chose the one in the middle as his chief protagonist.

The narrator of the film is much more distant than the narrator of the book. The choice to have him speak in Norwegian accentuates the distance. On the other hand, the camera is often turned towards Ivan's face, while he is not much described in the novel. We also see both Tsesar and Alyoshka as sharply as Ivan. In some episodes, the point of view of the film is Ivan's point of view, as during the march or when he looks at Tsesar's tobacco. Still, Ivan of the film remains more distant.

Many scenes have a strong black-and-white contrast. A strong scene is where you see dark men working in the white snow with their pickaxes. The scene reminds you of Platonov's *Kotlovan* and other Soviet novels where work is the main theme. Solzhenitsyn also shows that work can be gratifying. I liked the way <the team's> work between lunch and evening was positively described. Simultaneously, the minimalist, depressing music created a slightly absurd atmosphere.

At the end of the day Alyoshka asks Ivan what he would do with freedom and the question remains as yet unanswered. In the film, the estrangement is made obvious also spatially, as the camera moves away from the lights of the camp. This diminishing electrical little island is like an ironical comment to the famous slogan – "Socialism is Soviet power plus the electrification of the whole country".

Student 6:

The film is in its own way even more moving than the book, perhaps because you can see all the horrors and suffering with your own eyes. Gopchik, who reminds Ivan Denisovich of his own son, remains rather invisible in the film.

Student 7:

The film is very true to the book. Just like the novel, it tells about life in the camp in a low-key tone. The only difference is how successfully the description of the ice-cold day actually reaches the audience. In many ways the film is successful. Especially the decoration, the clothing and the music create a good illusion of Siberia. The reader of the book must make all this up himself.

Still the film remains somehow empty, something is never rendered. The decision to have the narrator talk in Norwegian is a failure, as it destroys the realistic illusion. Already the English language does not sound credible in this connection. Simultaneously the narrator, who in the novel is all but omniscient, is in the film somewhere high above the story, losing his contact with Ivan and the camp. You cannot but wonder why the narrator was needed.

The characters of the film remain more distant, you are not able to identify yourself with any of them. The whole story is just a stretch of every day events. The directing of the film could have been more experimental.

III MIKHAIL DEMIN'S DRAWINGS FOR THE SET OF CASPER WREDE'S *ONE DAY IN THE LIFE OF IVAN DENISOVICH* (for explanatory descriptions, see the Pre-production section)

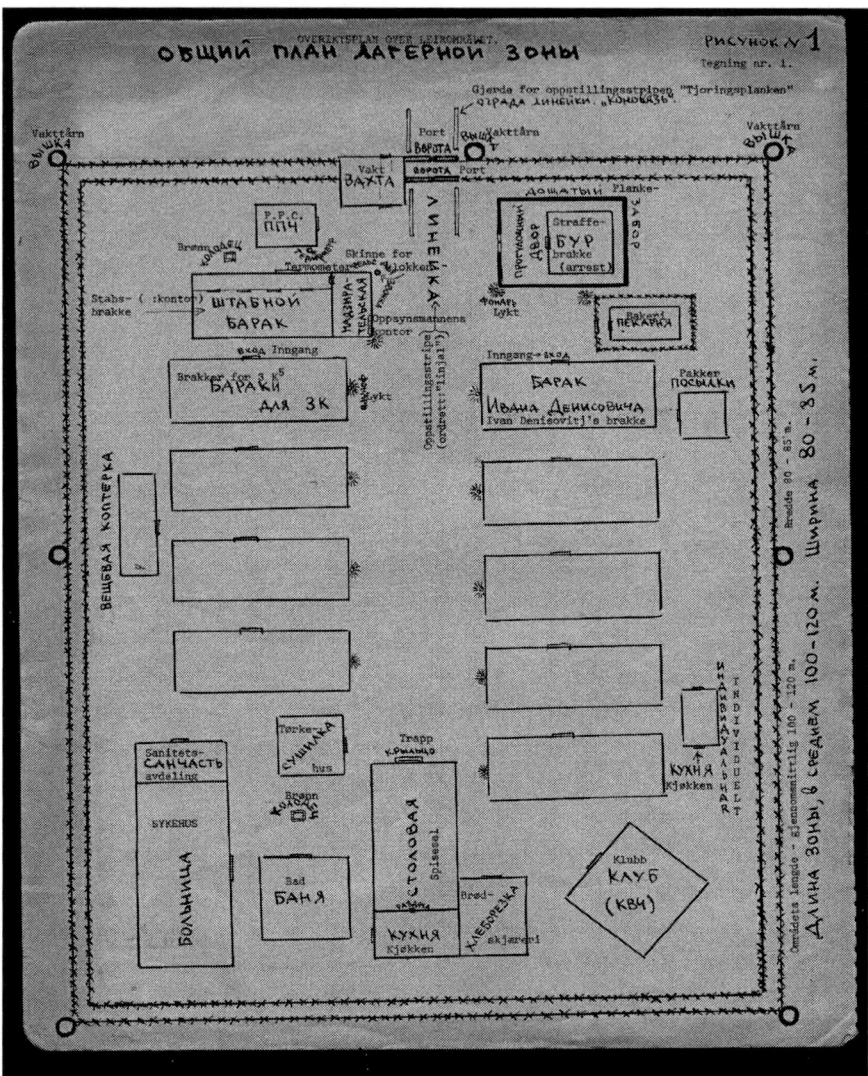

Pic. 1

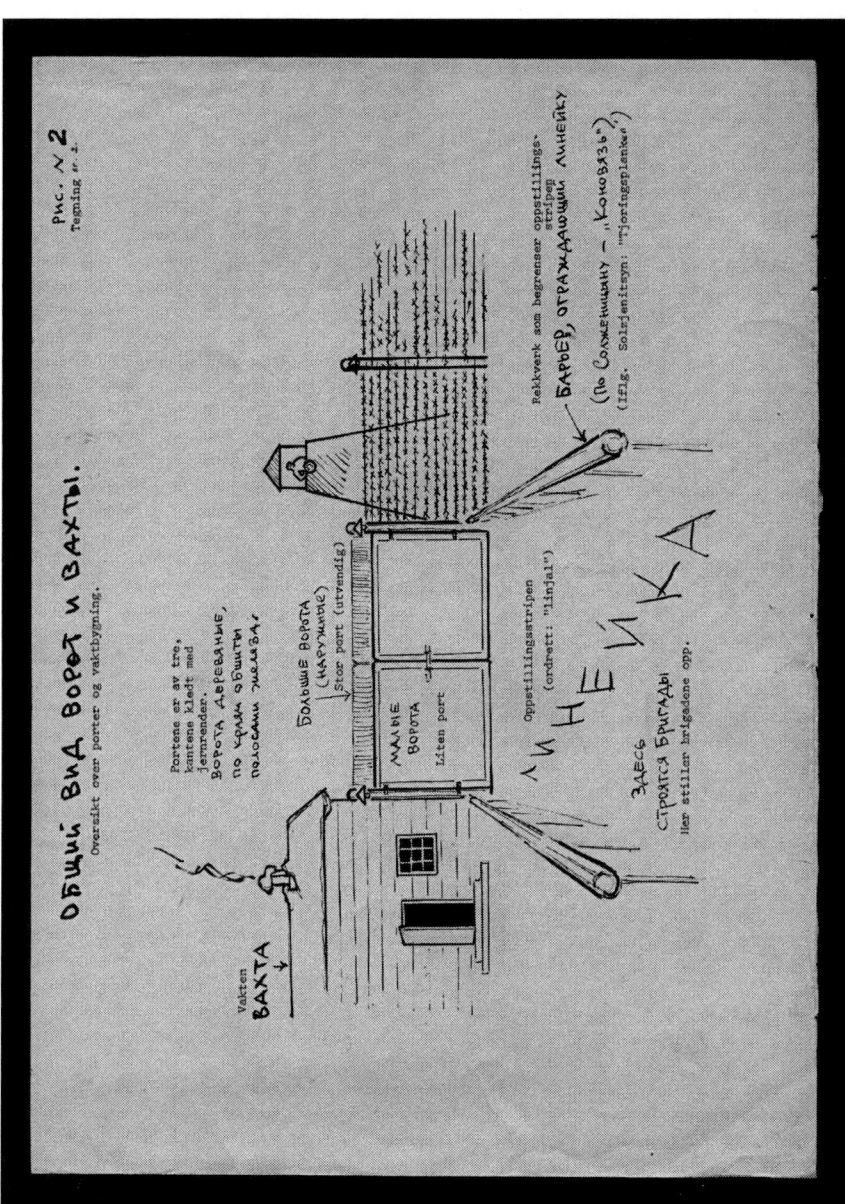

Pic. 2

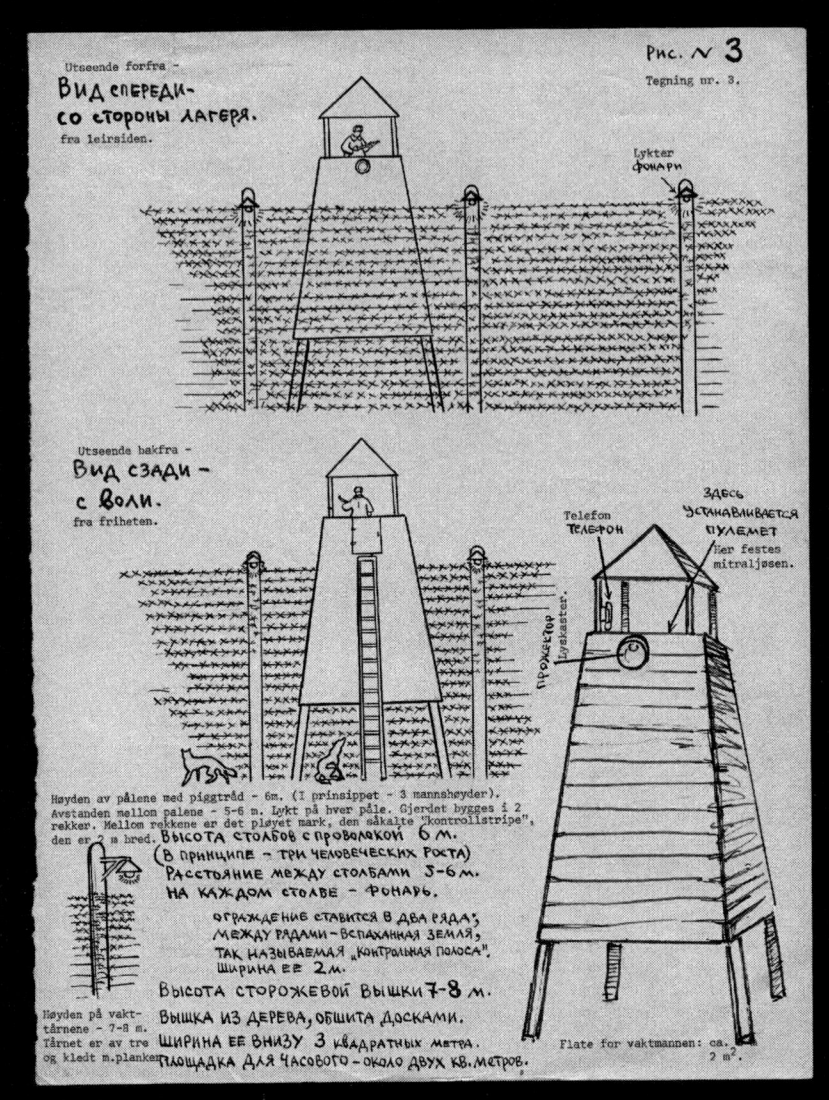

Pic. 3

FILMING THE UNFILMABLE 191

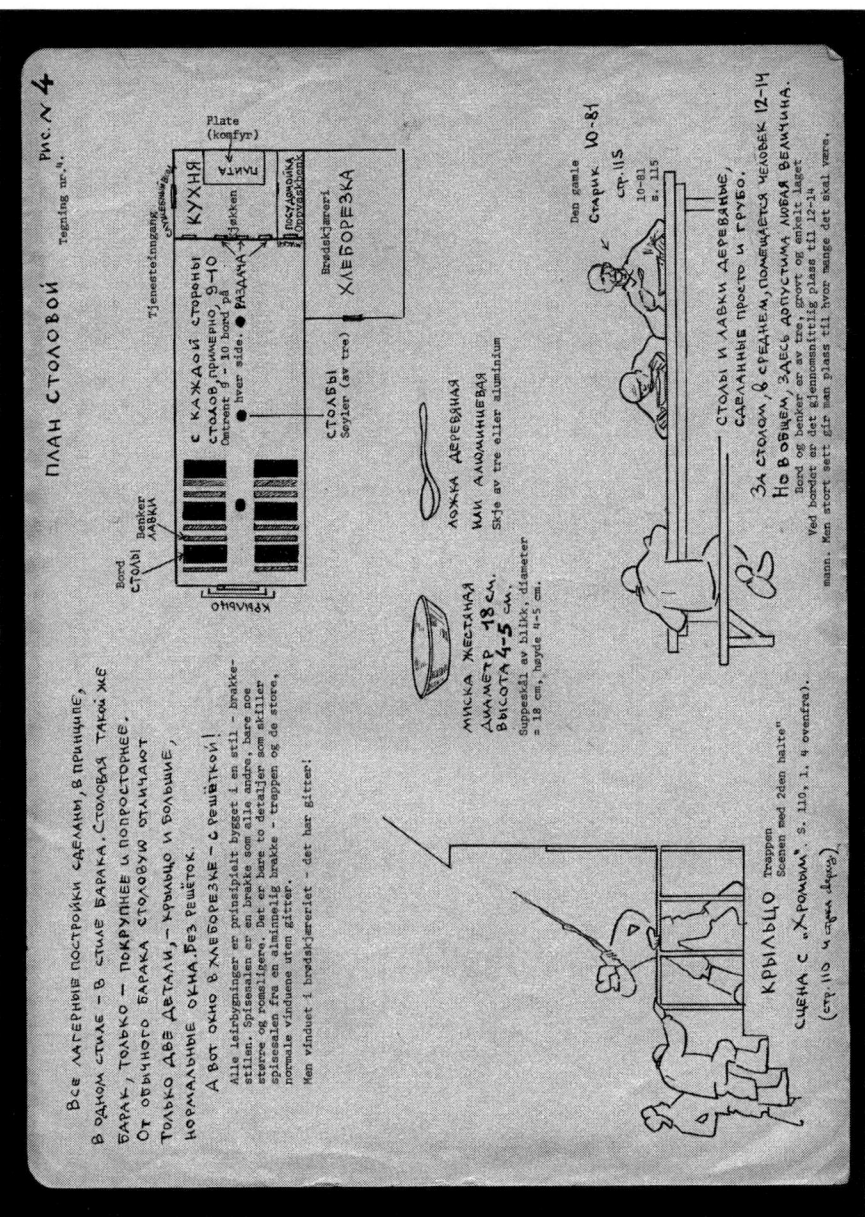

Pic. 4

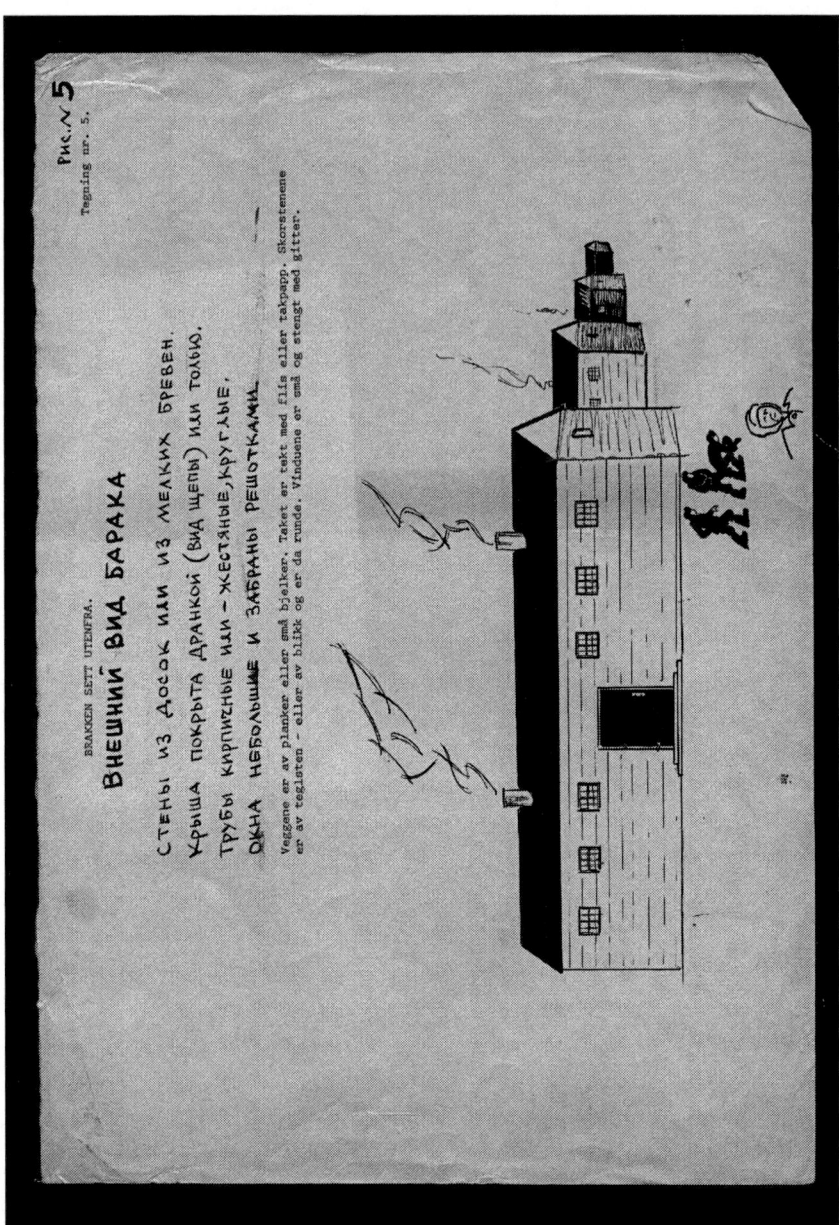

Pic. 6

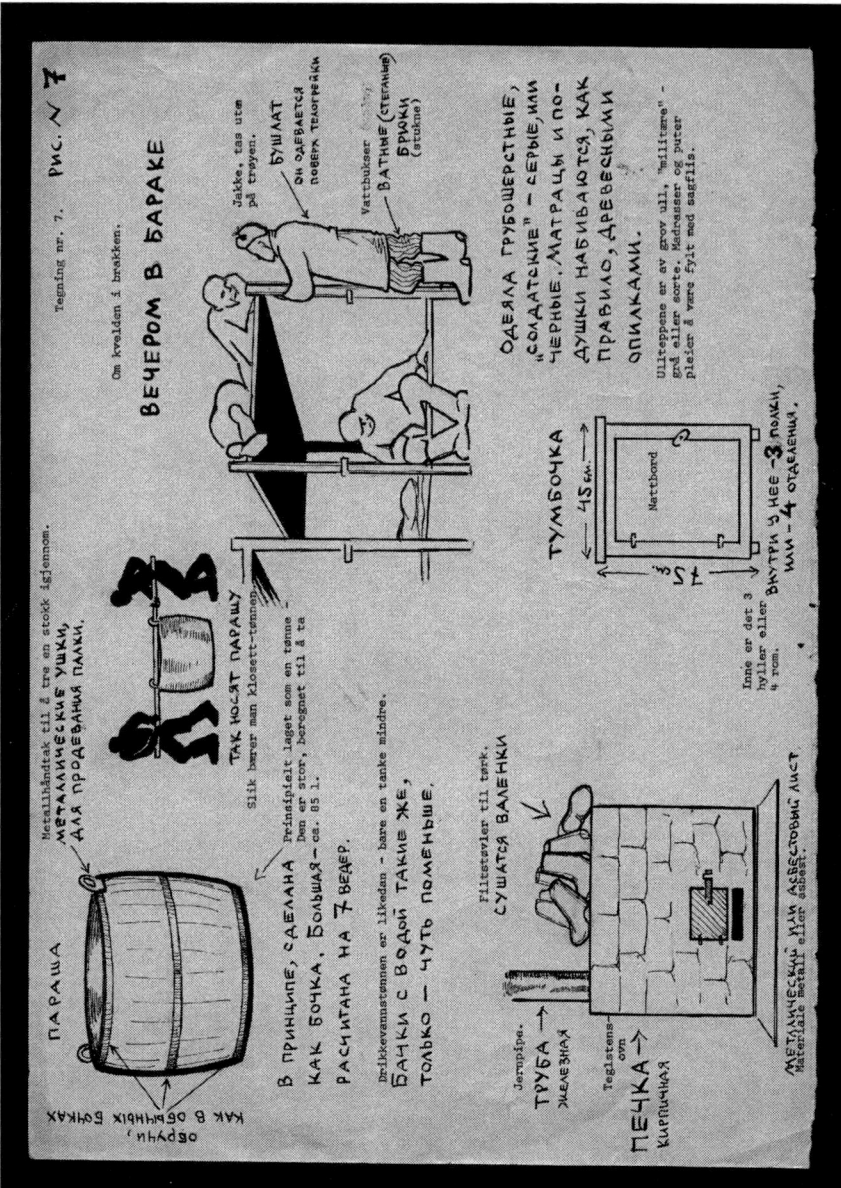

Pic. 7

FILMING THE UNFILMABLE

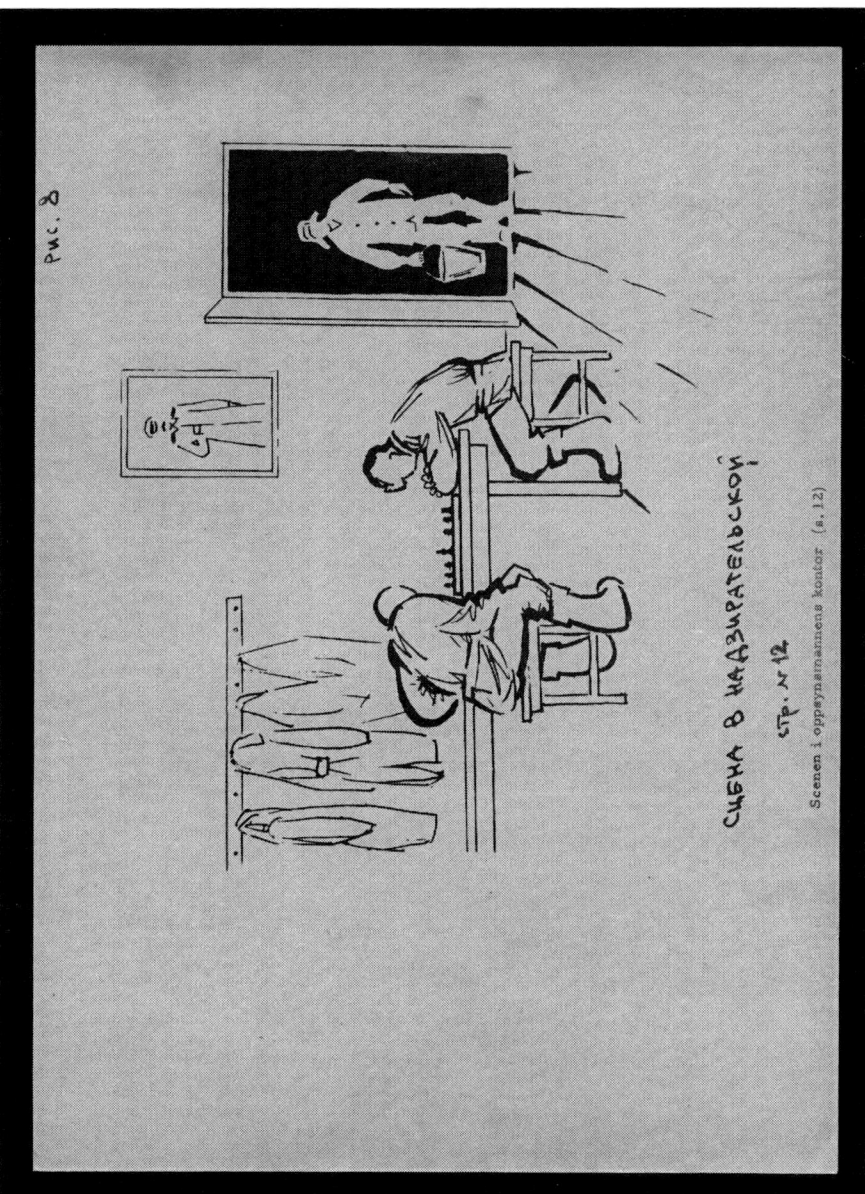

Pic. 8

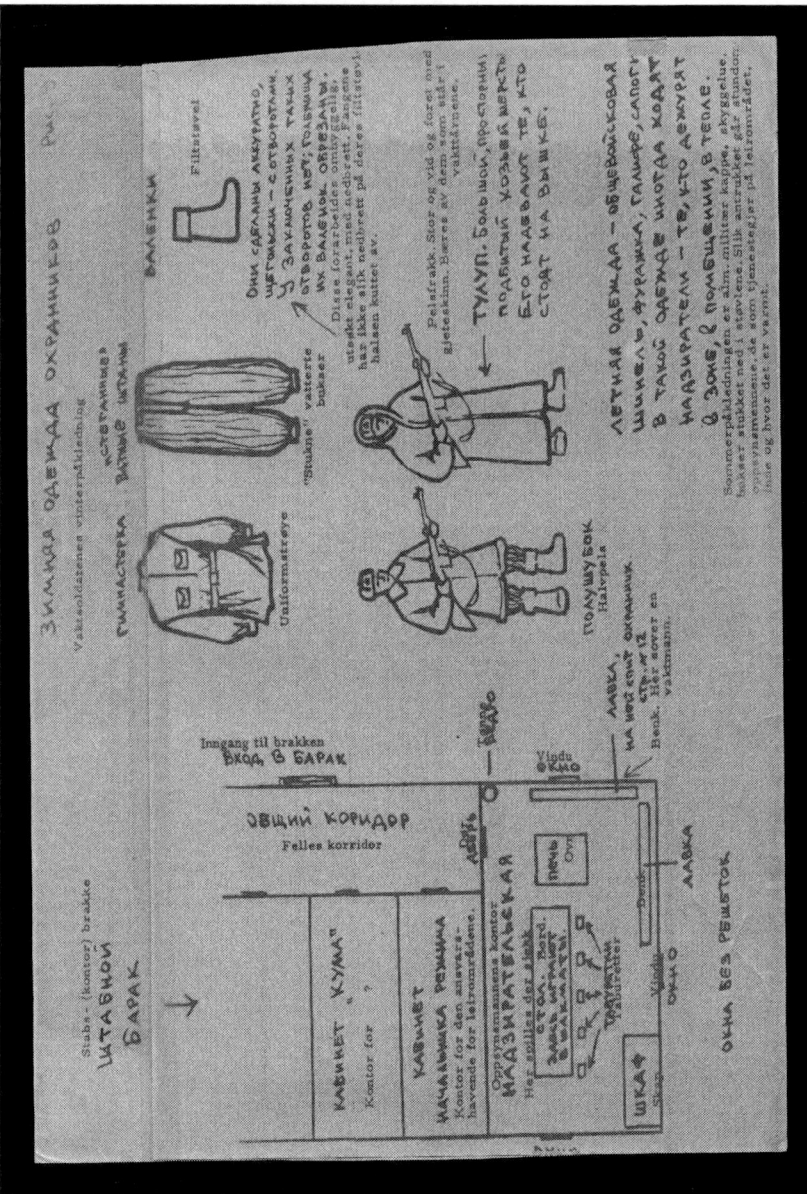

Pic. 9

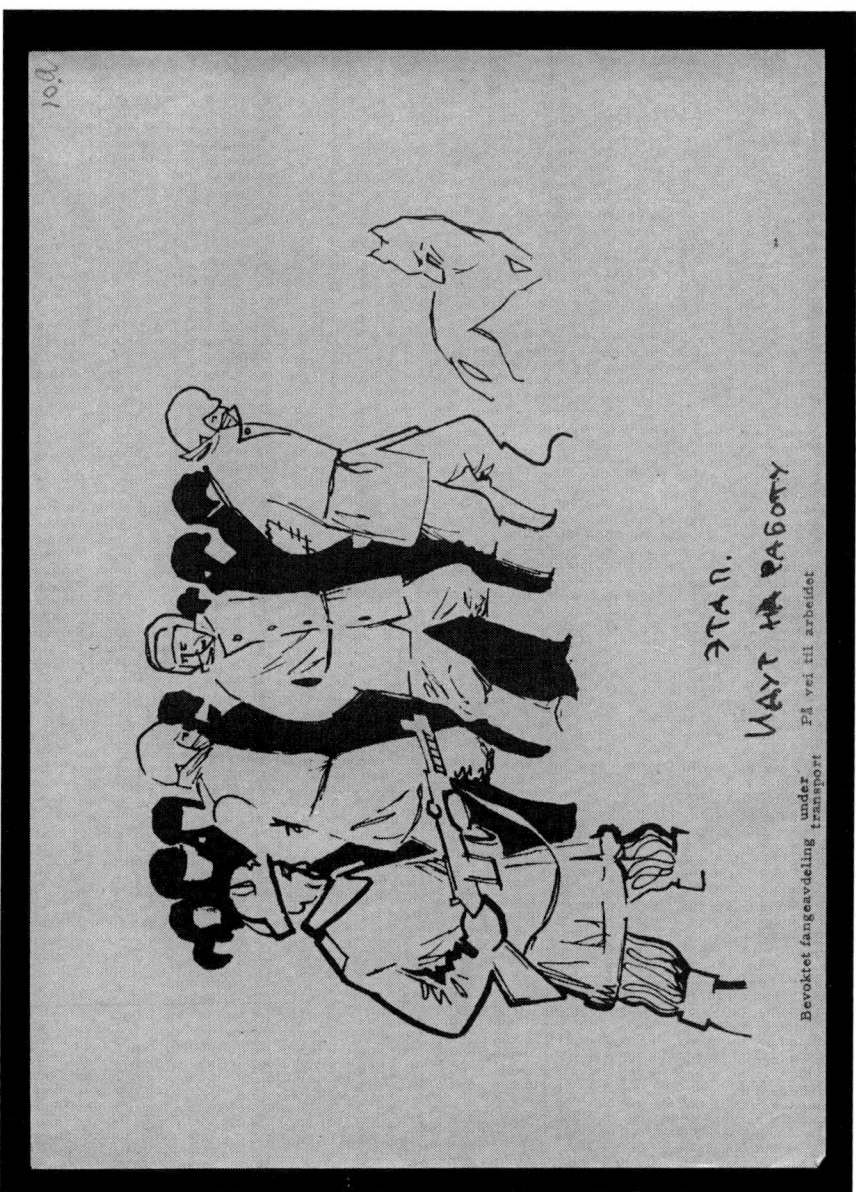

Pic. 10

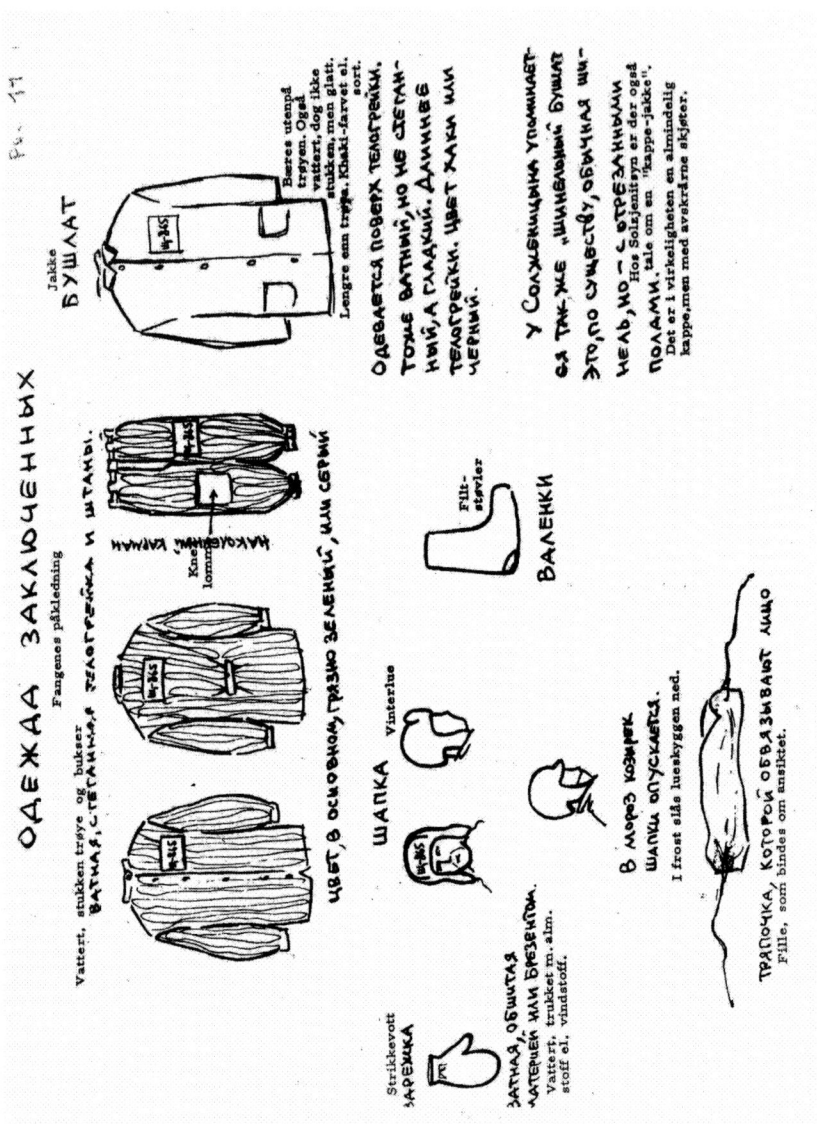

Pic. 11

Pic. 12

Pic. 13

Pic. 14

Pic. 15

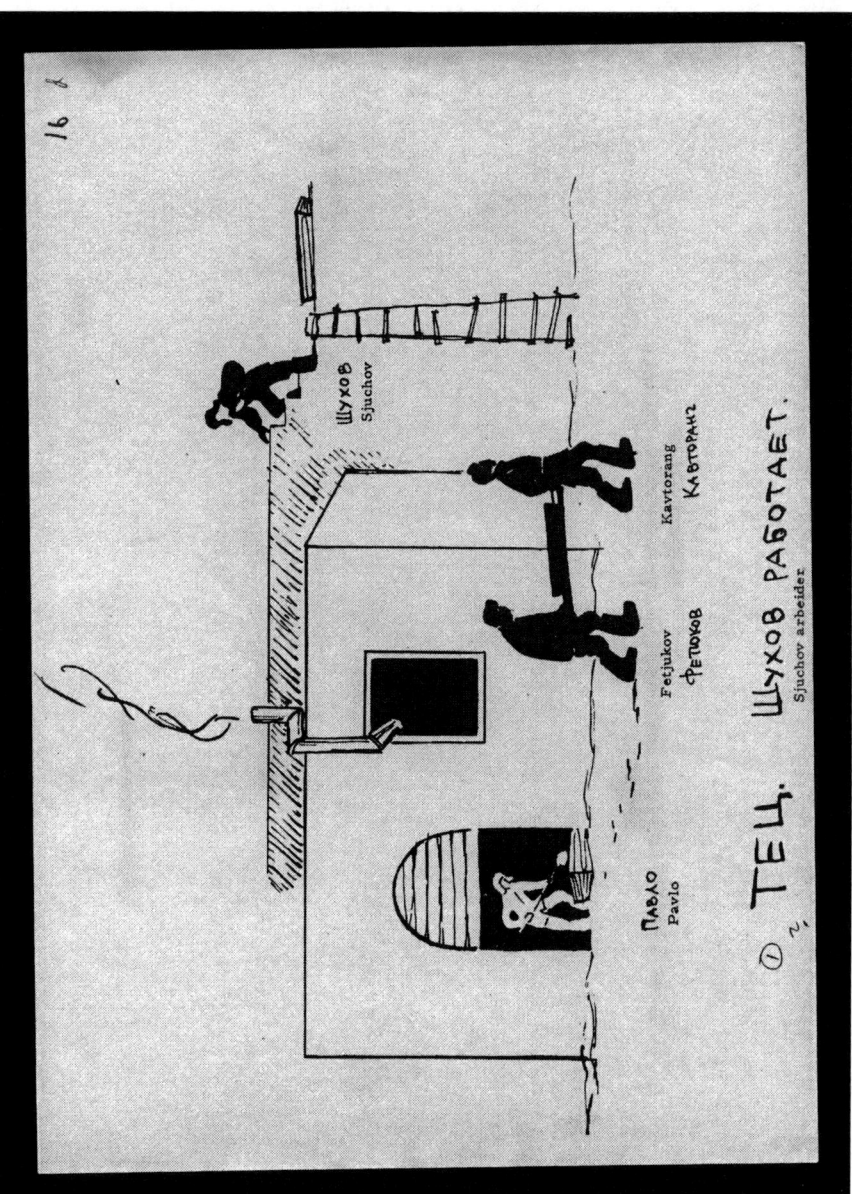

Pic. 16

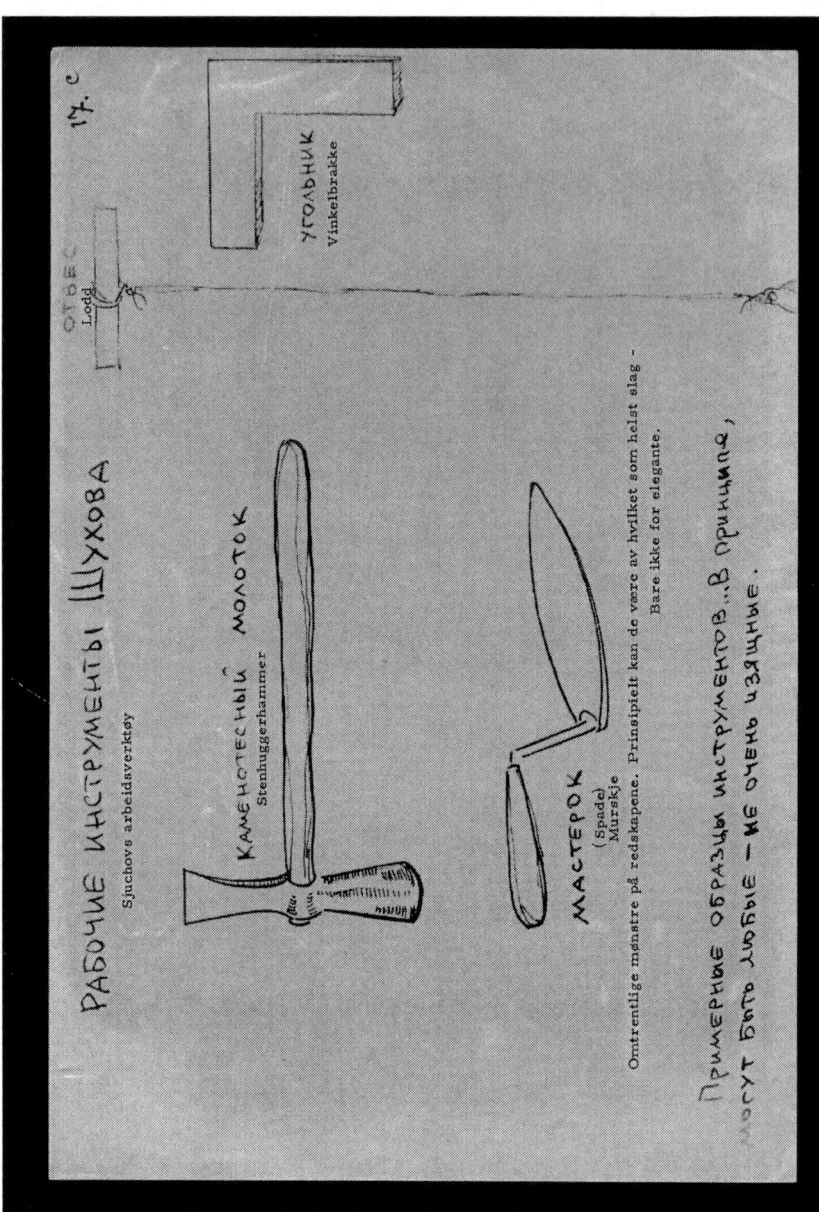

Pic. 17

Pic. 18

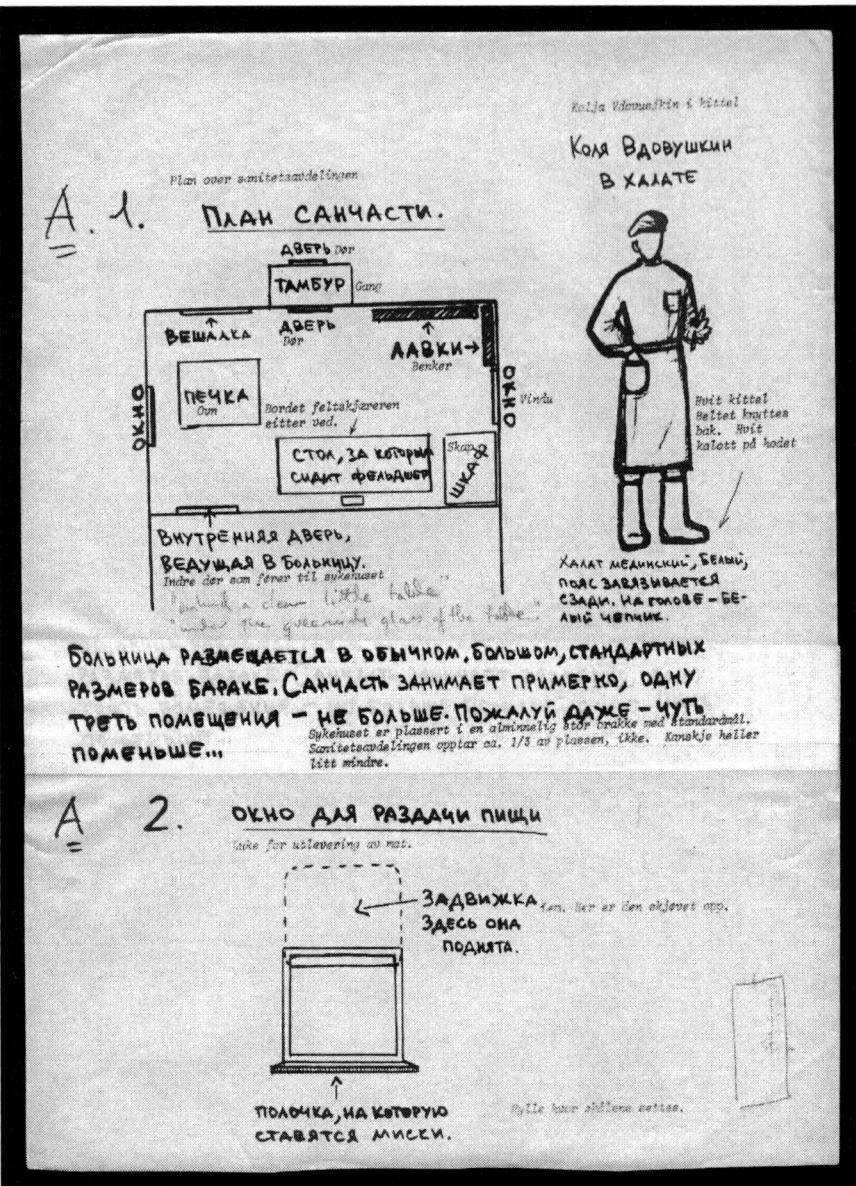

Pic. 19

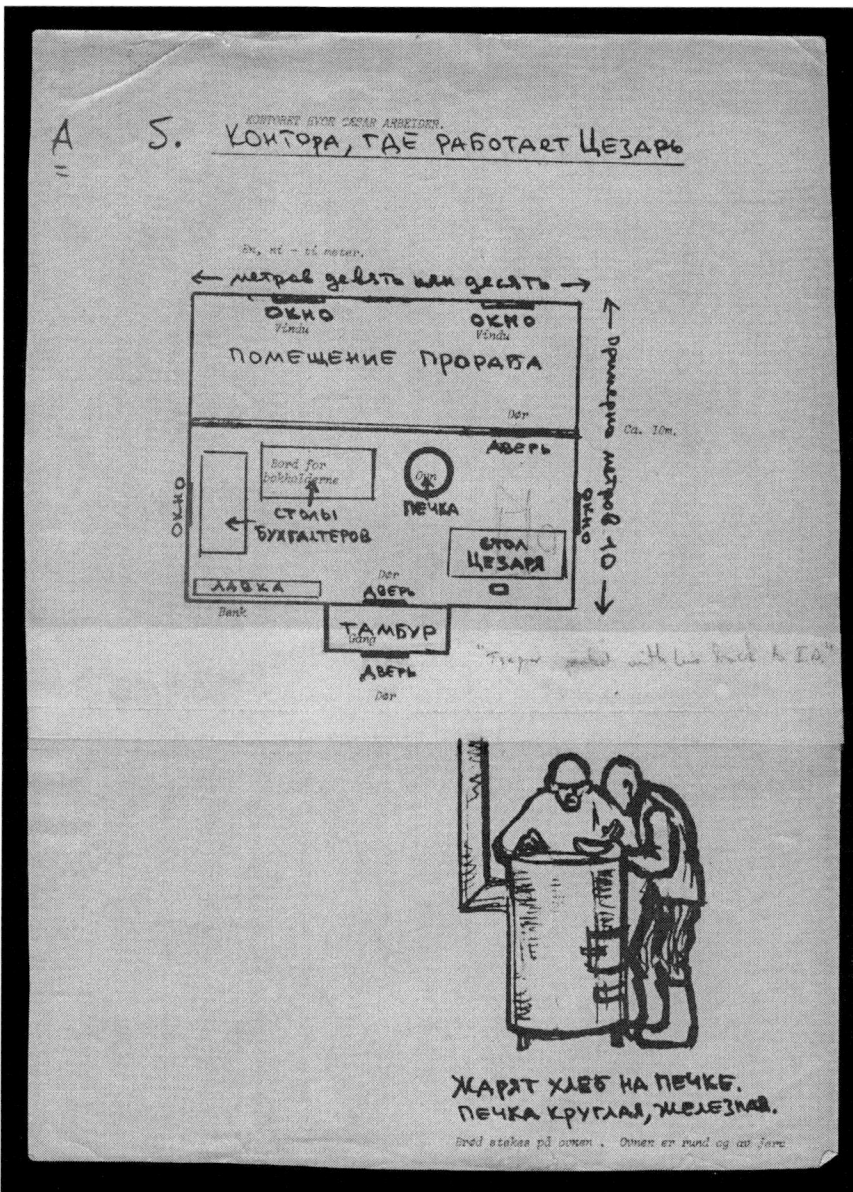

Pic. 20

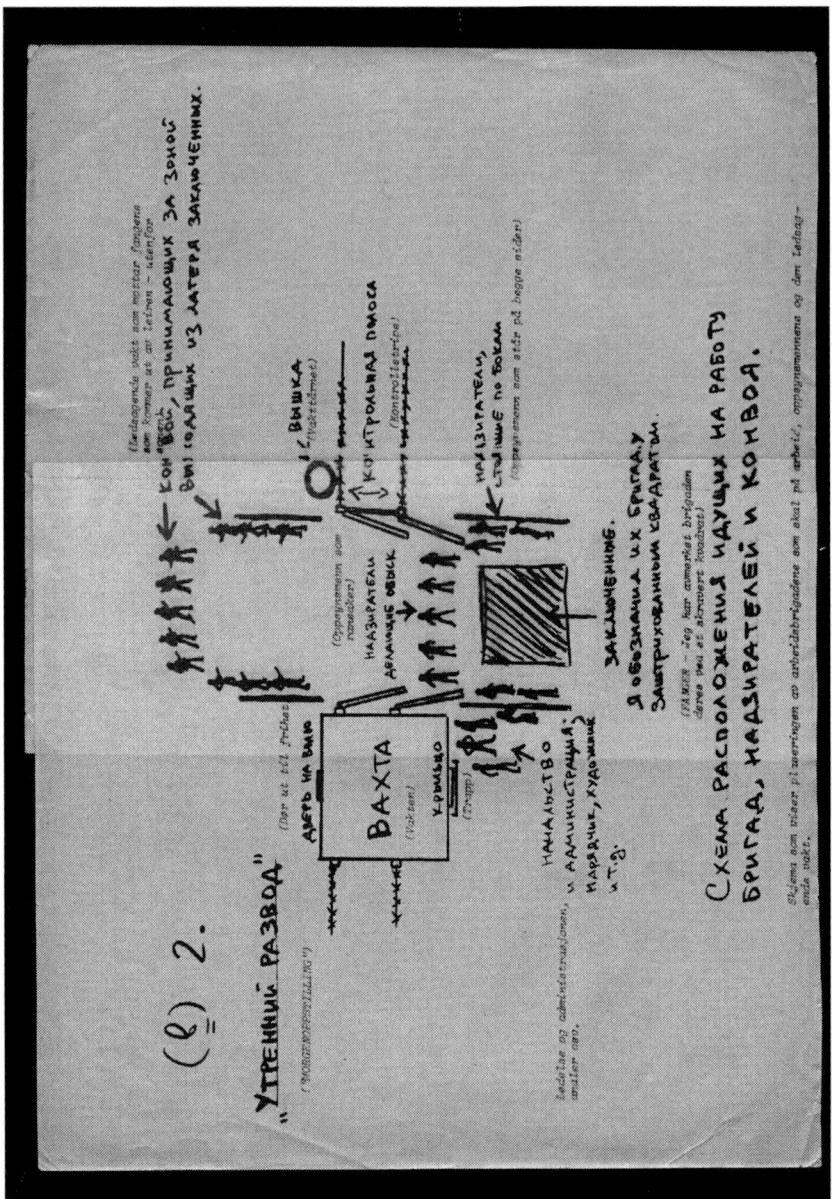

Pic. 21

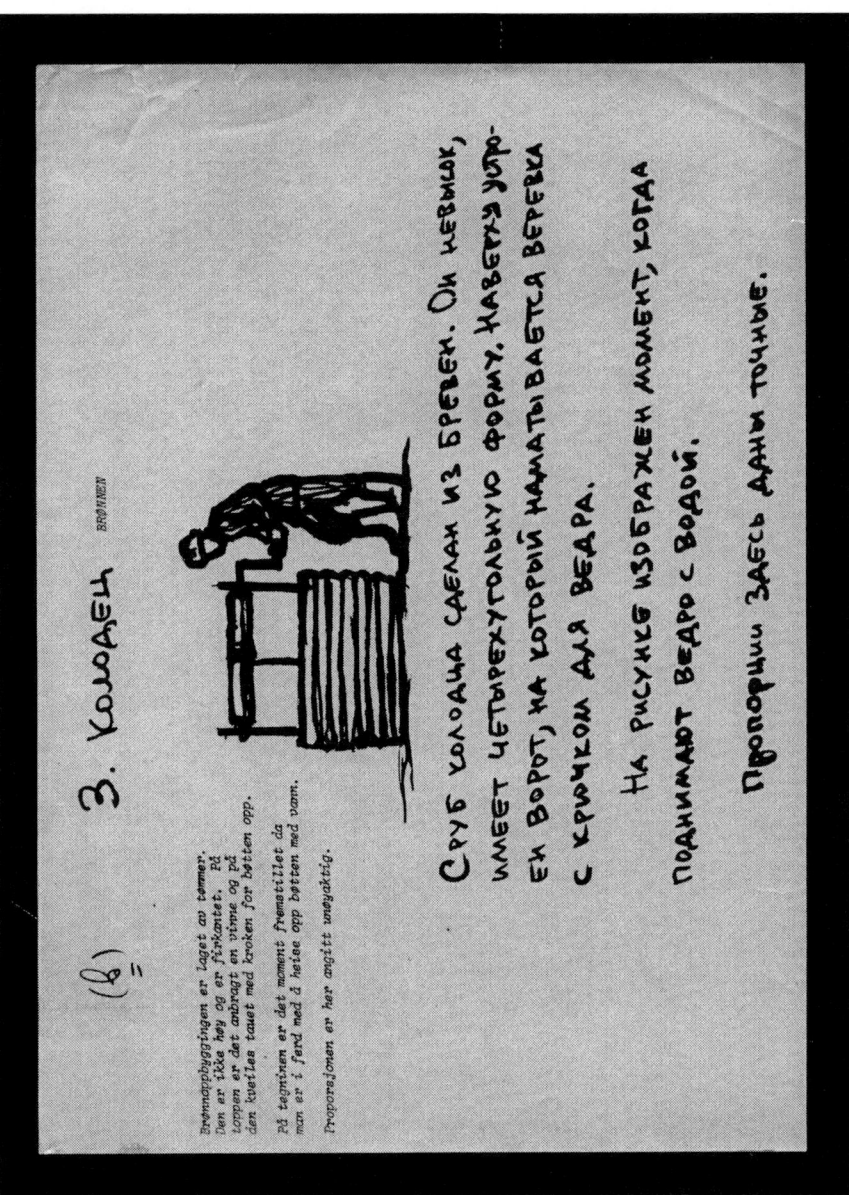

Pic. 22

Pic. 23

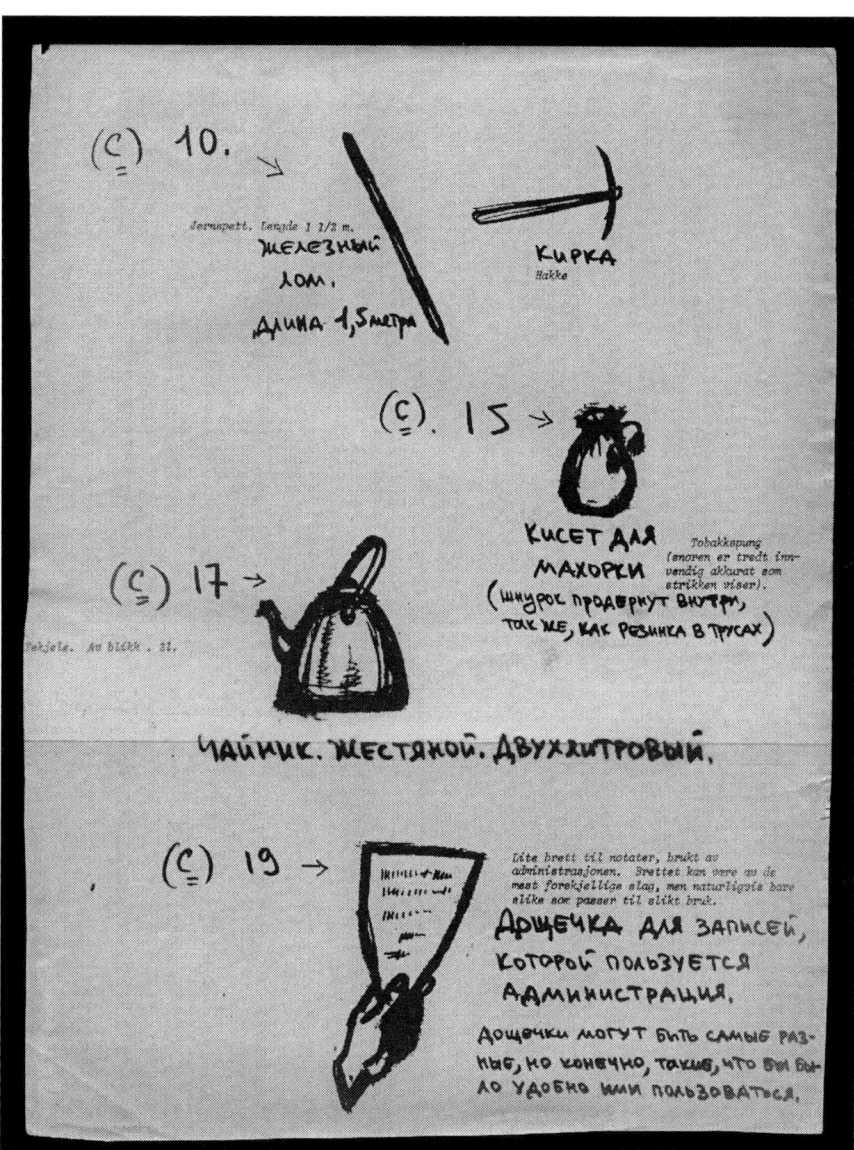

Pic. 24

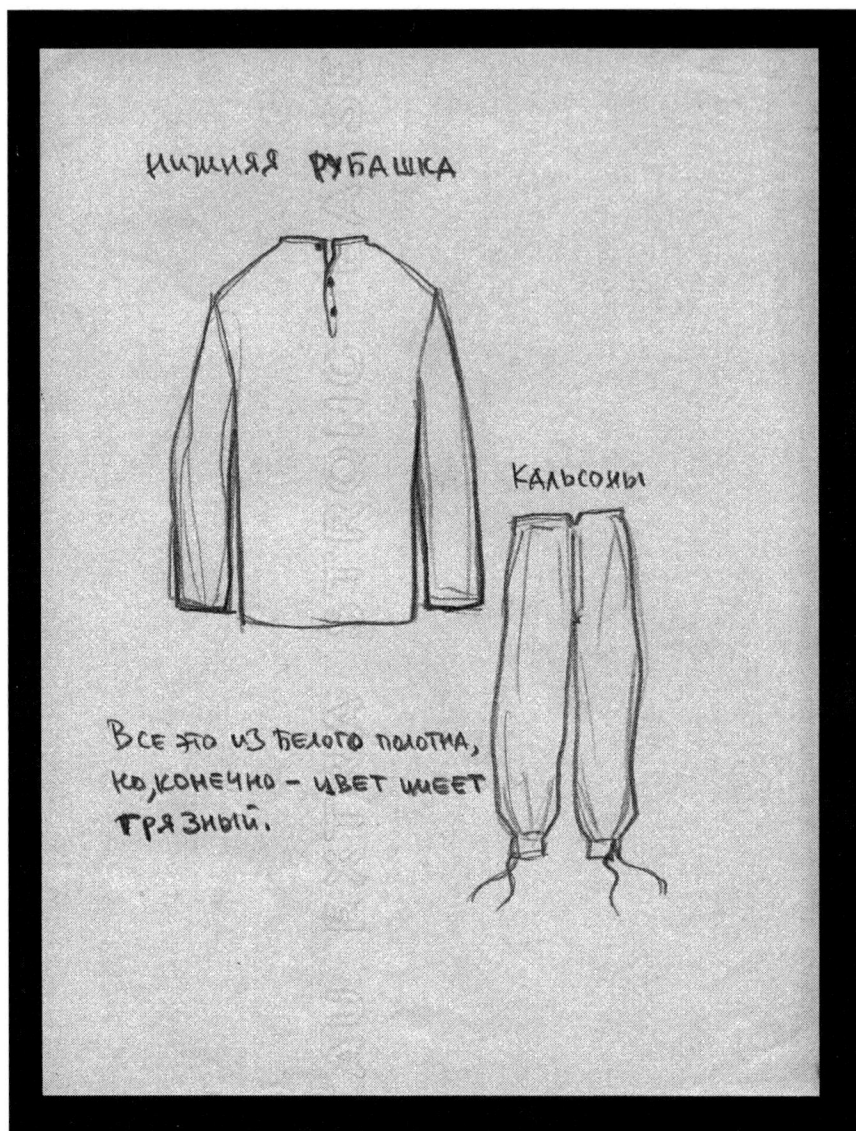

Pic. 25

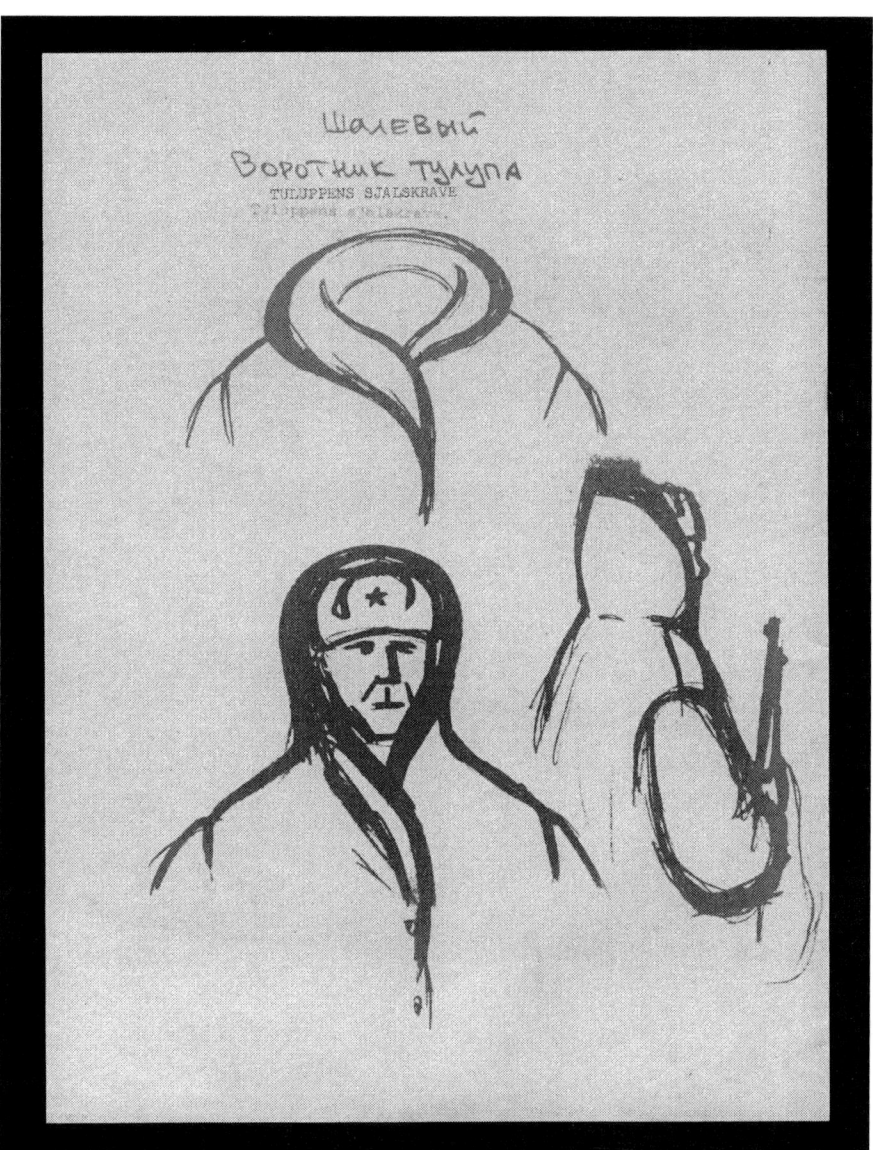

Pic. 26

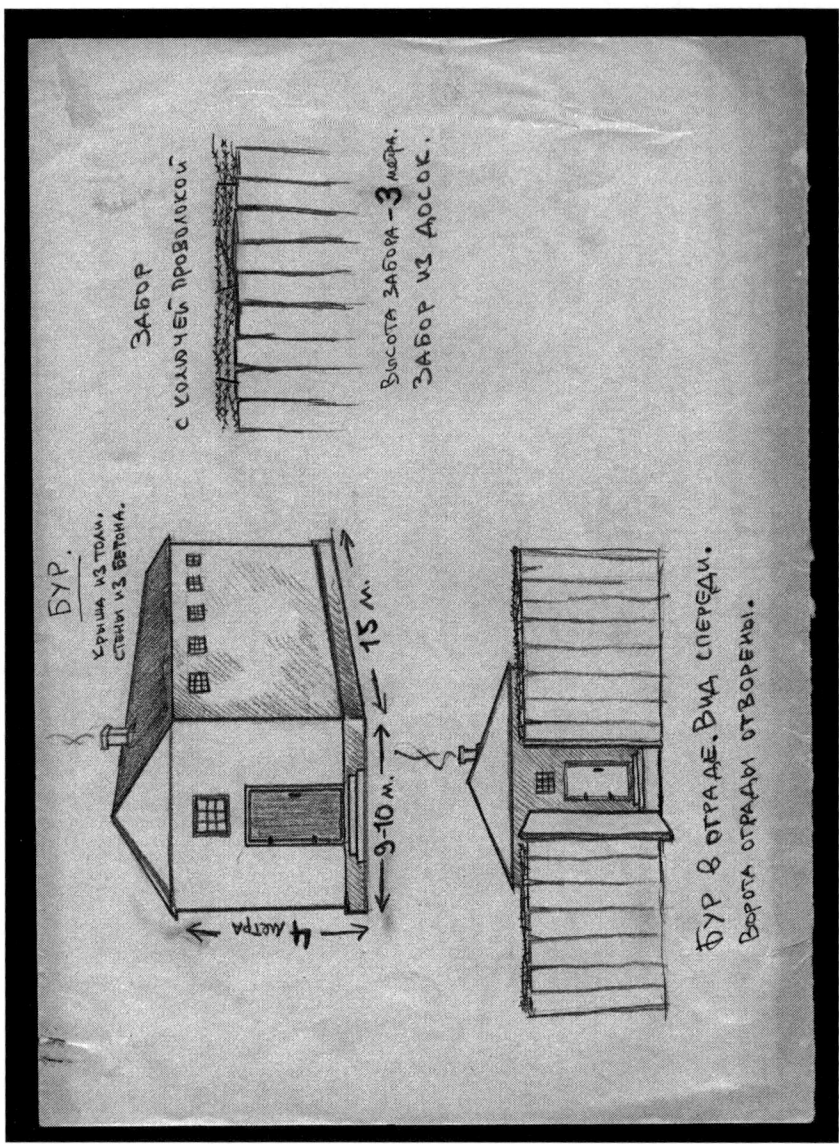

Pic. 27

Pic. 28

IV   OTHER ILLUSTRATIONS

Pic. 1. Wrede Coat of Arms

Pic. 2. A portrait of the young Casper Wrede, by Leif Knudsen (1928-75)

Pic. 3. Amund Hønningstad

Pic. 4. A leaflet advertising the Turisthotell in Røros, where the crew of *Ivan Denisovich* stayed when filming on location in Norway

Pic. 5. A model of the labour camp based on Mikhail Demin's drawings

FILMING THE UNFILMABLE 221

Pic. 6. A barbed wire fence erected on location near Røros

Pic. 7. Casper Wrede on location scouting near Røros

Pic. 8. On the set of *Ivan Denisovich*. Left to right: Casper Wrede, Espen Skjønberg, Tom Courtenay, Sven Nykvist, Alf Malland and Frimann Falck Clausen.

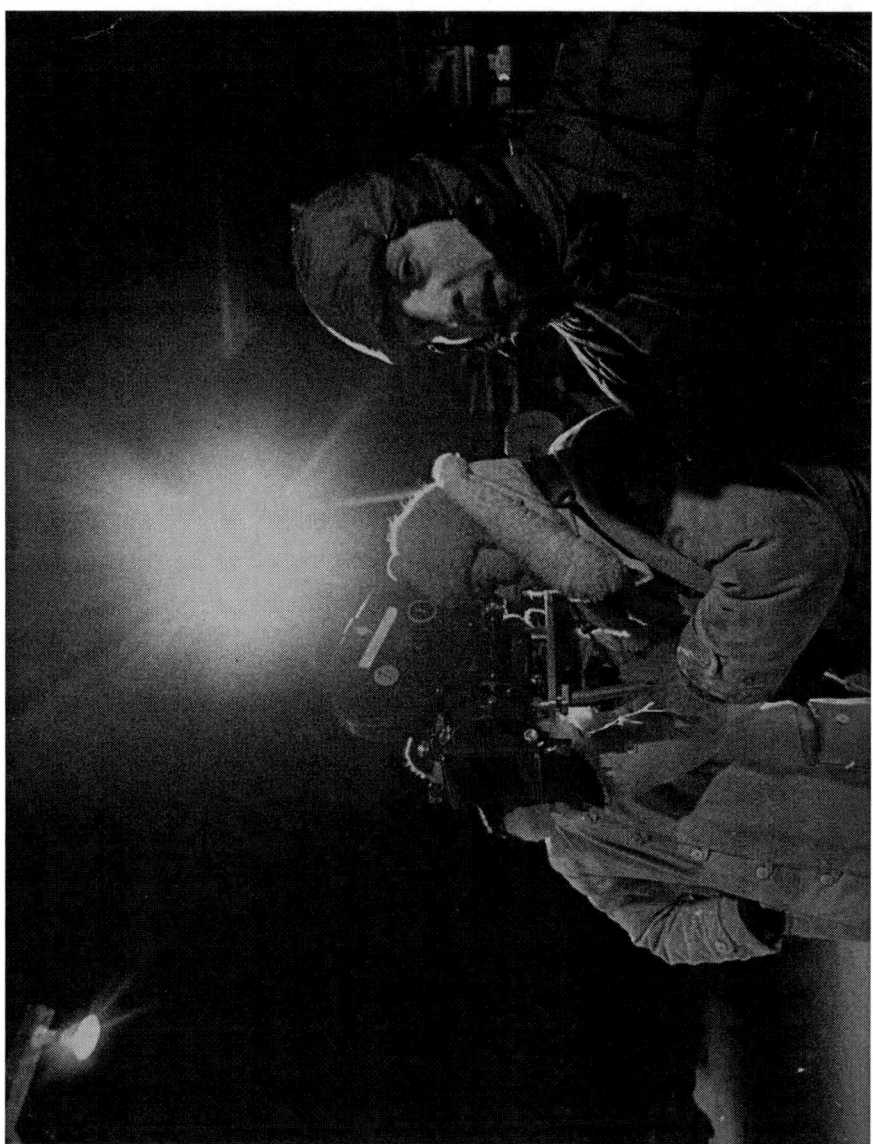

Pic. 9. Sven Nykvist and Casper Wrede filming at night on the set of *Ivan Denisovich*

Pic. 10. Tom Courtenay as Ivan Denisovich (photographed by Sven Åsberg)

Pic. 11. Casper Wrede's son David, photographed in the winter of 2007-08, wearing a prison guard's coat from the set of *Ivan Denisovich*

Pic. 12. An *Ivan Denisovich* film poster

V   STAGING THE UNSTAGEABLE: CASPER WREDE'S PRODUCTION OF *HOPE AGAINST HOPE* AT THE ROYAL EXCHANGE THEATRE (1983)[1]

The biographical notes to Donald Rayfield's 1973 translation of a chapter from Nadezhda Mandelstam's memoirs *Hope Against Hope* and sixteen poems by Osip Mandelstam, state that Rayfield 'has been obsessed with [Osip] Mandelstam for ten years' and 'has written an unpublished book on Mandelstam's poetry'.[2] A decade later, Rayfield's reputation as an expert on Mandelstam led, among other things, to his involvement in the theatrical adaptation of *Hope Against Hope* at the Royal Exchange Theatre in Manchester, by the renowned director Casper Wrede. The aim of the present article is to piece together the story of this remarkable production, including Rayfield's contribution.[3]

Casper Wrede (1929-98) was a Finn of Swedish extraction who underwent training at the Old Vic Theatre School in London and at the BBC, and co-founded the 69 Theatre Company, now known as the Royal Exchange Theatre. The Company's decision to set up camp in Manchester was prompted by their desire to provide a counterbalance to what can be termed a nihilistic theatre of despair, popular at the time. In the words of another co-founder, Braham Murray, this was only possible to achieve 'outside of London, a) where you get the right to fail, and b) where you don't have to be in the trend

---

1   This text by Andrei Rogachevskii initially appeared in a slightly different form in *When the Elephant Broke Out of the Zoo: A Festschrift for Donald Rayfield*, ed. by Andreas Schönle, Olga Makarova and Jeremy Hicks (Stanford 2012, pp. 108-28).
2   See *Chapter 42*, by Nadezhda Mandel'shtam, and *The Goldfinch and Other Poems*, by Osip Mandel'shtam; introduction and translations by Donald Rayfield (London: The Menard Press, 1973), p. 39.
3   I would like to express my profound gratitude to Casper Wrede's son David, for letting me see many relevant documents from his family archive; and to the Carnegie Trust for the Universities of Scotland, as well as John Goodfellow, Michelle Hickman, Stella Lowe and Vicky Bloor at the Royal Exchange Theatre, for facilitating my archival research trips to Manchester. In the instances where previously unpublished material has been reproduced, every effort has been made to contact copyright holders to obtain permission. Where this has not been possible, I wish to tender my apologies and thanks.

in order to be successful'.[4] The 69 Theatre Company/Royal Exchange's motto has been described by Murray as follows: 'Life is wonderful... Hard – you might have to go right into the darkness to find the light, but it's wonderful'.[5] This resonated well with Wrede's own understanding of what art should be about. An example is his 1970 film version of Alexander Solzhenitsyn's *One Day in the Life of Ivan Denisovich* depicting life in a labour camp under Stalin. According to Wrede, he selected the book for adaptation because it 'created the first living bond between the Russia of the future and the people in the world outside who chose to believe in forces stronger than violence and murder'.[6]

The release of Wrede's *One Day* roughly coincided with the publication of the first book of Nadezhda Mandelstam's memoirs in English translation.[7] The second part followed duly.[8] Both books took the literary world by storm. There was a feeling that Nadezhda's 'courageous and spine-chilling record of how (and by whom) her husband was hounded to his death in the years 1934-38... deserves to be read by the widest possible circle'.[9] Donald Rayfield rightly pointed out that Osip Mandelstam 'was unique as a poet in having a wife who has composed not a hagiography, not an idyll, but an objective memoir'.[10] This memoir's significance went far beyond the Mandelstams' personal story. The influential British theatre critic Ossia Trilling called it 'one of the most tragic documents about human courage in the face of evil ever to

---

4 Braham Murray's interview for the Theatre Archive project, www.bl.uk/projects/theatrearchive/murray4.html (last accessed on 16 March 2011). For more on the 69 Theatre Company and the Royal Exchange Theatre, see Braham Murray, *The Worst It Can Be Is a Disaster* (London: Methuen Drama, 2007).
5 Braham Murray's interview for the Theatre Archive project.
6 See p. 167 of the present edition.
7 See Nadezhda Mandelstam, *Hope Against Hope: A Memoir*, translated from the Russian by Max Hayward (New York: Atheneum, 1970). The English title of the book is a play on words: Nadezhda means 'hope' in Russian.
8 See Nadezhda Mandelstam, *Hope Abandoned: A Memoir*, translated from the Russian by Max Hayward (New York: Atheneum, 1973).
9 N. J. Anning, 'The Wolfhound Age', *The Times Literary Supplement*, 7 February 1971.
10 Donald Rayfield, 'Introduction', in Nadezhda and Osip Mandelstam, *Chapter 42 and The Goldfinch*, p. 3.

have found its way out of Russia'.[11] In his view, the two books 'give not only a faithful picture of [the Mandelstams'] life together as man and wife, but also an analysis of the nature of the creative artist against the background of the turbulent years of the Russian revolution and the years that followed. They introduce us not only to the events, but also to their causes, not only to some of the people – both friends and foes – who played an important role in [the Mandelstams'] lives, but also to their way of thinking'.[12] In short, the memoirs' 'real theme is the prison house of Russia under Stalin. Osip Mandelstam was a great poet full stop. If such torments can befall a totally non-political victim, consider the lives of his fellow citizens'.[13]

Given the proximity of this subject to Solzhenitsyn's *One Day in the Life of Ivan Denisovich*,[14] it was only a matter of time before Wrede took notice of Nadezhda's memoirs and recognised their lasting importance.[15] In an interview, he said of *Hope Against Hope* and *Hope Abandoned*: 'I read the books when they were first published and they made a terrific impact on me... Mandelstam always believed in speaking the truth as he saw it and he was persecuted for it. This is the best personal description I know of how life was, and is today, for people like that'.[16] In his memoirs, Wrede further elaborated on the subject:

---

11 A transcript of Ossia Trilling's review of Wrede's production of *Hope Against Hope*, first broadcast by the BBC on 4 February 1983 and kept at the Royal Exchange Theatre Archive in the *Hope Against Hope* file.
12 Ibid.
13 Irving Wardle, 'Defiant Survival', *The Times*, 4 February 1983.
14 To quote an American critic, Wrede's adaptation of *One Day* had 'man hoping against hope' (Hubert Norton, 'Courtenay Is Ideal Ivan', *The Miami News*, 16 October 1971).
15 In his unpublished undated handwritten notes on the back of the loose sheets from an early draft of *Hope Against Hope*, Wrede acknowledges a personal significance that both Solzhenitsyn and the Mandelstams had for him: 'I remember at the time when Solzhenitsyn was "hot", a distinguished literary person wrote an open letter to him to the effect that his life and its issues were clear-cut and "simple". And that by comparison our lives here in the West were infinitely more complex and therefore more difficult. In this falsehood I recognised myself... This is what attracted me to Solzhenitsyn and to the Mandelstams: [a desire] to keep company with those who have led "simple" lives, and find a perspective and a meaning in the life we lead' (David Wrede's private archive).
16 Alan Hulme, 'Revolutionary – a Russian Tragedy', *Manchester Evening News*, 27 January 1983.

> I lived with [Nadezhda Mandelstam's] books for years, immersed myself in them and extended my reading in order to understand how Russia had arrived at its present state and what had happened there to people like myself. These two voices, Nadezhda's and Osip's, have spoken to me more directly and clearly about the fundamental experiences of our times than any living person I have met. I think this is because in education and in vocation and in their personalities they were already intimately familiar to me – not that their characters are easy to penetrate; and because, highly sophisticated and intelligent people that they were, they lived – in fear – the lives of the poor and the persecuted, treasuring every moment, suffering every human want and weakness; and above all because – refusing to flee the land – they stubbornly maintained their integrity in the face of events which swept away even the idea of the right of an individual to have his own thoughts and feelings – let alone express them. Osip Mandelstam died for his right to be a poet. Nadezhda said she lived on in order to hide and save her husband's illegal poetry, but that is only the half of it: her own writing makes up the other half. Here is true agreement between life and work. Two lives: one in poetry, the other in prose; naked witnesses to the times they lived through and died in.[17]

Before long, Wrede started thinking about adapting Nadezhda's memoirs too – on this occasion, for the stage. He referred to this adaptation as 'a labour of love'.[18] Convinced that the Mandelstam-related material should speak for itself, he embarked on an almost impossible task of turning it into a play without adding a word of his own.[19] To complicate things further, Wrede's extreme 'documentary-style approach',[20] perhaps uniquely, merged with 'the ruthless inexorability of a Greek tragedy',[21] as Osip Mandelstam could appear reminiscent of a 'classical Greek tragic hero, a noble man who through a fault in his own character [– an inability to stay silent –] is destroyed by the gods [of the Kremlin]'.[22]

---

17 See pp. 169-70 of the present edition.
18 Hulme, op. cit.
19 According to Wrede, 'every word on stage was either spoken or written by the people involved... I haven't invented a syllable' (Hulme, op. cit.).
20 Pete Searson, 'To Siberia with Hope!', *Grip* [a UMIST student periodical], 8 February 1983.
21 Trilling's review of the *Hope Against Hope* production, broadcast by the BBC on 4 February 1983.
22 The unsigned article 'Za chto – Why?' from the 1983 theatrical programme for *Hope Against Hope* (p. 7); see also Marie-Louise Fock, 'Casper Wredes giv om Osip M.', *Hufvudstadsbladet* (Helsinki), 23 February 1983.

Years passed before the details of the adaptation finally crystallized in Wrede's mind. As he admitted himself on 8 August 1981 in a draft letter to James Greene, his other projects kept interfering on a regular basis: 'not only are my processes v[ery] slow but I am also obliged to earn a living'.[23] The letter's addressee – the son of the Director General of the BBC and nephew of the famous writer Graham Greene – happened to be a translator of Osip Mandelstam's poetry into English,[24] as well as the author of a dramatisation of the Mandelstams' relationship called *The Buzz of the Earth*, performed in London at the Mermaid Theatre in the summer of 1981, and at the Riverside Studios in the autumn of the same year. It might well be possible that a competition from James Greene (whose dramatisation benefitted from Wrede's advice and engaged, in its Mermaid version, Wrede's actress ex-wife, Dilys Hamlett) – in addition to Nadezhda Mandelstam's demise at the end of 1980 – helped Wrede to decide that it was a now or never moment, and to complete his own adaptation of *Hope Against Hope* in time for the 1982-83 season at the Royal Exchange.

A draft of Wrede's letter, written in mid-1981 to Clarence Brown of the Department of Comparative Literature at Princeton (a Mandelstam expert who supplied an introduction to *Hope Against Hope* in Max Hayward's translation), affords us an insight into Wrede's technique of assembling a suitable 'collection of fragments by which a camel might, in very fine pieces, pass through the eye of a needle'[25] (or, in other words, a successful piecing together of the adaptation's jigsaw puzzle). In the letter, Wrede uses a different metaphor to describe his creative processes – one that comes from a Scandinavian lifestyle rather than the Scriptures:

> I am at present in the throes of building a boat, so to speak, for the stage, out of the books of N[adezhda] Y[akovlevna] M[andelstam]... and M[andelstam]'s poetry. The keel of this vessel is the story of M[andelstam]'s last years. I have to confess that I have been thinking of <u>how</u> to do this for a few years now... The poetry of the theatre has, as you know, its own laws, although they are in-

---

23 David Wrede's private archive.
24 See, for example, Osip Mandelstam, *Poems*, chosen and translated by James Greene; with forewords by Nadezhda Mandelstam and Donald Davie (London: Elek, 1977).
25 Anonymous, 'Za chto – Why?', p. 7.

> frequently invoked at present... There is a blueprint in my mind. The ribs are in place, and I put my trust in M[andelstam] for a mast, his poetry for sails and N[adezhda] Y[akovlevna] M[andelstam]'s words for boards. However, I feel I am short of the odd length of deck-planking and my attention has for some time now rested on an essay of yours, which, I must confess, tempts me no end as a source for pilfering some durable New England material. I refer to "Into the Heart of Darkeness", which I have not read... Indeed, you could with your own voice become an actor in the play. If you approve my bold approach, please send me a photostat of the article.[26]

Wrede obtained Brown's consent and an offprint of his article 'Into the Heart of Darkness: Mandelstam's "Ode to Stalin"', which discussed Mandelstam's unsuccessful attempt to stave off persecution by singing praises to his principal persecutor, thus seeking to undo the adverse effects of his earlier anti-Stalin poem 'My zhivem, pod soboiu ne chuia strany' / We Live, Without Feeling Ground Beneath Our Feet. Subsequently Wrede used several passages from it in the play. In the adaptation, they are pronounced by a bespectacled character called 'An American University Professor':

> On the 12th of January 1937 Mandelstam decided that the time had come to sell out, that further resistance was simply not in him, that his choice was to give in or perish... And so he attempted – to the best of my knowledge, for the only time in his life – to dragoon his muse into writing a poem of which he felt a kind of preliminary revulsion and shame... It would not come. It is an extraordinary spectacle to contemplate: Mandelstam, one of the most gifted masters of verse technique and at the height of its powers, being unable to accomplish what was, to judge by the reams of similar stuff that marked Soviet letters for many years, well within the capacities of any moderately handy hack. If that were the end of it, there would be little left to say. But it was not the end...[27]

Using research publications as a verbatim source for a character's lines would not be considered standard practice and was undoubtedly a less obvious move than introducing Nadezhda and Osip as two chief protagonists. However, adding a third principal character – the Mandelstams' poet friend Anna Akhmatova, entrusted with 'the difficult task of holding the play together

---

26 David Wrede's private archive.
27 Casper Wrede, *Hope Against Hope*, a 1983 typescript kept in David Wrede's private archive, 73-74; cf. Clarence Brown, 'Into the Heart of Darkness: Mandelstam's "Ode to Stalin"', *Slavic Review*, 26.4 (1967), p. 586.

almost in the role of a narrator'[28] – proved to be a truly inspired choice. Akhmatova's own poetry (in Richard McKane's translations) featured prominently in the production,[29] complementing that of Mandelstam (translated by James Greene),[30] and this, according to some reports, 'significantly increased the adaptation's insight'.[31] Excerpts from Akhmatova's reminiscences of Osip, a fellow Acmeist whom she had known since 1911 (witnessing, *inter alia*, his arrest by the OGPU in May 1934), made their way into Wrede's play too.[32]

For female leads, Wrede relied on Dilys Hamlett as Akhmatova and Avril Elgar as Nadezhda Mandelstam. Both were trained at the same Old Vic Theatre School as Wrede. 'These two ladies have been in my mind for a long time in relation to these parts – two splendid actresses well cast', he said to a journalist.[33] Hamlett's previous appearances at the Royal Exchange included

---

28 GEI, 'Not Everyone's Taste, But...', *The Ellesmere Port Pioneer*, 10 February 1983. Unlike other characters, Akhmatova 'had a chair and a small table of her own and was seldom absent from the stage', Wrede, 'Note' (item 9) in the *Hope Against Hope* typescript, no pagination.

29 E.g. 'Voronezh', 'Nemnogo geografii' (A Bit of Geography) and fragments from *A Poem Without a Hero* ('Kak odnu muzykal'nuiu frazu' / Like a single musical phrase; 'Belykh nochenek khorovod' / The White Nights Pass Over You) and *Requiem* ('Tikho l'etsia tikhii Don' / The Quiet Don Flows Quietly; 'Uznala ia, kak opadaiut litsa' / I Found Out How Faces Droop; 'Pered etim gorem gnutsia gory' / The Mountains Bend Before this Grief; 'Opiat' pominal'nyi priblizilsia chas' / The Hour of Remembrance Has Drawn Close Again; 'I upalo kamennoe slovo' / The Stone Word Fell).

30 Such as 'Za gremuchuiu doblest' griadushchikh vekov'' (For the Resonant Virtue of Eras to Come), 'Morgulis – on iz Narkomprosa' (Old Man Margulis from Narkompros), 'Slukh chutkii parus napriagaet' (Ears Stretch a Sensitive Sail), 'Lishiv menia morei, razbega i razleta' (You Took Away My Seas and Running Jumps, and Sky), 'Eto kakaia ulitsa?' (What Street Is This?), 'Eshche ne umer ty, eshche ty ne odin' (I [sic] Still Have Not Died: Still Not Alone), 'Chto delat' nam s ubitost'iu ravnin?' (What Can We Do with the Murderous [sic] Plains?), 'V litso morozu ia gliazhu odin' (I Look into the Frost's Face, Alone), 'I ia vykhozhu iz prostranstva' (I Walk out of Space), 'Esli b menia nashi vragi vziali' (If Our Enemies Take Me), 'Kuda mne det'sia v etom ianvare?' (Where Can I Go This January?), 'Sokhrani moiu rech' navsegda za privkus neschast'ia i dyma' (Preserve My Words Forever for Their Aftertaste of Misfortune and Smoke), 'Nashedshii podkovu' (He Who Has Found a Horseshoe) and *The Ode* [to Stalin], either in full or in part – some twenty in total.

31 Marie-Louise Fock, op. cit.

32 Cf., for instance, Anna Akhmatova, 'Mandelstam: (Pages from a Journal)' / translated by Kristin de Kuiper, *Russian Literature Triquarterly*, 9 (1974), pp. 250, 252; and Wrede, the *Hope Against Hope* typescript, pp. 39-40, 80.

33 Hulme, op. cit.

the wife in *Have You Anything to Declare?* by Maurice Hennequin and Pierre Véber, Paulina in Shakespeare's *Winter's Tale*, the Countess in *The Deep Man* by Hugo von Hofmannsthal and Mme Ranevskaya in Chekhov's *Cherry Orchard*. Elgar was seen at the Royal Exchange in *The Family Reunion* by T S Eliot and *The Corn is Green* by Emlyn Williams. Osip's part went to David Horovitch, who had been trained at the Central School of Speech and Drama and associated with the 69 Theatre Company since its inaugural production of *Hamlet* (in which he played Rosencrantz). Less than a year before *Hope Against Hope*, he appeared at the Royal Exchange as Willum in *The Nerd* by Larry Shue.

The three principal actors were additionally supported by a cast of twelve (five women and seven men), representing a cross-section of Soviet people, now functioning as a Greek chorus of sorts (not only commenting on the unfolding events but also explaining peculiar Soviet terms, such as Cheka/OGPU/NKVD, and introducing historical figures, such as Abel Yenukidze and Lidia Seifullina), now playing individualised bit parts (usually several per actor or actress, in quick succession). Thus, Bill Leadbitter played the American University Professor – as well as Akhmatova's son Lev Gumilev, who comes to the Mandelstams for his morning coffee shortly after Osip's arrest and is immediately told to go away by Nadezhda. Sybil Allen impersonated, among others, Elena Bulgakova and Zinaida Pasternak, while Melanie Kilburn acted as a nurse, a telegraph girl, a Housing Committee secretary and Vassilissa Shklovski.

Wrede instructed the actors to directly 'address the audience as well as play scenes in the usual way. Addressing the audience [should be] different in poetry and in prose... The most important factor of the performance is the flow of it. Every character, however brief their appearance, brings with them a contribution of feeling and vitality which builds the momentum for Osip and Nadezhda to play their jail, poetry and parting sequences at the pace which is appropriate to each. A lifeless and uncommitted company would place an intolerable burden on the principal actors. If all the parts are not acted, the play degenerates into a lecture'.[34]

Yet, when less than a week before the opening night Wrede came down with bronchial pneumonia and asked Braham Murray to see *Hope Against Hope* through for him, Murray – who had no previous knowledge of the piece but agreed to step in with a proviso that he would be allowed to impose alterations if necessary – found that 'the production was as cold as ice. The actors confirmed that they had been instructed to repress all emotions. Presumably this was to ensure that nothing would intrude between the audience and their understanding of the text. For a director like Casper who detested Brecht this was a bit odd. It was also anathema to me. I gathered my courage and let the actors off the leash. For this they were profoundly grateful. The play came alive.'[35]

Another problem encountered by Murray was that Wrede's script 'was far too long, well over three and a half hours'.[36] It was an extremely important project for Wrede, whose family sought refuge in Norway and Sweden after his home town of Viipuri (now Vyborg) had been annexed by the USSR in the course of the 1939-40 Winter War. This childhood trauma appeared to have formed Wrede's attitude to communist Russia, which combined sympathy towards ordinary Russians with aversion to totalitarianism. The stage version of *Hope Against Hope* became, to a substantial degree, a manifestation of this trauma, a 'deeply felt personal account of [Wrede's] relationship with Communism… His absorption in the rehearsals and his concentration were quite terrifying'.[37] That is probably why it proved very difficult for Wrede to leave anything out of the final draft of his adaptation (although, as the minutes of the production meeting of 18 January 1983 demonstrate, he did cut the parts of the Mandelstams' flatmate Kostyrev and the Electrician, meant to be played by Roy Sampson and Paul Batterworth respectively).

---

34   Wrede, 'Note' (items 1 and 5) in the *Hope Against Hope* typescript, no pagination.
35   Murray, *The Worst It Can Be*, p. 195.
36   Ibid., p. 194.
37   Ibid.

David Horovitch recalls that, upon receiving the script, he told Wrede 'honestly that I considered it had exciting dramatic possibilities but that, if I were to undertake the role of Osip, I would need an assurance that cuts in the text would be negotiable as it seemed, on first reading, to be much too long... <Wrede> immediately became defensive saying that he had shown it to the other directors of the company, none of whom had expressed any doubts as to its length. It was a conversation without a resolution but I swallowed my doubts and accepted what seemed to me a huge challenge... I repeatedly pleaded with Casper to cut but he was immovable. I remember bumping into Michael Elliott[38] halfway through rehearsals and telling him it was much too long and Michael saying "Oh, he must cut it"... but he wouldn't'.[39]

When Murray took over and discovered that (not entirely out of keeping with some Greek tragedies) the play ran for a little under four hours, possible cuts – to 'at most, three hours'[40] – were discussed by him and the leading actors 'over a meal in the theatre restaurant, and the following morning Braham presented them to Casper. <Wrede> was understandably still reluctant to lose anything and of one lovely poem about a boy in the snow[41] he reportedly said "But that is my childhood!" Eventually, however, he agreed and we performed the new slim-line version that night for the first time before the press.'[42]

What the press – and, subsequently, other theatregoers – saw, as soon as they entered the magnificent commodities exchange building that houses a futuristic spider-like seven-sided module of Britain's most famous theatre-in-the round (designed by Wrede's fellow student at the Old Vic Theatre School, Richard Negri), was a surprise transformation of the venue's outer hall into a Kremlin look-alike. *The Times Literary Supplement* reported: 'Busts of Marx and Lenin at either end of the Royal Exchange piazza flank a gigantic banner portrait of Stalin. Hewn megaliths from Red Square and the polished marble of Victorian capitalism stand in sharp juxtaposition, modifying the impact of

---

38 An artistic director at the Royal Exchange.
39 David Horovitch's email to Andrei Rogachevskii of 20 March 2011.
40 Murray, *The Worst It Can Be*, p. 195.
41 'Liubliu moroznoe dykhan'e' (I Like Emitting a Frosty Breath) of 24 January 1937.
42 David Horovitch's email to Andrei Rogachevskii of 20 March 2011.

the steel modular structure that is the interior space of the Royal Exchange Theatre'.[43] Before the play's start and during the interval, members of the audience could avail themselves of an 'exhibition highlighting the period, and the sound of insistent propaganda... In the theatre the floor [was] covered with rough-hewn stained pitch pine, and high tech of the Royal Exchange module deadened by blanketing, the normal clear line between stage and audience blurred'.[44] As a further evidence of staging being 'aimed at breaking down the barriers between audience and actors... some of the latter [were] sitting among the former at various points',[45] 'anonymously dressed to represent in turn party functionaries, peasants, minor writers or secret police. They [would] emerge from the fringes of the round stage to remind us that the figures in this private drama are representative of a million others, each symptomatic of the social disintegration that accompanied Stalinistic communism'.[46] Positioning actors among the spectators was of course partly necessitated by the theatre's shape, 'to obviate lengthy entrances and exits, [although the company members] did also at times leave the auditorium. Most of the furniture and properties were stored at the edge of the stage and among the audience and were taken out of the theatre when no longer required. Most objects served several purposes'.[47]

Some critics did not fail to notice that the props were somewhat thin on the ground,[48] pointing at the 'parallels between Orwell's vision of the future in 1984 and [*Hope Against Hope*'s] version of the past... as starkly obvious as the Spartan set. Luxuries like props are at a minimum – even the costumes have been recycled from previous Exchange excursions into the Russian

---

43   Simon Berry, 'The Memory of Poetry', *The Times Literary Supplement*, 18 February 1983.
44   See the unsigned note 'Look-alike Kremlin' in *The Chester Chronicle* of 28 January 1983.
45   Hulme, op. cit.
46   Berry, op. cit.
47   Wrede, 'Note' (item 4) in the *Hope Against Hope* typescript, no pagination.
48   Despite the presence of a 'magnificently authentic train, [taking the Mandelstams' to their exile and] represented by three railway baggies made of steel, pushed onto the boards of the stage with all the accompanying noise that no special effects could achieve' (Berry, op. cit.).

wastes'.⁴⁹ Certain observers felt that there was 'something dispiritingly makeshift about the bare boards'.⁵⁰ Others, however, stated that the 'greyness of the set, the peasants' clothing and the soldiers' uniforms only added to the sombre grim reality of the life of betrayal and exile through which Mandelstam continued to write'.⁵¹

Wrede spared no effort in making his 'composite recreation of Stalin's Russia'⁵² as authentic as possible.⁵³ This was not easy to achieve, considering that he had not visited the USSR by that point in time,⁵⁴ and did not speak any Russian (although he was fluent in several European languages). Still, his previous experience in recreating Stalin's Russia (or the GULAG aspect of it, to be precise), when working on *One Day in the Life of Ivan Denisovich*, proved rather helpful.⁵⁵ Wrede's versions of *One Day* and *Hope Against Hope* were quite predictably linked together by the critics.⁵⁶ However, sometimes Solzhenitsyn's obvious influence on Wrede's perception of Russia and the

---

49   Robin Duke, 'Uneasy Hope', *West Lancashire Evening Gazette* of 7 February 1983. The critic may have meant Chekhov's *Uncle Vanya*, Dostoevsky's *Crime and Punishment* (directed by Elliott in 1977-78), Chekhov's *Cherry Orchard* (directed by Wrede in 1979) or Maxim Gorky's *Lower Depths* (directed by Murray in 1980).
50   Michael Coveney, 'Hope Against Hope / Royal Exchange, Manchester', *The Financial Times*, 4 February 1983. Generally speaking, Wrede's 'style of directing was not flamboyant… so what you saw was pretty unadorned when you saw it… [He] wanted the audience to receive what the play was about, straight' (Braham Murray, interviewed by Andrei Rogachevskii on 11 March 2011).
51   GEI, op. cit.
52   An unsigned notice in the Arty Facts section of *The Cheshire Observer* of 25 February 1983.
53   Cf. 'There is no naturalism implied in this script, yet every person, place and thing in it are authentic' (Wrede, 'Note' (item 6) in the *Hope Against Hope* typescript, no pagination).
54   He went there for the first time in 1989.
55   And so did Wrede's very successful attempt to reconstruct the life of London's famous Jewish quarter in his film version of Ronald Harwood's play *The Barber of Stamford Hill* (1962). Mandelshtam was Jewish, of course, although it took some critics 'three quarters of [*Hope Against Hope*] to discover that' (Daniel Scott, 'Hopeless Odes to Stalin', *Mancunion*, 9 February 1983).
56   Cf. the stage version of *Hope Against Hope* 'could not have a more authentic ring. And Wrede – whom many people may remember as the director of the film version of Solzhenitsyn's *One Day in the Life of Ivan Denisovich* – could hardly have given his production a more authentic appearance' (Trilling's review of *Hope Against Hope*, broadcast by the BBC on 4 February 1983).

Russians went, perhaps subconsciously, a touch too far. As Andrew Jameson, a Russianist at the University of Lancaster, observed in his review of the *Hope Against Hope* production, 'David Horovitch as Mandelstam himself does not particularly resemble the Mandelstam of the 1930s (who was usually clean shaven, with somewhat prominent ears and a narrow chin). In this production David Horovitch's whiskers bear an unfortunate resemblance to those of Aleksandr Solzhenitsyn'.[57]

On the whole, however, the production did please this particular expert: 'I was struck immediately with the totally authentic impression given by the design – in particular the costumes... Some of the characters were marvellous recreations of Soviet types, so familiar to me – I must mention in particular Paul Imbusch[58] with double-breasted suit and perfect, incredible hair-style, and Brigid Mackay as the Tatar writer Lidiya Seifullina. And I experienced a curious thrill of recognition at the brief appearances of the characters Boris Pasternak and Demyan Bednyi...[59] Russian names were well pronounced (though it would be worth practicing the names "Nadezhda" and "Demyan Bednyi" a little more).[60] I also found the props well-chosen, although if I wanted to be picky, I could say that the teapot sitting on top of the Mandelstams' kettle should be about half the size that it is. (But it is a tribute to the designer that that is the only comment I have.)'[61]

However, a *Daily Telegraph* critic ventured an opinion that Wrede's unwavering pursuit of authenticity could at times dominate detrimentally over all the other features of the show: 'An insistence on scene changing and realistic properties further emphasises the authenticity though tending to break concentration, and detracts from the atmosphere of intense sorrow and loss at

---

57 A transcript of Jameson's talk at the Red Rose Radio, Preston, on 10 February 1983, kept in the Royal Exchange Theatre archive.
58 In his role as the Interrogator.
59 Played by Roy Sampson and David Bauckham respectively.
60 A separate list of about a hundred Russian personal and geographical names, used in the adaptation, survived among the *Hope Against Hope* papers in the Royal Exchange Theatre archive.
61 Andrew Jameson, speaking at the Red Rose Radio, Preston, on 10 February 1983. *Hope Against Hope*'s set was designed by Stephen McCabe, and costumes, by David Short.

the heart of the production'.[62] The chorus's elucidatory function came under fire repeatedly. Daniel Scott of the student periodical *Mancunion* found it 'highly obtrusive, smashing our belief in the drama'.[63] Andrew Jameson echoed this sentiment: 'Wrede's device of stopping the play at intervals and making the cast shout in unison explanations of some of the Soviet terms used, [is] crude and intrusive in the extreme... Apart from this, Wrede fails to follow through his own logic, and leaves a number of important terms unexplained (such as The Terror, or Article 58)'.[64]

While recognising the merits of Wrede's unconventional and rather innovative approach to the material chosen for adaptation,[65] a number of critics harboured reservations about its suitability specifically for the stage. Thus, Jim Howie of *The Chester Chronicle* said: 'There is a danger in using extracts of this nature to make up a play. The production can tend to become "bitty" and borrowed prose and verse do not necessarily make good theatre. Sometimes inherent faults show up in this production despite sound acting. *Hope Against Hope* would possibly come off better as a radio play – but many who see it will doubtless cross swords with me over this'.[66]

The reception was, indeed, mixed. In the BBC World Service Arts programme Meridian of 10 February 1983, Natalie Anglesey said: 'Casper Wrede's loving adaptation of *Hope Against Hope* and his excellent production does make this absolutely riveting theatre'. *The Salford City Reporter* of 21 January 1983 called *Hope Against Hope* 'a fierce yet profoundly touching theatrical experience'. Chris Eakin of *The Birkenhead News* referred to the show as 'entertaining. In an attempt to avoid a static production and keep as much in line with Nadezhda's memoirs as possible, the Exchange has worked

---

62 Stella Flint, 'Hope Against Hope', *The Daily Telegraph*, 4 February 1983.
63 Scott, op. cit.
64 Andrew Jameson, speaking at Red Rose Radio, Preston, on 10 February 1983.
65 All sorts of comparisons were drawn in an effort to categorize Wrede's *Hope Against Hope*, from the ITV's *Crossroads* soap opera of the 1960s-80s (*The Mancunion* of 9 February 1983) and *Modern Times* by Chaplin (the Mandelstams as 'Charlie Chaplin and Paulette Goddard endlessly fleeing the bullies', David Horovitch in his email to Andrei Rogachevskii of 20 March 2011) to the David and Goliath and the Orpheus and Eurydice legends, as well as Shakespeare's King Lear (see Berry, op. cit.).
66 J. L. H., 'Banished Poet: Play's Theme', *The Chester Chronicle*, 11 February 1983.

on periods of rapidly changing short scenes, [such as a slap in the face given by Osip to the author Alexei Tolstoy, Osip's arrest and suicide attempt, as well as Stalin's telephone call to Pasternak about Osip's case]. This is a good try at keeping the action flowing'.[67]

Other critics begged to differ. Michael Coveney of *The Financial Times* branded *Hope Against Hope* a 'gloomy and ponderous saga on a worthy theme, delivered in an uneasy mixture of direct address, awkwardly staged fugitive episodes and repetitive brushes with the Stalinist bureaucracy... The perfunctoriness of the staging... is matched by the perfunctoriness of the storytelling and it is impossible to feel anything resembling involvement in the tragic tale'.[68] To *The Warrington Guardian*, the style of presentation did not seem understated enough: 'The playwright can call upon various tools of the trade to convey message and meaning to his audience. Unfortunately Casper Wrede opts for the sledgehammer (and sickle?) approach... There is drab monotony and despair a-plenty in this true-life account of Russian poet Osip Mandelstam'.[69] In fact, the word 'sledgehammer' was invoked more than once in connection with the play,[70] and so was the word 'propaganda' (e.g., 'Art and propaganda have always been unhealthy but frequent bedfellows and with the current production... their uneasy relationship continues with uncompromising conviction'[71]).

An extreme view was expressed by *The Mancunion*, whose critic ranked *Hope Against Hope* as 'definitely the most dreadful Royal Exchange presentation I have ever seen... The manner of production is the only thing of any

---

67 Chris Eakin, 'Hopeful Play at Exchange', *The Birkenhead News*, 18 February 1983.
68 Coveney, op. cit.
69 Anonymous, 'Wielding the sledgehammer and sickle', *The Warrington Guardian*, 11 February 1983.
70 Cf. 'The subject... was not intended to be comfortable. But it was hammered home to wring every ounce of sympathy from the audience with all the subtlety of a sledgehammer' (Anonymous, 'Hope Against Hope', *The Swinton and Pendlebury Journal*, 24 February 1983).
71 Duke, op. cit. For his part, Robin Thornber defined the production as a 'propagandist sob story' (quoted from Bernard Levin, 'Hope Springs Eternal But Not from This Inky Hand', *The Times*, 25 February 1983).

interest, apart from other members of the audience'.[72] A more moderate stance was represented by a reviewer at *The Ellesmere Port Pioneer*: 'The play will certainly not suit everyone's tastes, but I strongly recommend seeing it because whether people love it or hate it, it will provide food for thought'.[73] The overall mood of the play was also subjected to different interpretations. The *Oldham Evening Chronicle* of 14 February 1983 thought it was 'powerful and depressing'. A *Times* critic, on the contrary, asserted that he had emerged 'from the theatre not cast down but uplifted, [as] the play also shows that the divine spark in the human spirit can never be extinguished'.[74] George Hall's music became a cause for polemic too, as a *Financial Times* critic mistook a Russian folksong for its imitation and praised how it came 'steaming... most effectively as the Mandelstams board the vessel for exile in the East'.[75] For his part, Andrew Jameson expressed his hope 'that the tuneless dirges sung by the cast in the later stages of the play can be replaced by one or two genuine folk melodies... The background music (played while the Mandelstams are waiting on the quayside at Perm to return to European Russia) is unfortunately a total travesty – it's a jazzed up, sentimentalised version of folk music, and should immediately be replaced by the genuine article'.[76]

A bit of controversy often goes a long way at the box office, and, despite the strong competition in both theatre and cinema that month,[77] the Royal Ex-

---

72 Scott, op. cit.
73 GEI, op. cit.
74 Levin, op. cit. This phrase corresponds well with the Royal Exchange's philosophy of theatrical experience (briefly discussed at the outset of the present article). It is tempting to speculate that the choice of the production title between *Hope Against Hope* and *Hope Abandoned* may well have been made in favour of the former to reflect precisely that.
75 Coveney, op. cit.
76 Andrew Jameson, speaking at the Red Rose Radio, Preston, on 10 February 1983.
77 In February 1983, the following plays and films were on show in Manchester: G B Shaw's classic *Heartbreak House* and Charles Strouse's musical *Annie* at the Palace Theatre; Stephen Sondheim's musical *Company* and Peter Whelan's World War One drama *Accrington Pals* at the Library Theatre; John Flanagan and Andrew McCulloch's comedy *Stiff Options* at the Coliseum Theatre and Dario Fo's farce *Can't Pay? Won't Pay!* at the University Theatre; Steven Spielberg's *E.T.* at the (multi-screen) Odeon, Roxy and ABC; George Romero's *Creepshow* at the Odeon and the ABC; Ken Finkleman's *Airplane II: The Sequel* at the ABC; and Franc Roddam's *Quadrophenia* (with The Who's soundtrack) at the Roxy.

change's loyal fan base, which tends to be 'interested in the unusual and the edgy, rather than the safe thing',[78] did attend in numbers, sufficient for a completely new and risky undertaking with a *recherché* subject: over 60% of the tickets were sold. Curiously, regardless of Murray's cuts and new instructions to actors, some critics still claimed that the show's 'long speeches... would have benefited from a kinder and more selective adaptation for the stage.[79] <...> Casper Wrede <...> has interspersed some scenes where his cast have the luxury of representing character, but in general it is a severely Brechtian world they inhabit'.[80]

Yet, when Wrede was finally able to rise from his sickbed to see the play for the first time, more than a week after the press night, he arguably became the show's severest critic, and the prospect of restoring the cuts suddenly appeared on the agenda. According to David Horovitch, one Saturday Wrede came into his dressing room,

> white with rage, and demanded that we reinstate the cuts. I was exhausted, my voice was going, I knew that Casper had not seen me at my best, I was about to drive back to London and in no mood for such a confrontation. I told him that my understanding was that Braham [Murray] had cleared them with him, and that I endorsed them, but he was intransigent. He called the whole

---

78 Braham Murray, interviewed by Andrei Rogachevskii on 11 March 2011.
79 Cf. 'The script is sensitively written... However, the second half would have been better condensed' (Sally Tomlinson and Sally Anderson, 'Hope Against Hope / Royal Exchange', *Pulp* of 18 February 1983).
80 Berry, op. cit. It has to be noted that the actors engaged in *Hope Against Hope* received a very good press, by and large. The *Daily Telegraph* review could serve as an illustrative example: 'David Horovitch gives an intensely theatrical performance... rising to hyper-dramatic moments in the second act as despair and helplessness take their toll... Avril Elgar is both tough and vulnerable, appearing so ordinary, but responsive, sensitive and persuasive. To Dilys Hamlett, more striking and romantic..., falls the difficult task of introducing the play, merging the actors' interrelationship with their audience' (Flint, op. cit.). The rare dissenting voices included *The Financial Times* ('in the scene where the artist is revealed hard at work in Voronezh, Mr Horovitch twitches and mumbles and dictates his allegedly complex poetic structures as if planning a shopping expedition') and *The Warrington Guardian* ('somehow all this horror and trudging and sighing fails to strike a cord... Hearty Avril Elgar stretches credibility even further with a strange jolly-hockey-sticks performance... The cast of *Hope Against Hope* could find themselves suffering from chronic depression after three weeks of appearing in a play like this').

company in on the following Monday to reinstate the cuts. [That Monday] I arrived a little early and Casper and I had a hurried and rather hushed discussion in the auditorium before the others joined us. I remember little of this except that I said at one point "Casper, you have no idea what it feels like playing this to an audience who are wondering if they will catch their last bus home", to which he replied "Fuck the audience!" The rest of the cast strolled in and when they had all assembled Casper addressed them to the effect that he and I were agreed that the cuts were to be reinstated. I said, in front of the company, that I thought that the show was better in its new version but that he was the boss and if he insisted then I would do his bidding. I can't quite remember what happened then but the upshot was that we never again played the piece in its entirety.[81]

It took Wrede quite a while to come to terms with the cuts. As Murray recalled, 'it was a long time before [Wrede] would so much as look at me and it was nearly two years before he took me aside and said, "You made my play possible. You saved me from myself. Thank you".'[82]

Wrede's intimate attachment to his source material[83] that made him so protective about 'the inordinate length of this splendid beast'[84] (i.e. his version of *Hope Against Hope*), did not escape the attention of certain critics. As the *West Lancashire Evening Gazette* put it, 'there is too often the feel that the play is the result of someone's personal desire to purge the past than speak for the entire 20,000,000 apparent victims of Stalin's totalitarianism'.[85] It appeared equally obvious to others that the play was not only about the past. Ossia Trilling, for one, stated that, even though Wrede's dramatic work dealt with the past, it also served 'to remind us that terror still stalks many corners of the world today, and that the price of freedom is eternal vigilance and personal integrity'.[86] Simon Berry went even as far as to claim that 'despite the

---

81   Horovitch's email to Rogachevskii of 20 March 2011.
82   Murray, op. cit, p. 195.
83   It is not coincidental that for Wrede's obituary notice in the Finnish *Hufvudstadsbladet* newspaper of 4 October 1998, a poem by Mandelstam, 'O, kak zhe ia khochu' / Oh How Much I Would Like (written in 1937 in exile in Voronezh and included in the *Hope Against Hope* adaptation), was chosen.
84   Horovitch's email to Rogachevskii of 20 March 2011.
85   Duke, op. cit.
86   Trilling's review of the *Hope Against Hope* production, broadcast by the BBC on 4 February 1983.

skilfully created documentary flavour..., the Mandelstams' story seems almost mythically ageless'.[87]

It is hard to argue with this particular point. Yet the question is why the Royal Exchange production remained, even at the height of the West's interest in Russia in the mid-1980s – early 1990s, to the best of my knowledge, the only stage version of *Hope Against Hope* (even though Wrede clearly aspired for more, sending a revised script of his adaptation, among others, to the Finnish actor, director and theatre manager Lasse Pöysti at the Royal Dramatic Theatre in Stockholm, to Espen Skjønberg at the Norwegian National Theatre, to the publisher H. R. Krygier in Australia and to Robert Gottlieb at Alfred A. Knopf Inc. in New York). One possible explanation is that the show was too expensive and technically complex, with a fifteen-strong cast and lots of scene and costume changing, for most companies to contemplate putting it on.[88] An additional explanation probably lies in the structural peculiarities of the play, which Donald Rayfield identified upon reading the script of *Hope Against Hope*, sent to him by Wrede for consultation.[89] In his letter to Wrede of 7 January 1983, Rayfield wrote: 'I am sorry to take so long to return your typescript which I felt was very effective. I only have two doubts: firstly, the chorus seems to have too heavy a burden of explanation; secondly, the Mandelstam drama seems to have been overplayed, to judge by audience boredom at the last performance of James Greene's *The Buzz of the Earth*'.[90] These and other related factors, many of which have already been named in

---

87   Berry, op. cit.
88   Braham Murray, interviewed by Andrei Rogachevskii on 11 March 2011. As summarised by an anonymous reviewer in the *Swinton and Pendlebury Journal* of 24 February 1983, the adaptation seemed 'too clever for its own good at times'.
89   Although in his email to Andrei Rogachevskii of 3 September 2007, Donald Rayfield admitted that he had 'only the dimmest recollection and no record of [his] collaboration' with Wrede, and thought 'all I did was to give consent for him to use my translation of Chapter 42 of the first volume of Nadezhda Mandelshtam's memoirs', it is clear from Wrede's *Hope Against Hope* papers that he tried to involve Rayfield in the process of translating Mandelstam's and Akhmatova's poems for the show. Among these papers, there is a typescript of fourteen poems by Mandelstam, dated 1931-37, in Rayfield's translation.
90   David Wrede's private archive. In the words of a *Swinton and Pendlebury Journal* reviewer, 'the devices used to tell the story became a hindrance rather than a help, at times distracting the audience' (the issue of 24 February 1983).

this article, provided an intense and persistent challenge for Wrede. In the opinion of a *Sunday Times* critic, the *Hope Against Hope* adaptation resulted in 'something short of a play but far more than a documentary. The inevitable space between what we see on the stage and what we can only try to imagine is always in the director's mind'.[91] If Wrede himself struggled to implement fully his own vision of *Hope Against Hope*, would it be reasonable to expect any other director, not necessarily captivated by the Mandelstams' story to the same degree as Wrede was, to fare any better? This is probably yet another reason why *Hope Against Hope* remains a 'collector's item'[92] to this day.

---

91 James Fenton, 'Making Art out of Terror', *The Sunday Times*, 6 February 1983.
92 Horovitch's email to Rogachevskii of 20 March 2011.

Index

Ä
Äikiä, Armas, 165

A
Aitken, Gillon, 11, 21, 26, 57, 71, 74, 146
Akhmatova, A. A., 138, 169
Aksnes, Hallgjerd, 84
Aldwinckle, Linda, 9
Aliakrinskii, P. A., 29
Allen, Jack, 13
Alov, Aleksandr, 111, 122
Andersen, Arvid, 59, 89, 90, 150
Andrew, Geoff, 106, 150
Arni, Erkki, 13, 150
Åsberg, Sven, 225
Ashton, Michael, 18

B
Babel, I. E., 174
Bachteler, James, 99, 110, 132, 150
Baines, Jennifer, 138
Bardach, Emilie, 132
Barker, Felix, 89, 105, 106, 150
Barnard, Ken, 132, 150
Barnes, Howard G., 30, 50, 71, 145
Beale, Lewis, 97
Becker, Edmond, 111
Beckett, Samuel, 17
Beierfield, Ann, 43, 95, 97, 151
Bell, Joseph N., 47, 84, 92, 95, 108, 109, 150
Bergman, Ingmar, 50, 52
Bergström, Lasse, 91, 151
Berliner, Milton, 95
Bez, 19, 150
Bilbow, Marjorie, 103, 151
Billington, Michael, 137, 151
Block, Bela von, 74
Borge, Erik, 25, 26, 145
Börge, Göran, 90, 91, 151
Bourne, Kay, 95
Bowman, Pierre, 96, 151
Braun, Eric, 82, 105, 107, 108, 151
Brazhnev (Trifonov), E. A., 29
Brecht, Berthold, 65, 180
Bredangen, Nurven, 54, 145
Brezhnev, L. I., 7
Brinchmann, Arild, 43
Brodkin, Herbert, 120
Brodsky, Joseph, 172
Brown, Clarence, 138
Büchner, Georg, 18
Burgess, Anthony, 132, 151
Burke, Alfred, 18, 43, 49, 54, 93, 97, 146
Burke, Barbara, 49
Burke, John, 18
Butcher, Maryvonne, 107, 151
Byam Shaw, Glen, 15
Byrne, Bridget, 97, 100, 151

C
Caine, Michael, 82
Carlson, Stig G., 113
Cashin, Fergus, 109, 132, 151
Cavett, Dick, 95
Champlin, Charles, 129, 151
Chazal, Robert, 114, 151
Chekhov, A. P., 16, 47, 137
Christie, Ian, 106, 107, 151
Chung, Hilary, 128, 148

Churikova, I. M., 133
Clark, Katerina, 127
Coleman, John, 104, 107, 108, 151
Collett, Miranda, 143
Connell, Thelma, 81, 82, 83, 145, 146
Connery, Sean, 26, 82, 116, 136
Conquest, Robert, 138
Cook, Fielder, 25
Cording, John, 45, 54, 136, 146
Courtenay, Tom, 12, 18, 19, 21, 22, 25, 26, 27, 42, 45, 47, 50, 52, 54, 55, 58, 82, 84, 88, 89, 90, 91, 92, 93, 94, 95, 96, 97, 98, 105, 107, 108, 109, 110, 114, 115, 117, 118, 136, 140, 146, 150, 151, 152, 153, 154, 155, 156, 157, 185, 223, 225
Coveney, Michael, 137, 139, 151
Crist, Judith, 94, 102
Crowley, Edward L., 88, 147
Crowther, Bosley, 51
Curtis, James M., 77, 105, 122, 123, 124, 125, 147
Cusack, Niamh, 137

D

Daniels, Marc, 25
Dante Alighieri, 174
Davies, Richard D., 143
Davies, Russell, 136, 151
Dejmek, Kazimierz, 43
Demin, Mikhail, 5, 29, 30, 32, 33, 38, 77, 82, 166, 220
Devine, George, 15
Dewar, Cameron, 16, 20, 89, 95, 97, 100, 120, 152
Dexter, John, 82
Dickens, Charles, 39
Dickey, Fred, 46, 55, 152

Dobrenko, E. A., 127
Donner, Jörn, 112, 113, 156
Dos Passos, John, 122, 133
Dzerzhinskii, F. E., 173, 174

E

Eglick, Peter, 51, 55, 58, 96, 99, 123, 152
Eisenstein, S. M., 68, 71, 74, 77, 125, 126, 127, 133
Ekstrand, Nils-Erik, 50, 109, 152
Elgar, Avril, 138
Elliott, Michael, 16, 21, 50, 135, 137
Ellis Miller, Robert, 82

F

Falck Clausen, Frimann, 25, 54, 146, 223
Falkberget, Johan, 41
Fenton, James, 139, 152
Fiene, Donald M., 10, 147
Filippenko, A. G., 124
Finney, Albert, 137
Fock, Marie-Louise, 13, 16, 135, 137, 139, 152
Ford, Aleksander, 120
Fordyce, Robin, 16
Francis, Damien, 7, 147
Fransberg, Klas, 152, 158
Fräntti, Mikael, 114, 152
Frayn, Michael, 137
Fredriksen, N., 43
Fromm, Erich, 13
Frost, David, 95
-ft, 115, 152

G

Geist, Kenneth, 130, 132, 152
Gelmis, Joseph, 93, 132, 153

Getz, Rannveig, 84
Gibbs, Patrick, 107, 109, 117, 133, 153
Gill, Claes, 132
Gilliatt, Penelope, 59, 93, 129, 153
Giniger, Susan, 99, 153
Gjessing, Gunvor, 88, 153
Goldovskaia, M. E., 125
Gorfinkle, Connie, 95
Gorky, Maxim, 124, 130
Gould Boyum, Joy, 114, 129, 130, 132, 153
Grammatikov, V. A., 124
Gran, Per, 54, 145
Gran, Sverre, 27
Greene, Graham, 104, 130
Greenspun, Roger, 92, 93, 134, 153
Grégoire, Jean, 111
Grieg, Edvard, 39
Guinness, Alec, 43
Guinness, Matthew, 43, 54, 146
Günther, Hans, 127

H

Hald, Jac, 46, 53, 145
Hamlett, Dilys, 15, 32, 49, 137, 138
Handeland, Ingrid E., 44
Harwood, Ronald, 11, 18, 19, 21, 26, 48, 50, 54, 57, 60, 71, 76, 82, 84, 92, 94, 103, 104, 111, 127, 136, 140, 145, 146, 153
Hasse, Camilla, 132
Hayward, Max, 20, 74, 88, 101, 147, 171
Hebert, Hugh, 26, 50, 153
Heeb, Fritz, 118
Hegge, Per Egil, 115, 116
Hellborn, Olle, 41
Henriksen, Morten, 41

Hermansen, Kari, 54, 145
Herridge, Frances, 93, 153
Herstad Røed, Liv, 88, 89, 153
Hingley, Ronald, 20, 74
Hinxman, Margaret, 106, 141, 153
Hitler, Adolf, 125, 162
Hjertén, Hanserik, 90, 91, 153
Holbaek-Hanssen, Hilde, 84
Holland, Barry, 8
Hønningstad, Amund, 13, 21, 22, 25, 26, 99, 218
Horovitch, David, 138
Hosking, Geoffrey, 128, 133, 147
Houston, Gary, 100, 151, 153
Hoyle, Martin, 138, 153
Hua, Bai, 119
Huddy, John, 100, 101, 153
Hurum, Eric, 53, 145

I

Iakovlev, V. L., 133
Ibsen, Henrik, 17, 18, 21, 132, 136, 156
Ionesco, Eugène, 17
Iuon, K. F., 29
Iurovskii, V., 123, 147

J

Jacob, Gilles, 114, 154
Jasný, Vojtěch, 119

K

Kalfus, Bob, 90, 110, 130, 154
Kanfer, Stefan, 52, 80, 91, 92, 93, 154
Kankkonen, Peter, 112, 154
Karmazin, E., 29
Katz, Peter S., 26, 27, 32, 71, 82, 145

Kaufman, Michael T., 7, 148
Keenan, George F., 8
Kern, Gary, 9, 58, 60, 71, 79, 80, 128, 148
Kevin, Alexander, 16, 81, 157
Khrushchev, N. S., 7, 21, 76, 128
Klein, Stewart, 98
Klimoff, Alexis, 9, 12, 98, 102, 148, 149
Knickerbocker, Paine, 42, 96, 102, 118, 154
Knudsen, Leif, 217
Kobets, Svitlana, 80, 148
Kochetov, Vsevolod, 11
Kochs, Anton, 111
Kohan, John, 122, 123, 148
Kopelev, Lev, 128
Kotcheff, Ted, 84
Kraineva, Elena, 143
Kristensen, Lars, 13
Kuleshov, L. V., 47
Küng, Andres, 113, 154
Kuniaev, S. Iu., 29
Kuusinen, Hertta, 164
Kuusinen, Otto Wille, 164

L

Lahtela, Markku, 21
Lakshin, V. Ia., 9, 148
Lavis, Arthur, 52
Lawrie, James H., 17
Lean, David, 50, 129
Lebedev, V. S., 76
Lee, John M., 88, 118, 154
Leighton, Lauren G., 75, 148
LeMare, Paul, 54, 145
Levin, Bernard, 139
Levin, Victor, 42, 149
Lewis, Anthony, 32, 82, 87, 97, 148, 150

Libaek, Sven, 83
Loriot, Patrick, 114, 154
Lunders, Léo, 111
Luplow, Richard, 8, 58, 148

M

M. E., 114, 154
Mackay, Fulton, 43
Madianov, R. S., 133
Magidoff, Robert, 59, 149
Mahar, Ted, 81, 97, 100, 132, 154
Makk, Karoly, 111
Malcolm, Derek, 89, 104, 107, 109, 133, 136, 141, 154
Malland, Alf, 43, 45, 54, 145, 146, 223
Mandelstam, Nadezhda, 138, 169, 170, 171, 174
Mandelstam, Osip, 138, 139, 152, 169, 170, 171, 174
Marlowe, Christopher, 16, 43
Marriage, Sophia, 111
Martin, Werner, 10
Maslin, Janet, 95
Mason, Brewster, 19
Maxwell, James, 15, 18, 19, 43, 54, 55, 89, 93, 97, 104, 107, 135, 136, 137, 146
May, Rachel, 75
Mazloum, Joseph, 111
McKern, Leo, 19
McKinnon, George, 20, 21, 22, 95, 140, 141, 154
McTeer, Janet, 137
Meisel, Myron, 96, 97, 101, 102, 129, 154
Melly, George, 89, 105, 154
Meta, 17, 154
Meyer, Michael, 15, 16, 21, 65, 132, 154

Michael, Ralph, 19
Mikoyan, A. I., 166
Miles, Patrick, 137
Miller, Jeanne, 110
Milligan, Spike, 49
Milne, Tom, 106, 150
Mitchell, Jolyon P., 111
Moilanen, Harri-Ilmari, 114, 155
Molière, Jean-Baptiste, 18, 136
Moor, D. S., 29
Moore, John, 105
Moskovich, W., 42, 149
Munch, Carsten E., 87
Murray Abraham, F., 133
Murray, Braham, 14, 18, 133, 135, 139, 140, 155

N

Nabokov, V. V., 30
Nathan, John W., 39
Naumov, V. N., 111
Negri, Richard, 15, 135
Nicholson, Michael, 128, 148
Nietzsche, Friedrich, 13
Nord, Hans, 51, 145
Nordheim, Arne, 66, 83, 84, 89, 90, 98, 116, 129, 145
Norman, Barry, 22, 47, 52, 108, 110, 134, 140, 155
Norton, Hubert, 98, 138, 153
Nørve, Ivar, 43
Nykvist, Sven, 39, 44, 50, 51, 52, 53, 54, 55, 88, 90, 91, 94, 97, 116, 136, 145, 155, 167, 223, 224

O

Orff, Carl, 129
Orr, Alicia B., 30, 32
Ortiz, Gaye, 111
Owen, Alun, 18

P

Pack, Richard M., 39, 41, 42, 44, 50, 51, 55, 71, 84, 110, 145
Pack, Robert, 55
Panfilov, G. A., 133
Panin, Dimitrii, 105, 155
Parker, Ralph, 20, 21, 74
Peacock, Trevor, 15, 43, 46, 155
Penn, Jean, 143
Peter, John, 138
Pflaum, H. G., 115, 155
Pike, David, 77, 148
Pinter, Harold, 17
Platonov, A. P., 186
Porter, Catherine, 127
Porter, Robert, 12, 123, 127, 141, 148
Powell, Dilys, 107, 155
Preece, Tim, 43
Prime, Cheryl, 138
Pudovkin, V. I., 130

Q

Quinlan, David, 141, 155

R

Ratcliffe, Michael, 137, 155
Rawley, Peter, 26, 30, 31
Reed, Carol, 39
Reshetovskaia, N. A., 7, 11, 20, 118, 119, 122, 149
Riazhskii, G. G., 29
Richie, Natasha, 18
Roberts, Celia, 106, 155
Robeson, Paul, 165
Robin, Régine, 16, 127, 139
Robinson, David, 105, 106, 126, 132, 155
Rogatchevskaia, Ekaterina, 143

Rogatchevski, Boris, 143
Rogatchevski, Ilia, 143
Rogers, David, 16
Rogovin Frankel, Edith, 9
Rus, Vladimir J., 59, 149
Russell Taylor, John, 104, 106, 126, 127, 155
Rustdal, Torstein, 54, 146
Rzhevskii, L. D., 59, 149

S

Sadie, Stanley, 84
Saint-Denis, Michel, 15
Sandsdalen, Odd Jan, 54, 146
Saraskina, L. I., 124, 128, 149
Savel'ev, L. I., 175
Scammell, Michael, 8, 149
Schapiro, Leonard, 20, 149
Schébéko, Marie, 30, 31, 32, 82
Scherr, Barry P., 75, 149
Schickel, Richard, 92, 93, 94, 156
Schmidt, Carol, 96
Schubeck, John, 94
Schwab, Per, 32, 94, 145
Scott, Robert, 104
Seale, Colleen W., 143
Segraves, John, 95
Sériot, Patrick, 123, 147
Shakespeare, William, 15, 16
Shalit, Gene, 110, 157
Sharp, Don, 25
Shaw, George Bernard, 48, 180
Shaw, Irwin, 17
Shaw, Maxwell, 43
Shchusev, A. V., 175
Sheldon, Larry, 133
Shevelov, George Y., 59, 149
Shneerson, M., 59, 149
Silvera, René, 112
Simmons, J. S. G., 59, 149

Sinobad, Zoran, 143
Skjønberg, Espen, 25, 43, 59, 97, 137, 146, 150, 223
Skliar, I. B., 133
Skønberg, Jo, 54, 146
Skouen, Arne, 41
Slonim, Marc, 87, 149
Smirnov, A. S., 133
Smith, J. Y., 8
Solbakken, Eric, 87
Solzhenitsyn, A. I., 7, 8, 9, 10, 11, 20, 21, 22, 25, 27, 36, 38, 39, 42, 53, 54, 55, 57, 58, 59, 60, 63, 67, 71, 73, 75, 76, 77, 79, 80, 81, 87, 88, 90, 91, 92, 93, 96, 97, 99, 101, 102, 104, 105, 109, 110, 111, 112, 113, 114, 115, 116, 117, 118, 119, 120, 121, 122, 123, 124, 125, 126, 127, 128, 130, 133, 141, 145, 146, 147, 148, 149, 150, 153, 154, 157, 167, 168, 174, 185, 186
Spechler, Dina R., 9
Stakhanov, A. G., 71
Stalin, I. V., 8, 10, 29, 38, 46, 76, 87, 88, 91, 99, 102, 116, 117, 120, 125, 126, 129, 133, 138, 139, 157, 162, 164, 166, 170, 171, 174, 175
Stapran, O. A., 175
Stark, Susan, 98, 100, 157
Steiger, Rod, 51
Stone, Andrew L., 39, 52, 96, 158
Stoppard, Tom, 180
Strauss, Ulf von, 90, 157
Strindberg, August, 16, 18, 21
Superfin, Gabriel, 143
Sweeney, Louise, 97, 98, 101, 157

T

Tallmer, Jerry, 42, 108, 110, 157
Taranovski, Kiril, 59, 149
Tarkovsky, Andrei, 111, 169
Taube, Sven-Bertil, 137
Taylor, Nora E., 45, 50, 57
Tempest, Richard, 98, 149
Tenno, G. P., 120
Thirkell, Arthur, 106, 107, 132, 157
Thomas, Kevin, 99, 101, 114, 129
Thompson, Eric, 19, 43, 48, 49, 53, 93, 97, 146, 157
Thornber, Robin, 139
Todhunter, E. J., 49
Toker, Leona, 42, 126, 149
Tolczyk, Dariusz, 102, 149
Trasatti, Sergio, 111
Trevor, William, 15, 43, 46, 133, 155, 157
Trifonov, Iu. V., 29, 166
Trilling, Ossian, 17, 157
Tsymbal, E. V., 124
Tung, Wong, 119
Tuomari, Paavo, 112
Turan, Kenneth, 95
Turtiainen, Arvo, 165

U

Uboldi, Raffaello, 87, 157
Unbegaun, Boris O., 59, 149

V

Varen, Torgny, 90, 157
Verr, 92, 94, 157
Viertel, Peter, 17

W

Wagner, Friedrich A., 115, 157
Wajda, Andrzej, 119, 120, 131
Walker, Alexander, 104, 106, 157
Wall, Michael, 17
Wardle, Irving, 138, 158
Wedman, Les, 89, 92, 105, 158
Weisman, John, 52, 80, 96, 158
Westdijk, Robert Jan, 41
Whitehead, Tom, 143
Whitney, Thomas P., 74
Willetts, H. T., 75
Williams, Carol J., 8
Willoughby, George W., 84
Wilson, Cecil, 108, 158
Wolf, William, 93, 158
Wrede, Casper, 5, 11, 13, 14, 15, 16, 17, 18, 19, 20, 21, 22, 25, 26, 27, 29, 30, 31, 32, 33, 39, 41, 42, 43, 45, 46, 48, 49, 50, 51, 52, 53, 54, 55, 57, 60, 65, 70, 71, 76, 81, 83, 84, 87, 88, 89, 90, 91, 92, 94, 95, 96, 97, 99, 100, 102, 104, 105, 106, 108, 110, 111, 112, 113, 114, 115, 118, 119, 120, 129, 130, 131, 132, 133, 135, 136, 137, 138, 139, 140, 141, 143, 145, 146, 147, 150, 151, 152, 155, 157, 161, 164, 166, 167, 175, 184, 216, 217, 222, 223, 224, 226
Wrede, David, 13, 21, 22, 27, 30, 33, 43, 60, 83, 143, 147, 226
Wrede, Gerda, 15
Wrede, Karin, 114
Wrede, Kenneth Alexander, 167

Z

Zanussi, Krzysztof, 111
Zhdanov, A. A., 163
Zil'berman, M. A., 124
Zimmerman, Paul D., 39, 55, 81, 93, 107, 129, 158

Zorin, Libushe, 7

SOVIET AND POST-SOVIET POLITICS AND SOCIETY

Edited by Dr. Andreas Umland

ISSN 1614-3515

1   Андреас Умланд (ред.)
    Воплощение Европейской
    конвенции по правам человека в
    России
    Философские, юридические и
    эмпирические исследования
    ISBN 3-89821-387-0

2   Christian Wipperfürth
    Russland – ein vertrauenswürdiger
    Partner?
    Grundlagen, Hintergründe und Praxis
    gegenwärtiger russischer Außenpolitik
    Mit einem Vorwort von Heinz Timmermann
    ISBN 3-89821-401-X

3   Manja Hussner
    Die Übernahme internationalen Rechts
    in die russische und deutsche
    Rechtsordnung
    Eine vergleichende Analyse zur
    Völkerrechtsfreundlichkeit der Verfassungen
    der Russländischen Föderation und der
    Bundesrepublik Deutschland
    Mit einem Vorwort von Rainer Arnold
    ISBN 3-89821-438-9

4   Matthew Tejada
    Bulgaria's Democratic Consolidation
    and the Kozloduy Nuclear Power Plant
    (KNPP)
    The Unattainability of Closure
    With a foreword by Richard J. Crampton
    ISBN 3-89821-439-7

5   Марк Григорьевич Меерович
    Квадратные метры, определяющие
    сознание
    Государственная жилищная политика в
    СССР. 1921 – 1941 гг
    ISBN 3-89821-474-5

6   Andrei P. Tsygankov, Pavel
    A.Tsygankov (Eds.)
    New Directions in Russian
    International Studies
    ISBN 3-89821-422-2

7   Марк Григорьевич Меерович
    Как власть народ к труду приучала
    Жилище в СССР – средство управления
    людьми. 1917 – 1941 гг.
    С предисловием Елены Осокиной
    ISBN 3-89821-495-8

8   David J. Galbreath
    Nation-Building and Minority Politics
    in Post-Socialist States
    Interests, Influence and Identities in Estonia
    and Latvia
    With a foreword by David J. Smith
    ISBN 3-89821-467-2

9   Алексей Юрьевич Безугольный
    Народы Кавказа в Вооруженных
    силах СССР в годы Великой
    Отечественной войны 1941-1945 гг.
    С предисловием Николая Бугая
    ISBN 3-89821-475-3

10 Вячеслав Лихачев и Владимир
    Прибыловский (ред.)
    Русское Национальное Единство,
    1990-2000. В 2-х томах
    ISBN 3-89821-523-7

11 Николай Бугай (ред.)
    Народы стран Балтии в условиях
    сталинизма (1940-е – 1950-е годы)
    Документированная история
    ISBN 3-89821-525-3

12 Ingmar Bredies (Hrsg.)
    Zur Anatomie der Orange Revolution
    in der Ukraine
    Wechsel des Elitenregimes oder Triumph des
    Parlamentarismus?
    ISBN 3-89821-524-5

13 Anastasia V. Mitrofanova
    The Politicization of Russian
    Orthodoxy
    Actors and Ideas
    With a foreword by William C. Gay
    ISBN 3-89821-481-8

14 Nathan D. Larson
Alexander Solzhenitsyn and the
Russo-Jewish Question
ISBN 3-89821-483-4

15 Guido Houben
Kulturpolitik und Ethnizität
Staatliche Kunstförderung im Russland der
neunziger Jahre
Mit einem Vorwort von Gert Weisskirchen
ISBN 3-89821-542-3

16 Leonid Luks
Der russische „Sonderweg"?
Aufsätze zur neuesten Geschichte Russlands
im europäischen Kontext
ISBN 3-89821-496-6

17 Евгений Мороз
История «Мёртвой воды» – от
страшной сказки к большой
политике
Политическое неоязычество в
постсоветской России
ISBN 3-89821-551-2

18 Александр Верховский и Галина
Кожевникова (ред.)
Этническая и религиозная
интолерантность в российских СМИ
Результаты мониторинга 2001-2004 гг.
ISBN 3-89821-569-5

19 Christian Ganzer
Sowjetisches Erbe und ukrainische
Nation
Das Museum der Geschichte des Zaporoger
Kosakentums auf der Insel Chortycja
Mit einem Vorwort von Frank Golczewski
ISBN 3-89821-504-0

20 Эльза-Баир Гучинова
Помнить нельзя забыть
Антропология депортационной травмы
калмыков
С предисловием Кэролайн Хамфри
ISBN 3-89821-506-7

21 Юлия Лидерман
Мотивы «проверки» и «испытания»
в постсоветской культуре
Советское прошлое в российском
кинематографе 1990-х годов
С предисловием Евгения Марголита
ISBN 3-89821-511-3

22 Tanya Lokshina, Ray Thomas, Mary
Mayer (Eds.)
The Imposition of a Fake Political
Settlement in the Northern Caucasus
The 2003 Chechen Presidential Election
ISBN 3-89821-436-2

23 Timothy McCajor Hall, Rosie Read
(Eds.)
Changes in the Heart of Europe
Recent Ethnographies of Czechs, Slovaks,
Roma, and Sorbs
With an afterword by Zdeněk Salzmann
ISBN 3-89821-606-3

24 Christian Autengruber
Die politischen Parteien in Bulgarien
und Rumänien
Eine vergleichende Analyse seit Beginn der
90er Jahre
Mit einem Vorwort von Dorothée de Nève
ISBN 3-89821-476-1

25 Annette Freyberg-Inan with Radu
Cristescu
The Ghosts in Our Classrooms, or:
John Dewey Meets Ceauşescu
The Promise and the Failures of Civic
Education in Romania
ISBN 3-89821-416-8

26 John B. Dunlop
The 2002 Dubrovka and 2004 Beslan
Hostage Crises
A Critique of Russian Counter-Terrorism
With a foreword by Donald N. Jensen
ISBN 3-89821-608-X

27 Peter Koller
Das touristische Potenzial von
Kam''janec'–Podil's'kyj
Eine fremdenverkehrsgeographische
Untersuchung der Zukunftsperspektiven und
Maßnahmenplanung zur
Destinationsentwicklung des „ukrainischen
Rothenburg"
Mit einem Vorwort von Kristiane Klemm
ISBN 3-89821-640-3

28 Françoise Daucé, Elisabeth Sieca-
Kozlowski (Eds.)
Dedovshchina in the Post-Soviet
Military
Hazing of Russian Army Conscripts in a
Comparative Perspective
With a foreword by Dale Herspring
ISBN 3-89821-616-0

29 Florian Strasser
    Zivilgesellschaftliche Einflüsse auf die
    Orange Revolution
    Die gewaltlose Massenbewegung und die
    ukrainische Wahlkrise 2004
    Mit einem Vorwort von Egbert Jahn
    ISBN 3-89821-648-9

30 Rebecca S. Katz
    The Georgian Regime Crisis of 2003-
    2004
    A Case Study in Post-Soviet Media
    Representation of Politics, Crime and
    Corruption
    ISBN 3-89821-413-3

31 Vladimir Kantor
    Willkür oder Freiheit
    Beiträge zur russischen Geschichtsphilosophie
    Ediert von Dagmar Herrmann sowie mit
    einem Vorwort versehen von Leonid Luks
    ISBN 3-89821-589-X

32 Laura A. Victoir
    The Russian Land Estate Today
    A Case Study of Cultural Politics in Post-
    Soviet Russia
    With a foreword by Priscilla Roosevelt
    ISBN 3-89821-426-5

33 Ivan Katchanovski
    Cleft Countries
    Regional Political Divisions and Cultures in
    Post-Soviet Ukraine and Moldova
    With a foreword by Francis Fukuyama
    ISBN 3-89821-558-X

34 Florian Mühlfried
    Postsowjetische Feiern
    Das Georgische Bankett im Wandel
    Mit einem Vorwort von Kevin Tuite
    ISBN 3-89821-601-2

35 Roger Griffin, Werner Loh, Andreas
    Umland (Eds.)
    Fascism Past and Present, West and
    East
    An International Debate on Concepts and
    Cases in the Comparative Study of the
    Extreme Right
    With an afterword by Walter Laqueur
    ISBN 3-89821-674-8

36 Sebastian Schlegel
    Der „Weiße Archipel"
    Sowjetische Atomstädte 1945-1991
    Mit einem Geleitwort von Thomas Bohn
    ISBN 3-89821-679-9

37 Vyacheslav Likhachev
    Political Anti-Semitism in Post-Soviet
    Russia
    Actors and Ideas in 1991-2003
    Edited and translated from Russian by Eugene
    Veklerov
    ISBN 3-89821-529-6

38 Josette Baer (Ed.)
    Preparing Liberty in Central Europe
    Political Texts from the Spring of Nations
    1848 to the Spring of Prague 1968
    With a foreword by Zdeněk V. David
    ISBN 3-89821-546-6

39 Михаил Лукьянов
    Российский консерватизм и
    реформа, 1907-1914
    С предисловием Марка Д. Стейнберга
    ISBN 3-89821-503-2

40 Nicola Melloni
    Market Without Economy
    The 1998 Russian Financial Crisis
    With a foreword by Eiji Furukawa
    ISBN 3-89821-407-9

41 Dmitrij Chmelnizki
    Die Architektur Stalins
    Bd. 1: Studien zu Ideologie und Stil
    Bd. 2: Bilddokumentation
    Mit einem Vorwort von Bruno Flierl
    ISBN 3-89821-515-6

42 Katja Yafimava
    Post-Soviet Russian-Belarusian
    Relationships
    The Role of Gas Transit Pipelines
    With a foreword by Jonathan P. Stern
    ISBN 3-89821-655-1

43 Boris Chavkin
    Verflechtungen der deutschen und
    russischen Zeitgeschichte
    Aufsätze und Archivfunde zu den
    Beziehungen Deutschlands und der
    Sowjetunion von 1917 bis 1991
    Ediert von Markus Edlinger sowie mit einem
    Vorwort versehen von Leonid Luks
    ISBN 3-89821-756-6

44 Anastasija Grynenko in
    Zusammenarbeit mit Claudia Dathe
    Die Terminologie des Gerichtswesens
    der Ukraine und Deutschlands im
    Vergleich
    Eine übersetzungswissenschaftliche Analyse
    juristischer Fachbegriffe im Deutschen,
    Ukrainischen und Russischen
    Mit einem Vorwort von Ulrich Hartmann
    ISBN 3-89821-691-8

45 Anton Burkov
    The Impact of the European
    Convention on Human Rights on
    Russian Law
    Legislation and Application in 1996-2006
    With a foreword by Françoise Hampson
    ISBN 978-3-89821-639-5

46 Stina Torjesen, Indra Overland (Eds.)
    International Election Observers in
    Post-Soviet Azerbaijan
    Geopolitical Pawns or Agents of Change?
    ISBN 978-3-89821-743-9

47 Taras Kuzio
    Ukraine – Crimea – Russia
    Triangle of Conflict
    ISBN 978-3-89821-761-3

48 Claudia Šabić
    "Ich erinnere mich nicht, aber L'viv!"
    Zur Funktion kultureller Faktoren für die
    Institutionalisierung und Entwicklung einer
    ukrainischen Region
    Mit einem Vorwort von Melanie Tatur
    ISBN 978-3-89821-752-1

49 Marlies Bilz
    Tatarstan in der Transformation
    Nationaler Diskurs und Politische Praxis
    1988-1994
    Mit einem Vorwort von Frank Golczewski
    ISBN 978-3-89821-722-4

50 Марлен Ларюэль (ред.)
    Современные интерпретации
    русского национализма
    ISBN 978-3-89821-795-8

51 Sonja Schüler
    Die ethnische Dimension der Armut
    Roma im postsozialistischen Rumänien
    Mit einem Vorwort von Anton Sterbling
    ISBN 978-3-89821-776-7

52 Галина Кожевникова
    Радикальный национализм в России
    и противодействие ему
    Сборник докладов Центра «Сова» за 2004-
    2007 гг.
    С предисловием Александра Верховского
    ISBN 978-3-89821-721-7

53 Галина Кожевникова и Владимир
    Прибыловский
    Российская власть в биографиях I
    Высшие должностные лица РФ в 2004 г.
    ISBN 978-3-89821-796-5

54 Галина Кожевникова и Владимир
    Прибыловский
    Российская власть в биографиях II
    Члены Правительства РФ в 2004 г.
    ISBN 978-3-89821-797-2

55 Галина Кожевникова и Владимир
    Прибыловский
    Российская власть в биографиях III
    Руководители федеральных служб и
    агентств РФ в 2004 г.
    ISBN 978-3-89821-798-9

56 Ileana Petroniu
    Privatisierung in
    Transformationsökonomien
    Determinanten der Restrukturierungs-
    Bereitschaft am Beispiel Polens, Rumäniens
    und der Ukraine
    Mit einem Vorwort von Rainer W. Schäfer
    ISBN 978-3-89821-790-3

57 Christian Wipperfürth
    Russland und seine GUS-Nachbarn
    Hintergründe, aktuelle Entwicklungen und
    Konflikte in einer ressourcenreichen Region
    ISBN 978-3-89821-801-6

58 Togzhan Kassenova
    From Antagonism to Partnership
    The Uneasy Path of the U.S.-Russian
    Cooperative Threat Reduction
    With a foreword by Christoph Bluth
    ISBN 978-3-89821-707-1

59 Alexander Höllwerth
    Das sakrale eurasische Imperium des
    Aleksandr Dugin
    Eine Diskursanalyse zum postsowjetischen
    russischen Rechtsextremismus
    Mit einem Vorwort von Dirk Uffelmann
    ISBN 978-3-89821-813-9

60 Олег Рябов
    «Россия-Матушка»
    Национализм, гендер и война в России XX
    века
    С предисловием Елены Гощило
    ISBN 978-3-89821-487-2

61 Ivan Maistrenko
    Borot'bism
    A Chapter in the History of the Ukrainian
    Revolution
    With a new introduction by Chris Ford
    Translated by George S. N. Luckyj with the
    assistance of Ivan L. Rudnytsky
    ISBN 978-3-89821-697-5

62 Maryna Romanets
    Anamorphosic Texts and
    Reconfigured Visions
    Improvised Traditions in Contemporary
    Ukrainian and Irish Literature
    ISBN 978-3-89821-576-3

63 Paul D'Anieri and Taras Kuzio (Eds.)
    Aspects of the Orange Revolution I
    Democratization and Elections in Post-
    Communist Ukraine
    ISBN 978-3-89821-698-2

64 Bohdan Harasymiw in collaboration
    with Oleh S. Ilnytzkyj (Eds.)
    Aspects of the Orange Revolution II
    Information and Manipulation Strategies in
    the 2004 Ukrainian Presidential Elections
    ISBN 978-3-89821-699-9

65 Ingmar Bredies, Andreas Umland and
    Valentin Yakushik (Eds.)
    Aspects of the Orange Revolution III
    The Context and Dynamics of the 2004
    Ukrainian Presidential Elections
    ISBN 978-3-89821-803-0

66 Ingmar Bredies, Andreas Umland and
    Valentin Yakushik (Eds.)
    Aspects of the Orange Revolution IV
    Foreign Assistance and Civic Action in the
    2004 Ukrainian Presidential Elections
    ISBN 978-3-89821-808-5

67 Ingmar Bredies, Andreas Umland and
    Valentin Yakushik (Eds.)
    Aspects of the Orange Revolution V
    Institutional Observation Reports on the 2004
    Ukrainian Presidential Elections
    ISBN 978-3-89821-809-2

68 Taras Kuzio (Ed.)
    Aspects of the Orange Revolution VI
    Post-Communist Democratic Revolutions in
    Comparative Perspective
    ISBN 978-3-89821-820-7

69 Tim Bohse
    Autoritarismus statt Selbstverwaltung
    Die Transformation der kommunalen Politik
    in der Stadt Kaliningrad 1990-2005
    Mit einem Geleitwort von Stefan Troebst
    ISBN 978-3-89821-782-8

70 David Rupp
    Die Rußländische Föderation und die
    russischsprachige Minderheit in
    Lettland
    Eine Fallstudie zur Anwaltspolitik Moskaus
    gegenüber den russophonen Minderheiten im
    „Nahen Ausland" von 1991 bis 2002
    Mit einem Vorwort von Helmut Wagner
    ISBN 978-3-89821-778-1

71 Taras Kuzio
    Theoretical and Comparative
    Perspectives on Nationalism
    New Directions in Cross-Cultural and Post-
    Communist Studies
    With a foreword by Paul Robert Magocsi
    ISBN 978-3-89821-815-3

72 Christine Teichmann
    Die Hochschultransformation im
    heutigen Osteuropa
    Kontinuität und Wandel bei der Entwicklung
    des postkommunistischen Universitätswesens
    Mit einem Vorwort von Oskar Anweiler
    ISBN 978-3-89821-842-9

73 Julia Kusznir
    Der politische Einfluss von
    Wirtschaftseliten in russischen
    Regionen
    Eine Analyse am Beispiel der Erdöl- und
    Erdgasindustrie, 1992-2005
    Mit einem Vorwort von Wolfgang Eichwede
    ISBN 978-3-89821-821-4

74 Alena Vysotskaya
    Russland, Belarus und die EU-
    Osterweiterung
    Zur Minderheitenfrage und zum Problem der
    Freizügigkeit des Personenverkehrs
    Mit einem Vorwort von Katlijn Malfliet
    ISBN 978-3-89821-822-1

75 Heiko Pleines (Hrsg.)
    Corporate Governance in post-
    sozialistischen Volkswirtschaften
    ISBN 978-3-89821-766-8

76 Stefan Ihrig
    Wer sind die Moldawier?
    Rumänismus versus Moldowanismus in
    Historiographie und Schulbüchern der
    Republik Moldova, 1991-2006
    Mit einem Vorwort von Holm Sundhaussen
    ISBN 978-3-89821-466-7

77 Galina Kozhevnikova in collaboration
    with Alexander Verkhovsky and
    Eugene Veklerov
    Ultra-Nationalism and Hate Crimes in
    Contemporary Russia
    The 2004-2006 Annual Reports of Moscow's
    SOVA Center
    With a foreword by Stephen D. Shenfield
    ISBN 978-3-89821-868-9

78 Florian Küchler
    The Role of the European Union in
    Moldova's Transnistria Conflict
    With a foreword by Christopher Hill
    ISBN 978-3-89821-850-4

79 Bernd Rechel
    The Long Way Back to Europe
    Minority Protection in Bulgaria
    With a foreword by Richard Crampton
    ISBN 978-3-89821-863-4

80 Peter W. Rodgers
    Nation, Region and History in Post-
    Communist Transitions
    Identity Politics in Ukraine, 1991-2006
    With a foreword by Vera Tolz
    ISBN 978-3-89821-903-7

81 Stephanie Solywoda
    The Life and Work of
    Semen L. Frank
    A Study of Russian Religious Philosophy
    With a foreword by Philip Walters
    ISBN 978-3-89821-457-5

82 Vera Sokolova
    Cultural Politics of Ethnicity
    Discourses on Roma in Communist
    Czechoslovakia
    ISBN 978-3-89821-864-1

83 Natalya Shevchik Ketenci
    Kazakhstani Enterprises in Transition
    The Role of Historical Regional Development
    in Kazakhstan's Post-Soviet Economic
    Transformation
    ISBN 978-3-89821-831-3

84 Martin Malek, Anna Schor-
    Tschudnowskaja (Hrsg.)
    Europa im Tschetschenienkrieg
    Zwischen politischer Ohnmacht und
    Gleichgültigkeit
    Mit einem Vorwort von Lipchan Basajewa
    ISBN 978-3-89821-676-0

85 Stefan Meister
    Das postsowjetische Universitätswesen
    zwischen nationalem und
    internationalem Wandel
    Die Entwicklung der regionalen Hochschule
    in Russland als Gradmesser der
    Systemtransformation
    Mit einem Vorwort von Joan DeBardeleben
    ISBN 978-3-89821-891-7

86 Konstantin Sheiko in collaboration
    with Stephen Brown
    Nationalist Imaginings of the
    Russian Past
    Anatolii Fomenko and the Rise of Alternative
    History in Post-Communist Russia
    With a foreword by Donald Ostrowski
    ISBN 978-3-89821-915-0

87 Sabine Jenni
    Wie stark ist das „Einige Russland"?
    Zur Parteibindung der Eliten und zum
    Wahlerfolg der Machtpartei
    im Dezember 2007
    Mit einem Vorwort von Klaus Armingeon
    ISBN 978-3-89821-961-7

88 Thomas Borén
    Meeting-Places of Transformation
    Urban Identity, Spatial Representations and
    Local Politics in Post-Soviet St Petersburg
    ISBN 978-3-89821-739-2

89 Aygul Ashirova
    Stalinismus und Stalin-Kult in
    Zentralasien
    Turkmenistan 1924-1953
    Mit einem Vorwort von Leonid Luks
    ISBN 978-3-89821-987-7

90　*Leonid Luks*
　　Freiheit oder imperiale Größe?
　　Essays zu einem russischen Dilemma
　　ISBN 978-3-8382-0011-8

91　*Christopher Gilley*
　　The 'Change of Signposts' in the
　　Ukrainian Emigration
　　A Contribution to the History of
　　Sovietophilism in the 1920s
　　With a foreword by Frank Golczewski
　　ISBN 978-3-89821-965-5

92　*Philipp Casula, Jeronim Perovic
　　(Eds.)*
　　Identities and Politics
　　During the Putin Presidency
　　The Discursive Foundations of Russia's
　　Stability
　　With a foreword by Heiko Haumann
　　ISBN 978-3-8382-0015-6

93　*Marcel Viëtor*
　　Europa und die Frage
　　nach seinen Grenzen im Osten
　　Zur Konstruktion ‚europäischer Identität' in
　　Geschichte und Gegenwart
　　Mit einem Vorwort von Albrecht Lehmann
　　ISBN 978-3-8382-0045-3

94　*Ben Hellman, Andrei Rogachevskii*
　　Filming the Unfilmable
　　Casper Wrede's 'One Day in the Life
　　of Ivan Denisovich'
　　Second, Revised and Expanded Edition
　　ISBN 978-3-8382-0044-6

95　*Eva Fuchslocher*
　　Vaterland, Sprache, Glaube
　　Orthodoxie und Nationenbildung
　　am Beispiel Georgiens
　　Mit einem Vorwort von Christina von Braun
　　ISBN 978-3-89821-884-9

96　*Vladimir Kantor*
　　Das Westlertum und der Weg
　　Russlands
　　Zur Entwicklung der russischen Literatur und
　　Philosophie
　　Ediert von Dagmar Herrmann
　　Mit einem Beitrag von Nikolaus Lobkowicz
　　ISBN 978-3-8382-0102-3

97　*Kamran Musayev*
　　Die postsowjetische Transformation
　　im Baltikum und Südkaukasus
　　Eine vergleichende Untersuchung der
　　politischen Entwicklung Lettlands und
　　Aserbaidschans 1985-2009
　　Mit einem Vorwort von Leonid Luks
　　Ediert von Sandro Henschel
　　ISBN 978-3-8382-0103-0

98　*Tatiana Zhurzhenko*
　　Borderlands into Bordered Lands
　　Geopolitics of Identity in Post-Soviet Ukraine
　　With a foreword by Dieter Segert
　　ISBN 978-3-8382-0042-2

99　*Кирилл Галушко, Лидия Смола
　　(ред.)*
　　Пределы падения – варианты
　　украинского будущего
　　Аналитико-прогностические исследования
　　ISBN 978-3-8382-0148-1

100　*Michael Minkenberg (ed.)*
　　Historical Legacies and the Radical
　　Right in Post-Cold War Central and
　　Eastern Europe
　　With an afterword by Sabrina P. Ramet
　　ISBN 978-3-8382-0124-5

101　*David-Emil Wickström*
　　"Okna otkroi!" – "Open the
　　Windows!"
　　Transcultural Flows and Identity Politics in
　　the St. Petersburg Popular Music Scene
　　With a foreword by Yngvar B. Steinholt
　　Second, Revised and Expanded Edition
　　ISBN 978-3-8382-0100-9

102　*Eva Zabka*
　　Eine neue „Zeit der Wirren"?
　　Der spät- und postsowjetische Systemwandel
　　1985-2000 im Spiegel russischer
　　gesellschaftspolitischer Diskurse
　　Mit einem Vorwort von Margareta Mommsen
　　ISBN 978-3-8382-0161-0

103　*Ulrike Ziemer*
　　Ethnic Belonging, Gender and
　　Cultural Practices
　　Youth Identitites in Contemporary Russia
　　With a foreword by Anoop Nayak
　　ISBN 978-3-8382-0152-8

104　Ksenia Chepikova
‚Einiges Russland' - eine zweite KPdSU?
Aspekte der Identitätskonstruktion einer postsowjetischen „Partei der Macht"
Mit einem Vorwort von Torsten Oppelland
ISBN 978-3-8382-0311-9

105　Леонид Люкс
Западничество или евразийство?
Демократия или идеократия?
Сборник статей об исторических дилеммах России
С предисловием Владимира Кантора
ISBN 978-3-8382-0211-2

106　Anna Dost
Das russische Verfassungsrecht auf dem Weg zum Föderalismus und zurück
Zum Konflikt von Rechtsnormen und -wirklichkeit in der Russländischen Föderation von 1991 bis 2009
Mit einem Vorwort von Alexander Blankenagel
ISBN 978-3-8382-0292-1

107　Philipp Herzog
Sozialistische Völkerfreundschaft, nationaler Widerstand oder harmloser Zeitvertreib?
Zur politischen Funktion der Volkskunst im sowjetischen Estland
Mit einem Vorwort von Andreas Kappeler
ISBN 978-3-8382-0216-7

108　Marlène Laruelle (ed.)
Russian Nationalism, Foreign Policy, and Identity Debates in Putin's Russia
New Ideological Patterns after the Orange Revolution
ISBN 978-3-8382-0325-6

109　Michail Logvinov
Russlands Kampf gegen den internationalen Terrorismus
Eine kritische Bestandsaufnahme des Bekämpfungsansatzes
Mit einem Geleitwort von Hans-Henning Schröder
und einem Vorwort von Eckhard Jesse
ISBN 978-3-8382-0329-4

110　John B. Dunlop
The Moscow Bombings of September 1999
Examinations of Russian Terrorist Attacks at the Onset of Vladimir Putin's Rule
Second, Revised and Expanded Edition
ISBN 978-3-8382-0388-1

111　Андрей А. Ковалёв
Свидетельство из-за кулис российской политики I
Можно ли делать добро из зла?
(Воспоминания и размышления о последних советских и первых послесоветских годах)
With a foreword by Peter Reddaway
ISBN 978-3-8382-0302-7

112　Андрей А. Ковалёв
Свидетельство из-за кулис российской политики II
Угроза для себя и окружающих
(Наблюдения и предостережения относительно происходящего после 2000 г.)
ISBN 978-3-8382-0303-4

113　Bernd Kappenberg
Zeichen setzen für Europa
Der Gebrauch europäischer lateinischer Sonderzeichen in der deutschen Öffentlichkeit
Mit einem Vorwort von Peter Schlobinski
ISBN 978-3-89821-749-1

114　Ivo Mijnssen
The Quest for an Ideal Youth in Putin's Russia I
Back to Our Future! History, Modernity, and Patriotism according to *Nashi*, 2005-2013
With a foreword by Jeronim Perović
Second, Revised and Expanded Edition
ISBN 978-3-8382-0368-3

115　Jussi Lassila
The Quest for an Ideal Youth in Putin's Russia II
The Search for Distinctive Conformism in the Political Communication of *Nashi*, 2005-2009
With a foreword by Kirill Postoutenko
Second, Revised and Expanded Edition
ISBN 978-3-8382-0415-4

116　Valerio Trabandt
Neue Nachbarn, gute Nachbarschaft?
Die EU als internationaler Akteur am Beispiel ihrer Demokratieförderung in Belarus und der Ukraine 2004-2009
Mit einem Vorwort von Jutta Joachim
ISBN 978-3-8382-0437-6

117   Fabian Pfeiffer
       Estlands Außen- und Sicherheitspolitik I
       Der estnische Atlantizismus nach der
       wiedererlangten Unabhängigkeit 1991-2004
       Mit einem Vorwort von Helmut Hubel
       ISBN 978-3-8382-0127-6

118   Jana Podßuweit
       Estlands Außen- und Sicherheitspolitik II
       Handlungsoptionen eines Kleinstaates im
       Rahmen seiner EU-Mitgliedschaft (2004-2008)
       Mit einem Vorwort von Helmut Hubel
       ISBN 978-3-8382-0440-6

119   Karin Pointner
       Estlands Außen- und Sicherheitspolitik III
       Eine gedächtnispolitische Analyse estnischer
       Entwicklungskooperation 2006-2010
       Mit einem Vorwort von Karin Liebhart
       ISBN 978-3-8382-0435-2

120   Ruslana Vovk
       Die Offenheit der ukrainischen
       Verfassung für das Völkerrecht und
       die europäische Integration
       Mit einem Vorwort von Alexander
       Blankenagel
       ISBN 978-3-8382-0481-9

121   Mykhaylo Banakh
       Die Relevanz der Zivilgesellschaft
       bei den postkommunistischen
       Transformationsprozessen in mittel-
       und osteuropäischen Ländern
       Das Beispiel der spät- und postsowjetischen
       Ukraine 1986-2009
       Mit einem Vorwort von Gerhard Simon
       ISBN 978-3-8382-0499-4

122   Michael Moser
       Language Policy and the Discourse on
       Languages in Ukraine under President
       Viktor Yanukovych (25 February
       2010–28 October 2012)
       ISBN 978-3-8382-0497-0 (Paperback edition)
       ISBN 978-3-8382-0507-6 (Hardcover edition)

123   Nicole Krome
       Russischer Netzwerkkapitalismus
       Restrukturierungsprozesse in der
       Russischen Föderation am Beispiel des
       Luftfahrtunternehmens "Aviastar"
       Mit einem Vorwort von Petra Stykow
       ISBN 978-3-8382-0534-2

124   David R. Marples
       'Our Glorious Past'
       Lukashenka's Belarus and
       the Great Patriotic War
       ISBN 978-3-8382-0574-8

125   Ulf Walther
       Russlands "neuer Adel"
       Die Macht des Geheimdienstes von
       Gorbatschow bis Putin
       Mit einem Vorwort von Hans-Georg Wieck
       ISBN 978-3-8382-0584-7

***ibidem*-Verlag**

Melchiorstr. 15

D-70439 Stuttgart

info@ibidem-verlag.de

www.ibidem-verlag.de
www.ibidem.eu
www.edition-noema.de
www.autorenbetreuung.de